"Doloc's book is a masterfully written and essential handbook for anyone involved in utilizing data to gain insights into their respective industries. With intellectual honesty, Doloc separates hype from reality, skillfully and intricately weaving a framework to harness the advances and recent developments in quantitative and computational finance. He challenges readers to adopt the best approaches for their applications, knowing the potential but also the limitations, and wisely problem solve. The author may have expertly designed this book for the trading community, but the takeaways are industry agnostic. A must-read for any academic or practitioner in data science, machine learning, and AI fields."

—Rob Friesen, president & COO, Bright Trading,
LLC; CEO & Director of Education, StockOdds, Inc.

"Cris Doloc's book is a great introduction to a fascinating field of Computational Intelligence and its applications to quantitative finance. Through examples and case studies covering a wide range of problems arising in quantitative finance from market making to derivative valuation and portfolio management the author demonstrates how to apply complex theoretical frameworks to solving practical problems. Using a sequence of case studies, Doloc shows quantitative researchers and practitioners the power of emerging Computational Intelligence and machine learning technologies to build intelligent solutions for quantitative finance."

—Yuri Burlakov, Ph.D., head of Proprietary Research,
Volant Trading

"Cris Doloc has created a valuable guide to Computational Intelligence and the application of these technologies to real-world problems. This book establishes a firm foundation to update the Financial Mathematics program curriculum and prac- titioners in this domain by presenting a systematic, contemporary development of data-intensive computation applied to financial market trading and investing. Using a sequence of case studies, Doloc shows quantitative researchers and practitioners the power of emerging Computational Intelligence and machine learning technologies to build intelligent solutions for quantitative finance."

—Jeff Blaschak, Ph.D., data scientist and co-founder,
Social Media Analytics, Inc.

"Cris Doloc has written a book that is more than just a solid introduction to the current state of the art in AI for quants; it is a solid introduction in how to *think about* AI for quants. In a field that is changing daily, the focus on application of techniques and critical thinking about the strengths and weaknesses of different approaches rather than on details of the latest tools makes time spent with this book a good investment in the future. The case studies in particular help ground the material in the real world of quantitative finance and provide powerful examples of the informed application of AI to finance."

—John Ashley, Ph.D., director of Global Professional Services,
Nvidia

"Doloc's book masterfully distills the complex world of quantitative trading into a clear guide that's an ideal starting point for new, would-be quants. It provides so many fresh insights into the space that even more seasoned practitioners can learn from it."

—James L. Koutoulas, Esq., CEO,
Typhon Capital Management

"Through a series of case studies, Doloc illustrates a number of examples of real-world problems designed to prepare the reader to work in the contemporary world of quantitative finance. I recommend this book to students of financial engineering and quantitative finance, and to all quantitatively oriented participants in all areas of finance."

—Ilya Talman, president,
Roy Talman & Associates, Inc.

Applications of Computational Intelligence
in Data-Driven Trading

Applications of Computational Intelligence in Data-Driven Trading

CRIS DOLOC

Published by John Wiley & Sons, Inc., Hoboken, New Jersey.
Published simultaneously in Canada.

For general information on our other products and services or for technical support, please contact our Customer Care Department within the United States at (800) 762-2974, outside the United States at (317) 572-3993, or fax (317) 572-4002.

Wiley publishes in a variety of print and electronic formats and by print-on-demand. Some material included with standard print versions of this book may not be included in e-books or in print-on-demand. If this book refers to media such as a CD or DVD that is not included in the version you purchased, you may download this material at http://booksupport.wiley.com. For more information about Wiley products, visit www.wiley.com/go/permissions.

Library of Congress Cataloging-in-Publication Data is Available:

ISBN 978-1-119-55050-1 (hardback)
ISBN 978-1-119-55052-5 (ePDF)
ISBN 978-1-119-55051-8 (ePub)

Cover Design: Wiley
Cover Images: © metamorworks/iStock.com, © BiksuTong/Shutterstock, © AVIcon/Shutterstock, © Classica2/Shutterstock

Printed in the United States of America

V10014401_100219

Dedicated to the memory of my father, Emil

Contents

About the Author

Cris Doloc holds a PhD in Computational Physics and worked for more than two decades at the intersection of Quantitative and Computational Finance. He is an accomplished technology leader, who designed and led the implementation of several firm-wide trading, valuation, and risk systems. Cris's expertise extends from enterprise software architecture to High Performance Computing and Quantitative Trading.

Cris is currently teaching at the University of Chicago in the Financial Mathematics program, and is the founder of FintelligeX, a technology platform designed to promote quantitatively data-driven education. He is very passionate about the opportunities that recent developments in Cognitive Computing and Computational Intelligence could bring to the field of Quantitative and Computational Finance.

Acknowledgments

The metamorphosis of my ideas into the format of a book would not have been possible without the participation and help of many people. Unfortunately, I will not be able to name all of them, but I would like to start by thanking Bill Falloon, my editor at Wiley, who was at the origin of this project. Bill believed in this project from the beginning and helped me tremendously to navigate through the very complex and time-consuming process of writing a book. I would also like to thank Michael Henton, Beula Jaculin and Elisha Benjamin from Wiley for all the editorial help they have provided me with throughout this process.

This project could not have been completed without the constant understanding and support of my beloved wife, Lida, and of my precious daughter, Marie-Louise.

I am extremely grateful to my reviewers for their time and invaluable feedback. I would like to thank Professor Dan Nicolae, the Chair of the Statistics Department at the University of Chicago, Professor Roger Lee, the director of the Financial-Mathematics program at the University of Chicago, and Linda Kreitzman, the Executive Director of the MFE program at UC Berkeley, for their guidance and suggestions throughout the review process. I feel privileged to have had among the reviewers of this book some very influential names from the practitioner's realm like:

- Robert Friesen, the President and COO of Bright Trading and the CEO and Director of Education at StockOdds in Vancouver, Canada.
- Dr. Gerald Hanweck, a pioneer in the field of GPU applications to finance, the CEO and founder of *Hanweck Associates, LLC, New York*, a leading provider of real-time risk analytics for global derivatives markets.
- James Koutoulas, Esq., the CEO of Typhon Capital Management, in Chicago.
- Dr. John Ashley, the Director of Global Professional Services at NVidia.
- Dr. Jeff Blaschak, data scientist and the co-founder of Social Media Analytics.
- Dr. Yuri Burlakov, head of the proprietary research group at Volant Trading, New York.
- Ilya Talman, the president of Roy Talman and Associates in Chicago.

I am profoundly grateful to a large group of people that helped me to grow in my career, both as a physicist, and as a quant-technologist. I am deeply grateful to my high school physics teacher, Constantin Vasile, and to my PhD thesis adviser, Dr. Gilles Martin, for instilling in me the love for physics and problem solving. I am also very thankful to many amazing entrepreneurs and business leaders who entrusted me with important projects throughout my career. I would like to acknowledge many of my colleagues and mentors who helped me to shape my current views on how to apply the latest technology to solve the most important problems at hand.

Finally, I would like to thank my students for helping me to understand the importance of promoting problem-solving skills over content acquisition or tools management. The complexity of modern financial markets demands a continuous assimilation of the newest technology available, and a new breed of quant workforce will have to emerge. The quant of the twenty-first century will have to combine classical quant skills with deep knowledge of computer science and hands-on knowledge of modern HPC technologies. My message to them is this: *There is no magic tool other than our own intelligence! Neither AI, nor any other "intelligence"-containing idiom could be a substitute for human intelligence! Our duty as educators is to kindle your interest in innovating, to nurture your problem-solving skills, and to guide your professional development.* My earnest hope is that this book will be a useful device for reaching this purpose!

Cris Doloc, PhD
August 2019, Chicago

About the Website

Additional materials for the book can be found at:

`https://www.fintelligex.com/book`

The website includes the following materials: book's cover and description, table of contents and weblinks to coding resources.

Introduction

"Life on earth is filled with many mysteries, but perhaps the most challenging of these is the nature of Intelligence."

–Terrence J. Sejnowski, computational neurobiologist

Two decades of participation in the digital transformation of the trading industry as a system architect, quant, and trader, coupled with the experience of teaching in the Financial-Mathematics program at the University of Chicago, provided me with a unique perspective that I will convey to the reader throughout this book. As both a practitioner and an educator, I wrote this book to assert the fact that the trading industry was, and continues to be, a very fertile ground for the adoption of cutting-edge technologies.

The central message of this book is that the development of *problem-solving* skills is much more important for the career advancement of a quantitative practitioner than the accretion and mastering of an ever-increasing set of new tools that are flooding both the technical literature and the higher education curricula. While the majority of these tools become obsolete soon after their release into the public domain, acquiring an adequate level of problem-solving expertise will endow the learner with a long-lasting *know-how* that will transcend ephemeral paradigms and cultural trends.

If the use of an exhaustive tool set is providing the solution architect with *horizontal* scalability, mastering the expertise of what tools should be used for any given problem will grant the user with the *vertical* scalability that is absolutely necessary for implementing *intelligent* solutions. While the majority of books about the application of *machine intelligence* to practical problem domains are focused on how to use tools and techniques, this book is built around six different types of problems that are relevant for the quantitative trading practitioner. The tools and techniques used to solve these problem types are described here in the context of the case studies presented, and not the other way around.

MOTIVATION

The impetus to write this book was triggered by the desire to introduce to my students the most recent scientific and technological developments related to the use of *computationally intelligent* techniques in quantitative finance. Given the strong interest of my students in topics related to the use of Machine Learning in finance, I decided to write a companion textbook for the course that I teach in the Financial-Mathematics program, titled Case Studies in Computing for Finance.

Soon after I started working on the book, I realized that this project could also benefit a much larger category of readers, the quantitative trading practitioners. An important motivation for writing this book was to create awareness about the promises as well as the formidable challenges that the era of data-driven decision-making and Machine Learning (ML) are bringing forth, and about how these new developments may influence the future of the financial industry. The subject of *Financial Machine Learning* has attracted a lot of interest recently, specifically because it represents one of the most challenging *problem spaces* for the applicability of Machine Learning.

I want to reiterate that the central objective of this book is to promote the primacy of developing problem-solving skills and to recommend solutions for evading the traps of keeping up with the relentless wave of new tools that are flooding the markets. Consequently the main purpose of this book is pedagogical in nature, and it is specifically aimed at defining an adequate level of engineering and scientific clarity when it comes to the usage of the term *artificial intelligence*, especially as it relates to the financial industry.

The term AI has become the mantra of our time, as this label is used more and more frequently as an *intellectual wildcard* by academicians and technologists alike. The AI label is particularly abused by media pundits, domain *analysts*, and venture capitalists. The excessive use of terms like AI disruption or AI revolution is the manifestation of a systemic failure to understand the technical complexity of this topic. The hype surrounding the so-called *artificial intelligence revolution* is nothing but the most noticeable representation of a data point on Gartner's *hype curve of inflated expectations*.

This hype could be explained eventually by a mercantile impulse of using any opportunity to promote products and services that could benefit from the use of the AI label. It is rather common that a certain level of misunderstanding surrounds novel technology concepts when they are leaving the research labs and are crossing into the public domain. The idea that we are living in an era where the emergence of *in silico* intelligence could compete with human intelligence could very well qualify as "*intellectual dishonesty*", as Professor Michael Jordan from Berkeley said on several occasions. Consequently, one of the main goals of this book is to clarify the terminology and to adjust the expectations of the reader in regard to the use of the term AI in quantitative finance.

Another very important driver behind this book is my own opinion about the necessity of updating the Financial-Mathematics curriculum on two contemporary topics: data-driven decision-making (trading and investing) and Computational Intelligence.

As a result, the first half of this book is dedicated to the introduction of two modern topics:

- *Data-driven trading*, as a contemporary trading paradigm and a byproduct of the fourth scientific paradigm of data-intensive computation.
- *Computational Intelligence*, as an umbrella of computational methods that could be successfully applied to the new paradigm of data-driven trading.

The general confusion created by the proliferation of the term AI is at the same time enthralling and frightening. While *mass fascination* comes from the failure to grasp the complexity of applying *machine intelligence* techniques to practical problems, the fear of an AI-world taking over humanity is misleading, distracting, and therefore counterproductive. Whether or not Science will be able any time soon to understand and properly model the concept of *Intelligence*, enrolling both computers and humans into the fight to enhance human life is a major challenge ahead.

While solving the challenge of understanding *general intelligence* will be quintessential to the development of *Artificial Intelligence* it may also represent the foundation of a new branch of engineering. I will venture to call this new discipline *Quantitative and Computational Engineering* (Q&CE). Like many other classic engineering disciplines that have emerged in the past (e.g. Civil, Electrical, or Chemical), this new engineering discipline is going to be built on already mature concepts (i.e. *information*, *data*, *algorithm*, *computing*, and *optimization*). Many people call this new discipline *Data Science*. No matter the label employed, this new field will be focused on leveraging large amounts of data to enhance human life, so its development will require perspectives from a variety of other disciplines: from quantitative sciences like Mathematics and Statistics to Computational, Business, and Social sciences. One of the main goals of writing this book is to acknowledge the advent and to promote the development of this new engineering discipline that I label *Quantitative and Computational Engineering*.

The intended purpose of this book is to be a practical guide for both graduate students and quantitative practitioners alike. If the majority of books and papers published on the topic of *Financial Machine Learning* are structured around the different types and families of tools, I decided to center this book on practical problems, or *Case Studies*. I took on the big challenge to bridge the perceived gap between the academic literature on quantitative finance, which is sometimes seen as *divorced from the practical reality*, and the world of practitioners that is sometimes labeled as being *short on scientific rigor*. As a result I dedicated the second half of the book to the presentation of a set of Case Studies that are contemporarily relevant to the needs of the financial industry and at the same time representative of the problems that practitioners have to deal with. For this purpose I will consider categories of problems such as trade execution optimization, price dynamics forecast, portfolio management, market making, derivatives valuation, risk, and compliance. By reviewing dozens of recently peer-reviewed publications, I selected what I believed to be the most practical, yet scientifically sound studies that could illustrate the current state-of-the-art in Financial Machine Learning. I earnestly hope that this review of recently published information will be useful and engaging for both Financial-Mathematics students as well as practitioners in quantitative finance who have high hopes for the applicability of Machine Learning, or more generally Computational Intelligence techniques in their fields of endeavor.

Last but not least I hope that other industries and sectors of the digital economy could use the financial industry's adoption model to further their business goals in two main directions: automation and innovation. Therefore, another important motivation in writing this book was to share with decision-makers from other industries (e.g. Healthcare and Education) valuable lessons learned by the financial industry during its digital revolution.

The message that I want to convey in this book is one of confidence in the possibilities offered by this new era of *data-intensive computation*. This message is not grounded on the current hype surrounding the latest technologies, but on a deep analysis of their effectiveness and also on my two decades of professional experience as a technologist, quant, and academic. Throughout my career I was driven by the passion to adopt cutting-edge technologies for as long as they could be useful in solving real-world problems. I wanted to convey this philosophy to my students as well as to the readers of this book. This book is an attempt to introduce the reader to the great potential offered by the new paradigm of Data-Intensive Computing, or to what is called the fourth paradigm of scientific discovery to a variety of industries. Throughout this book I am going to promote the concept of Computational Intelligence as an umbrella of new technologies aimed at augmenting human performance (through automation) and engendering intelligence (via innovation and discovery) with examples from the emerging field of data-driven trading. The use of computer systems to analyze and interpret data, coupled with the profound desire to learn from them and to reason without constant human involvement, is what Computational Intelligence is all about. As a means to convey the message I chose to introduce the reader to the realm of Computational Intelligence by presenting a series of Case Studies that are actionable and relevant in today's markets, as well as modern in their data-driven approach.

TARGET AUDIENCE

This book is primarily intended for students and graduate students who contemplate becoming practitioners in the field of Financial Machine Learning and Computational Intelligence as well as for more-seasoned trading practitioners who are interested in the new paradigm of data-driven trading by using *machine intelligence* methodologies.

Another possible target audience is represented by technologists and decision-makers from other sectors of the economy that currently undergo structural digital transformations and could have a major societal impact, like Education and Healthcare. This very large potential audience could learn extremely useful lessons from the digital revolution that shaped the financial industry in the last 10 to 15 years and could apply similar approaches for the successful early adoption of the newest technology available.

As mentioned before, the main goal of this book is to promote and advocate for the use of Computational Intelligence framework in the field of data-driven trading. Since this is a quite novel and technically advanced topic, I choose to embed this message into a more readable narrative, one that will not exclude readers who may not be very fluent in the language of quantitative and computational sciences. By embedding the main message into a more readable narrative, I hope it will make it more appealing to nontechnical people.

BOOK STRUCTURE

The first part of the book is dedicated to introducing the two main topics of the book: Data-Driven Decision-Making and Computational Intelligence. As such:

- Chapter 1 describes the historical evolution of trading paradigms and the impact that technological progress had on them. A good portion of this chapter is spent on describing the new paradigm of data-driven trading.
- Chapter 2 introduces the reader to the role that data is playing in trading and investing, especially in light of the new data-driven paradigm. This chapter will guide the reader through a fascinating journey from Data to Intelligence.
- Chapter 3 endeavors to *de-noise* the AI hype by introducing an adequate level of scientific clarity for the usage of the term *Artificial Intelligence*, especially as it relates to the financial industry.
- Chapter 4 introduces the framework of Computational Intelligence, as a more realistic and practical framework compared to the AI narrative. Novel approaches to the *solvability* problem are presented and the Probably Approximately Correct framework is introduced.
- Chapter 5 exemplifies the use of Computational Intelligence in Quantitative Finance. It starts with assessing the viability of this methodology in the context of financial data and it presents a brief introduction to Reinforcement Learning as one of the most promising methods used in the next chapters on case studies.

The second part of the book introduces the reader to a series of Case Studies that are representative of the needs of today's financial industry. All the Case Studies presented are structured as follows: an introduction to the problem, a brief presentation on the state-of-the-art in that specific area, a description of the implementation methodology employed, and a presentation of empirical results and conclusions.

- Chapter 6, Case Study 1: *Optimizing trade execution*. This chapter gives a short introduction to the Market Microstructure topic, specifically as it relates to Limit Order Book dynamics in a high-frequency trading context, and then it describes a series of methods for optimizing the Market *impact* problem.

- Chapter 7, Case Study 2 – *Price dynamics forecast*. Several practical examples that use Reinforcement Learning and a variety of Deep Neural Networks are presented.
- Chapter 8, Case Study 3 – *Portfolio management*. This chapter compares the more traditional methods for portfolio construction and optimization with the more modern approaches like Reinforcement Learning and Deep Learning.
- Chapter 9, Case Study 4 – *Market making*. Reinforcement Learning and Recurrent Neural Network algorithms are applied to the problem of liquidity provisioning and several practical examples are presented.
- Chapter 10, Case Study 5 – *Valuation of derivatives*. This chapter introduces the reader to a fascinating new set of applications of ML. Well-established valuation models like Black-Scholes are becoming outdated by the use of Deep Neural Networks and Reinforcement Learning.
- Chapter 11, Case Study 6 – *Financial risk management*. This last chapter dedicated to Case Studies exemplifies understanding and controlling credit, market, operational, and regulatory risk with the help of ML techniques.

The book concludes with Chapter 12, a summary of the three main goals of this book, namely to:

- Describe the new paradigm of Data-Driven Trading and the application of Computational Intelligence techniques to implement it.
- Present from both a scientific and an engineering perspective a critical opinion on the use of the term *Artificial Intelligence* attempting to *de-noise* it.
- Draw the blueprint of a new engineering discipline that in my opinion will be absolutely quintessential to furthering the progress of Computational Intelligence and its applications in Finance and other sectors of the digital economy.

CHAPTER 1

The Evolution of Trading Paradigms

"You never change things by fighting the existing reality. To change something, build a new model that makes the existing model obsolete."

— *Buckminster Fuller, inventor, system theorist*

1.1 INFRASTRUCTURE-RELATED PARADIGMS IN TRADING

Since the beginning of human civilization, commerce has been the main engine of progress. The Cambridge dictionary defines commerce as "the business of buying and selling products and services." The exchange of valuables has been the main driver of progress in any type of economy throughout history, and it was primarily accomplished through trading. The mechanism of trading is considered to have been the main instrument that linked different peoples and acted as the main channel of communication for cultural and intellectual exchange. The primal forms of trade appeared when prehistoric peoples started exchanging valuables for food, shelter, and clothing. The concept of exchange for sustenance became a reality in a physical space known as the *marketplace*. The concept of a *marketplace* as an area designated for the exchange of goods or services became associated with a set of rules to operate within it. As human civilization progressed and the sophistication of trading practices advanced, the need for more modern avenues to trade have become prevalent, and the world of financial instruments was created. Pioneering markets, like the Dojima Rice Market or the Amsterdam Stock Exchange, were the early promoters of modern trading, transacting products such as equities, futures contracts, and debt instruments.

The long history of trading (Spicer 2015) as the main vehicle to exchange valuables and information could be studied by considering the evolution of different trading paradigms. Since a paradigm is a conceptual representation for looking at, classifying, and organizing a specific human endeavor, one can look at trading paradigms from two different perspectives:

- The *infrastructure* required to establish a marketplace, and
- The *methods* required to support and generate trading decisions.

Since the dawn of the financial markets, trading was strongly associated with the technological progress of the time, by heavily employing the most recent break-throughs. This section is meant to be a very brief history of the *love affair* between trading and technology.

1.1.1 Open Outcry Trading

In its earliest manifestation, trading took place in a setting called the *open outcry* system. This mechanism of transacting involved the matching of buyers and sellers through direct, face-to-face verbal communication, where the information exchanged consisted of bids and offer prices that were shouted out loud, thus the *outcry* designation. This primal system of trading developed out of the necessity for market partic-ipants to see and verbally communicate with one another. The technology-enabling direct communication had yet to be invented. Within this early paradigm of trad-ing, the process of price discovery was initiated by an oral auction for a certain asset. As supply and demand forces interplayed, the debate over the value of the auctioned asset was settled. The access to this kind of marketplace was limited both by monopolistic associations and by capital requirements. However, over time the transactions taking place in the *open outcry* system became more securitized and the appetite to engage in speculative trading increased. In order to service the growing demand, the nascent *trading industry* had to consolidate into so-called exchanges, and it started using more and more of the *technology* available at the time. As the demand to access these markets increased, new marketplaces and financial products came into being. The creation of futures and forward contracts enabled extensive hedging practices for agricultural producers. The introduction of bonds serviced corporate and government debt and satisfied the desire of investors and speculators to grow their capital. From the mid-nineteenth century to the late-twentieth century, open outcry markets commenced trading on a large scale and became the backbone of the financial industry.

1.1.2 Advances in Communication Technology

As the vast majority of trading operations remained largely contained to the traditional open outcry marketplaces, the technological progress achieved during the nineteenth and twentieth centuries generated growth in market participation. Inventions like the telegraph, the ticker tape, and the telephone established the foundations for today's computerized trading systems. The invention of the telegraph by Samuel Morse in 1832 was quickly adopted by the trading industry. As a result, financial information was quickly disseminated to areas far away from the usual marketplaces. By the mid-1850s, broker-assisted financial transactions of exchange-based securities became a reality by using the telegraph.

The first *stock ticker* was implemented by the New York Stock Exchange in 1867. Edward Callahan invented the stock ticker by adapting the telegraph technology to transmit up-to-the-minute stock quotes originating at the NYSE nationwide. This new technology created a new service that facilitated the reception of streaming market data by remote traders. The invention of the telephone in 1876 augmented the potential of the telegraph by providing bi-directional means of communication between market participants. As such, the telephone became a fundamental component for the infrastructure of the financial industry as it developed into the industry's standard for interacting remotely with a marketplace.

The development of the *Electronic Numerical Integrator and Computer* (ENIAC) in 1946 marked the beginning of the computer age. This was also a major development in the history of the financial markets. The ENIAC was one of the first digital general-purpose computers that were able to solve a *large class of numerical problems* via reprogramming. The financial industry recognized immediately this event as a technological breakthrough that could be readily adapted to perform many market-related tasks. By the early 1960s, computer-based market data services started to replace the traditional ticker-tape quotation services.

The inventions of the telegraph, ticker tape, and telephone all contributed to the growth of marketplaces and exchanges in both the United States and Europe. When coupled with the computational power developed by the breakthroughs in information systems technology, the stage was set for the rapid evolution of computerized trading systems and electronic trading.

1.1.3 The Digital Revolution in the Financial Markets

With the development of the first computerized stock quote delivery system in the early 1960s, the financial markets began the transition toward full automation. The availability of streaming real-time market quotes made possible the democratization of the financial markets as the dissemination of market information in real-time was a far more efficient medium than using ticker tapes or the telephone.

Instinet was developed in 1969 as the first fully automated system to trade US securities, and this was done by leveraging the digital exchange-based streaming quote technology developed a decade earlier. By using the Instinet trading system, large institutional investors were able to trade *pink sheet* securities directly with one another in a purely electronic over-the-counter (OTC) manner. This event marked the birth of the electronic trading era and the departure from the ancient practice of open outcry. Many new competitors jumped into this very hot market where technology was the name of the game. All traditional *brick-and-mortar* exchanges started automating their trade processing in order to be able to compete in this brave new world where Electronic Communications Networks (ECNs) gained so much traction.

ECNs are digital networks that facilitate the trading of financial products outside traditional exchanges (see Figure 1.1). These digital systems disseminate orders originated by market makers to third parties and allow these orders to be executed against

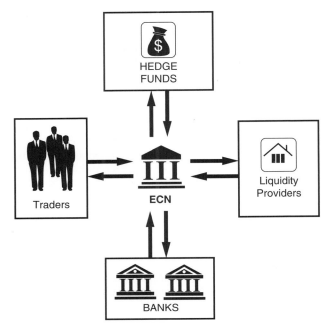

FIGURE 1.1   The ECN concept.

either partially or completely. ECNs are generally passive computer-driven networks that could internally match limit orders by charging a very small transaction fee, making them extremely competitive in the marketplace.

The year 1971 saw the birth of NASDAQ as a fully automated OTC trading system. As Instinet did a few years earlier, NASDAQ employed state-of-the-art information technology systems to create a 100% digital trading infrastructure. This innovative model was soon followed by NYSE, which in 1976 created the Designated Order Turnaround (DOT) system, allowing their member firms to connect electronically direct to the exchange. The SuperDOT system launched in 1984 marked a disruptive leap in equities trade execution in terms of both speed and volume. Ten years later, the SuperDOT system was capable of processing trading volumes of one billion shares per day, with a standard response time from floor to firm of 60 seconds or less.

With all the progress achieved in the digitization of the US equity markets, the open outcry remained the preferred way of trading in many futures and options markets until the turn of the twenty-first century. But as Internet connectivity technology evolved and personal computers became more powerful and affordable, the push toward market automation took over the last open outcry holdovers. During the last decade of the twentieth century, the digital revolution of the financial markets went on full gear driven by both institutional investors as well as individual retail traders.

The diminishing demand for open outcry trading in the United States coupled with the direct competition from the electronic trading markets in Germany and the United

Kingdom provided the conditions for a global move toward the full automation of financial markets. Leading global exchanges like the Chicago Mercantile Exchange launched web-based trading applications (the Globex platform) that enabled clients to trade exclusively using online trading platforms. Just during the last decade of the twentieth century, one billion futures contracts have been traded electronically on the CME Globex platform. This electronic trading paradigm increased the overall efficiency of the marketplace in ways that were not foreseeable just a few decades before. As a result, greater liquidity, narrower bid-ask spreads, lower commissions and fees, and especially the ease to access the markets represented the main gains that the new trading paradigm made possible.

At the same time the critics of the new electronic trading paradigm claimed that the advent of electronic markets enhanced market volatility, facilitated operational fragility due to technology failure, induced a lack of transparency, and created the conditions for market manipulation. Nevertheless it is undeniable that with the advent of the Internet and the personal computer era, the financial markets have become a very dynamic environment where change was the only constant. The pace of change has accelerated so much that all market participants need to stay abreast of the latest technological developments in order to survive in the marketplace. Being at the leading edge of the technology game has become a survival instinct.

1.1.4 The High-Frequency Trading Paradigm

The *High-Frequency Trading* (HFT) paradigm emerged as the result of the very swift technological progress coming from areas such as communication infrastructure and hardware accelerators. It started at the turn of the twenty-first century with the advent of the 10-gigabit ethernet and the PCI Express cards, and it continued later with the availability of ultra-fast fiber-optic lines, wireless towers, and transatlantic submarine cables linking the biggest US financial centers to London, Tokyo, or Hong Kong.

The so-called *race-to-zero* had as an ultimate goal the almost instantaneous end-to-end transmission of market data with the goal of preserving or even enhancing a trader's edge. Expensive collocations facilities enabled trading firms to locate their order processing hardware in very close proximity of financial exchanges. The communication infrastructure had to be paired to extremely fast hardware accelerators that could consume huge amounts of market data in time intervals compatible with the speed of light. Hardware appliances such as Field Programmable Gate Arrays (FPGAs) have been developed to obtain sub-micro-second end-to-end market data processing. HFT became not just a technology consumer but also a major contributing factor to the rapid development of fiber and wireless technology, networking switching appliances, and the importance of developing specialized coding skills.

But the rise of HFT has also created some serious side effects. Because the vast majority of financial transactions are executed by machines in an automated and lightning-fast fashion, a huge barrier of entry was erected for a large majority of market participants, making HFT a very expensive and sometimes unaffordable game.

Some opponents of this trading paradigm believe that HFT preyed on investors and caused flash crashes. These critics claim that HFT created the conditions that traditional market participants are very likely to be transacting against very powerful algorithms with very little chance to profit. Even for the tech-savvy trading firms this high-speed game is converging very rapidly to the law of diminishing returns. Small- to medium-sized trading firms are struggling to profit from investing in the newest technology that will allow an incremental gain in speed. This effect is compounded across the markets by reduced volumes and market volatility. If the 2009 HFT revenues were in the $7 billion to $8 billion range, in 2017 they were below the $1 billion mark.

The combination of exploding operational costs and low volatility has created the conditions for the onset of a new trading paradigm. As visionary traders quickly adopted novel technology several decades ago to conquer the electronic trading landscape, today's traders are in the process of enlisting not just the latest technology, but also the power of Data Science and Computational Intelligence to drive trading decisions that rely more on the power of data than on very expensive technology.

1.1.5   Blockchain and the Decentralization of Markets

Technology and modern financial markets have a good track record of double-feedback: great technology has fueled the progress of financial markets through the creation of new products and even the advent of new trading paradigms; and conversely, the quick progress achieved in the financial markets has enabled and accelerated the development of advanced technologies that have been in turn applied to domains and industries well beyond the financial sector. The so-called *blockchain revolution* is nevertheless a quite unique development in the sense that it changes in a fundamental way the archetype of financial transactions. Some consider the advent of blockchain similar in magnitude and impact to the introduction of the Internet many decades ago. Although the effects will be undeniably long-reaching, it is quite difficult to see all its potential yet. The blockchain technology is undoubtedly an ingenious invention, which has grown to become one of the biggest digital transformations to date. Financial firms and banks have already invested large amounts of resources into this new technology with the goal to maintain or differentiate their competitive edge.

Through a transparent *digital ledger* of transactions and records that are immune to any tampering (change or deletion), the notion of ownership, transfer of value, and payment has gained profoundly new meanings. Through its decentralized environment, the blockchain technology offers increased security, lowers costs, time efficiency, and error resistance, and therefore promises a great impact on a variety of industries. Blockchain's security and transparency promise to protect businesses and investors alike, and it represents the enabling force to removing the middle layers, administration, and reconciliation steps currently hampering the global markets. Modern-day markets need to be built with the interests of all participants at their core. The goal is for trading to become a more seamless experience and for the individual investor to regain trust in the markets. Through decentralization and the use of cryptocurrency, blockchain can provide a safer and more transparent network for trading from both parties.

Currently all financial transactions have to go through a complex chain of clearing houses, banks, and exchanges. This process may take days to verify the ownership of the securities being transacted. The process of trading is quite complex and is involving settlement risk for both parties. There is an inherent lack of trust between parties, and it is by eliminating this type of uncertainty that blockchain can add value. Blockchain provides security and invokes trust mechanisms. By providing heightened visibility it will change how we carry out trade settlements and how we manage counterparty risk. Over $2 trillion is transacted via trading every single day. As the transactions associated with this volume of trading involve the physical exchange of many documents, the large-scale implementation of blockchain could completely revolutionize the whole financial industry. Both post-trade costs as well as settlement times could decrease in a quite dramatic manner. Although there is a lot of optimism already invested in the *blockchain revolution*, the technology is still in its infancy. There are a great number of moral, practical, and technical questions that need to be answered about the organization and the functioning of this new breed of markets, as well as the legal framework to be considered.

1.2 DECISION-MAKING PARADIGMS IN TRADING

As in practically any business endeavor, decision-making is a central aspect of trading and investing. But because the financial markets operate in a fast-changing and extremely competitive environment, the process of making decisions accrues an ever-increased importance. What is markedly different in trading compared to other industries is that the decision to be taken (buy, sell, or hold) is generated by a complex optimization process between a series of trade-offs in order to achieve a given objective. The choices are simply not binary and they are usually more complex than just being *right* or *wrong*. Choosing one trade-off over another is the result of an optimization process that is supported by a series of different paradigms.

The process of decision-making generally involves navigating the problem space instinctually or on autopilot, and by doing so, more often than not, one fails to consider all potential implications and unintended consequences. What behavioral psychology research has shown is that it is vital to recognize that every time one makes a decision, one also makes a trade-off. But with the advent of modern technology, especially as it pertains to the era of *Big Data*, the dynamics of certain trade-offs could be dramatically altered. By better understanding the parameters of the problem space, one could potentially make better decisions. Since change is the only constant in today's business landscape, the decision-making process needs to be data dependent.

What makes today's decision-making process much more amenable to optimization is the availability of an extremely wide range of technology choices, the availability of various types of data at scale, as well as recent advances in understanding the psychology of the behavioral process involved in decision-making. Behavioral Finance is a well-established field of research, and it studies the psychology of irrationality in human decision-making in the area of financial markets. Experimental psychologists have already built a substantial body of knowledge demonstrating biases and shortcomings in expert decision-making in general, and their applications to the financial markets are already available.

From a decision-making perspective, the history of the financial markets could be classified into several periods:

- Discretionary trading
- Systematic trading
- Algorithmic trading
- Data-driven trading

These periods correspond to the adoption of different scientific and engineering paradigms: from largely ignoring systemic experimental evidence by relying on our own biases or a set of empirical rules (in discretionary trading), to the use of rule-based systems (as in systematic trading), and from the use of computationally implemented algorithms (as in algo-trading), to the more recent paradigm of data-driven trading – a parallel to a fourth paradigm introduced by computer scientist Dr. Jim Grey (Hey, Tansley, and Tolle 2009).

1.2.1   Discretionary Trading

Discretionary trading is commonly defined as a paradigm of trading based on a set of empirical rules that traders tend to follow throughout their trading career. These rules could be modified or replaced based on a trader's experience, performance, and their survivability. Some discretionary traders follow these rules rigorously while others tend to experiment until the time they feel they have cracked the code and continue to make required modifications in their strategy. A discretionary trader makes decisions based on a large variety of *signals*: from pure *gut-feeling* to news-driven signals or the study of market charts. The trader makes all decisions in discretionary trading (i.e. when to enter or exit positions). In discretionary trading, maximum risk originates from decisions taken under the influence of uncontrolled emotions by the trader. In most cases, these emotions can lead to decisions (trades) which cannot be logically defended. Hence in order to make a profit, it becomes extremely important not to just have a profitable strategy, but also have a check on one's emotions.

1.2.2   Systematic Trading

Systematic trading is a trading paradigm that defines specific trade goals and the associated set of rules and the ways and means to control the risk associated. This trading style is also known as *mechanical trading* because all investment and trading decisions are made in a methodical fashion (Carver 2015).

Systematic trading covers both manual trading and fully or partially automated trading. This style of trading relies mostly on technical rules but also on using fundamental analysis. Systematic trading is pretty much the antithesis of discretionary trading that could be influenced by emotions, could not be easily back tested, and where the control of risk is less rigorous. Systematic trading represents a large umbrella of methods that cover also the field of quantitative trading.

An example of a systematic trading approach will be the replication of an equity index using futures and stocks. Starting with the creation of a replication basket and analyzing the correlations between different components, the systematic trading strategy will be first back-tested on historical data, and then a profit and loss (P&L) analysis will be generated to include transaction costs, rollovers, stop-loss orders, and all other wanted risk controls. After the historical back-test was performed and the P&L report was analyzed, the strategy will be used *live* for signal generation while trying to optimize the P&L and controlling continuously the risks.

In general any systematic trading strategy should include components for:

- Data management – for both real-time and historical data.
- Signal generation – create buy and sell signals according to predefined strategies.
- Portfolio and P&L tracking.
- Risk management – defining portfolio exposure.
- Execution and routing of the orders.

A key component of any systematic trading system is the back-testing module that is used to verify the fitness of different strategies before being traded live. A prerequisite is to have easy and robust access to historical trading data. A very good review for all these techniques could be found in de Prado's recently published book (de Prado 2018). Any systematic trading strategy should take seriously the importance of risk management by using a methodical approach to quantify the trading risk and the quantity limits and to define how to close excessively risky positions. This approach lends itself very well to controlling the risk because it allows portfolio managers to define profit targets, allowable losses, and trade size objectively and in advance of entering any trade.

1.2.3 Algorithmic Trading

Algorithmic trading (algo-trading) is one of the progenies of the third industrial revolution and of the new era of digital computers. Also known as automated trading or black-box trading, algo-trading is the process of using a proprietary set of instructions (an algorithm) implemented on a digital computer in order to generate a profitable trade at a speed and frequency that is beyond the ability of a human trader (Aldridge 2010).

The algorithmic trading rules are based on timing, price, quantity, or any mathematical model. Aside from creating profit opportunities for traders, algo-trading contributes to the generation of impressive amounts of liquidity in the financial markets and makes trading more systematic by ruling out the impact of human emotions on trading activities.

Among the wide variety of trading strategies employed by algorithmic traders the most common ones are:

- Trend following
- Arbitrage trading
- Mathematical-based models (e.g. delta-neutral)
- Mean-reversion or range trading
- Volume-weighted and time-weighted average price trading
- Implementation shortfall

The main benefits of algorithmic trading are:

- Execution of transactions is done at the best possible prices
- Instant and accurate trade order placement
- Reduced transaction costs and risk of manual errors in placing orders
- The possibility to back-test strategies on historical and real-time data
- Reduced impact of human errors based on emotional and psychological factors

Algorithmic trading is used nowadays in a variety of forms by the trading and investment community. The main categories are:

- Mid- to long-term investors like buy-side firms – pension funds, mutual funds, insurance companies – are using algo-trading to purchase securities in large quantities in such a way that prices are not influenced by large-volume purchases.
- Short-term traders and sell-side participants like market makers, speculators, hedgers, and arbitrageurs. They could also benefit from automated trade execution.
- Systematic traders like trend followers, hedge funds, or pair traders find algo-trading to be much more efficient to implement their trading rules and let the program trade automatically.

Algorithmic trading is also exhibiting some drawbacks, specifically as it relates to how quickly an algorithmic error could escalate into a systemic problem for most of the market participants. Since a single algorithm can trigger a very large amount of transactions in a very short amount of time, when for some reason something goes wrong, considerable amounts of money could be lost in that same time frame. There have been multiple incidents of *flash crashes* on global markets resulting from problems with algorithmic trading.

One example is the so-called Flash Crash of 2010, which led US stock indexes to collapse for a short period of time after recovering. Algorithmic trading has also been linked to significant market volatility. While quality control measures could help prevent losses due to poorly defined or coded algorithms, market participants are keenly aware of the dangers of fully automating the trading workflow.

1.3 THE NEW PARADIGM OF DATA-DRIVEN TRADING

The globalization of asset trading, coupled with the emergence of ultrafast communications and high-performance computing technology, has made it impossible for humans to efficiently compete with algorithms in the low-level decision-making process. Nowadays most of the micro-level trading decisions in the listed markets are made by algorithms that define how to execute a trade (at what price and quantity) and where to route the order. Given the very complex nature of the modern financial markets, trading algorithms have to operate on multiple levels of granularity. The decision-making process is generally driven by market data and quantitative models. Up until very recently the trading algorithms were a mixture of quantitative models expressing a *scientific* view of the world, and heuristic rules which expressed the very *practical experience* and preferences of human traders. The logic of a traditional trading algorithm is generally encapsulated in tens of thousands lines of code. These *human-coded* algorithms have to be continuously maintained, tweaked, or improved to handle the ever-changing nature of the markets. The financial industry is also heavily regulated by placing some very specific requirements on the participants. Achieving the desired efficiency in trading while conforming to all the regulatory constraints is becoming a huge challenge for most of the trading firms. The possibility of using a data-centric approach to this problem presents itself as a very attractive opportunity to the financial industry.

As computing technologies are developing at an exponential rate and data generation is completely transforming our society, the financial industry is sensing the powerful impact that data could have in its own future. And this impact seems to be more of a splash than a ripple. Historically, the financial industry has relied on very accurate and timely inputs into its decision-making models. Traditionally, numbers were crunched by humans and decisions were made based on inferences drawn from these computations and models. Nowadays, computers are operating in this environment by using inputs from a multitude of sources and performing computations at a massive scale in order to generate more accurate outcomes almost instantaneously.

The history of trading is intertwined with the history of human civilization. No matter what paradigm was driving the trading style of a certain epoch, the success in trading was always dependent on three attributes that transcend time:

- Good knowledge of the market – what to trade
- Acute sense of timing – when to trade
- Ability to adjust quickly to the most current market conditions

If the first attribute – market knowledge – could be acquired through education and experience, the second one – market timing – is more of an aptitude that is characteristic to successful traders and therefore has an important survivorship bias. The third attribute, the ability to rapidly adapt to changing market conditions, is what one calls nowadays data-driven trading.

As a relatively new field of research and as a new paradigm, data-driven trading draws inspiration from a vast repository of trading knowledge as well as from

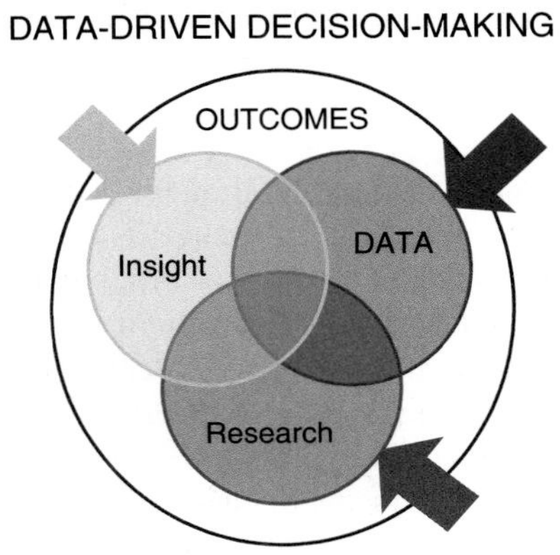

DATA-DRIVEN DECISION-MAKING

FIGURE 1.2   The data-driven trading concept.

the multidisciplinary field of Data Science (see Figure 1.2). The *wisdom* of markets claims that past performance is not indicative of future performance – or in other words, one should not care much about past performance, but instead try to forecast how well a strategy is going to perform in the future. On the other hand, Data Science teaches that historical data is the only vehicle that one could utilize to train the learning models on. Equally important is the fact that not all aspects of past data are likely to occur in the future.

Adapting to current market conditions is not a new endeavor. What is really new is the ability of market participants to tap into a huge data pool, be it pure market data (historical or real-time), or what one calls alternative data. The world of alternative data is developing at a very rapid pace, and it is becoming a very fashionable tool for investment management firms that are seeking alpha. From geolocation information to credit card transactions, from social media content to product reviews and customer feedback, the market for alternative data is growing very fast and is expanding the realm of traditional market data sources.

But the availability of large amounts of data to assist in the decision-making process is not enough. A complex algorithmic infrastructure is also required to extract actionable information from this data. The advent of Computational Intelligence techniques to perform this knowledge extraction was a major step forward in the development of data-driven trading.

Nevertheless, there are still major hurdles that need to be addressed:

- Given the very nature of financial markets, which are fundamentally nonlinear and nonstationary processes, the learning process from past data needs to be coupled with other exogenous techniques that could signal major departures from *stable* conditions, and the need to retrain the learning algorithms on more relevant data sets.
- Sometimes the algorithms that properly model a current market situation could not be coded, either because their algorithmic complexity is too high or because

they are not *encode-able* using current *hard* computing techniques. This subject
will be addressed in Chapter 4 when we will introduce the concepts of Computational Intelligence and *soft* computing.

Having foresight of market directionality is every investor's dream, and this is
driving financial investment firms to mine for data in the digital information economy
(rather than for gold). Traders and investors have traditionally based their decisions
on fundamentals, intuition, and analysis drawn from traditional financial data sources.
In the new data-driven paradigm, High Performance Computing and Computational
Intelligence tools offer a more robust framework to generate data-driven profits.

Computational Intelligence techniques differ fundamentally from the ubiquitous
factor-driven style used by traditional quantitative methods that account nowadays
for about $1.5 trillion in total assets under management (AUM). These *factor-driven*
approaches model the markets through a simplified, linearly constrained lens.
Computational Intelligence, on the other hand, could integrate a multidimensional
set of perspectives into each investment decision through an ensemble of different
models by synthesizing the most pertinent information to guide decision-making.
Compared to a stylized and simplistic traditional quantitative approach, Computational Intelligence has more in common with a human-driven approach by
combining the most appropriate aspects of data-driven modeling techniques with
guiding human-like rationales.

Traders and investors value information above everything else. The difference
between success and failure depends heavily on what information they may have
available to reach the proper decisions: from what they see on their screens to how to
search through the right information at the right time in order to make the right trade
in a fast-paced financial market. Relying only on traditional sources of financial data
is no longer sufficient to ensure success in the markets.

Using alternative data in their decision-making processes is becoming increasingly
common for traders and investors alike. The use of alternative data offers market participants a firsthand glance into the markets beyond the traditional lenses, highlighting
new information and dynamics to complement their existing knowledge. Even more
so, the access to real-time information from alternative data sources gives traders a
competitive advantage to quickly harness new insights, assess situations, and make
critical business decisions as events unfold. One of the shortcomings of this universe
of alternative data sets is represented by its expanse and the speed at which it is bom-
barding the users with hundreds of data streams at once.

The primary source of alternative data is represented by the social media. A single
tweet from a prominent figure could roil the markets. Other sources of publicly available alternative data are blogs, satellite information, or even retail sites that could
provide a wealth of contextual information. But because the range of alternative
data sources is incredibly broad, the intrinsic value of each source is highly dependent on context. Most of the time, combining multiple data points from a variety of
sources could provide traders and investors with significant insights to sharpen their
competitive edge. The use of alternative data provides traders and investors with a
more complete picture of the market. The more traditional pricing data sets and press

releases lack critical, real-time context. By incorporating time-sensitive information into their execution workflows, market participants could expand and deepen their views of market events. There are situations in which alternative data could explain recent market movements in or could even forecast a market move. By the time information is widely publicized it is usually too late to profit from that information.

Despite the growing adoption by traders and investors alike, the data-driven approach is still in its infancy. Major challenges remain to be addressed by both individual users and the financial firms that are looking to incorporate this new paradigm into their existing processes. The users of this new trading paradigm need to learn how to derive actionable insights from all data available and ultimately how to drive better trading decisions. With an enormous amount of data currently available, it's becoming increasingly difficult and expensive for trading firms, and especially for individual market participants, to capture it, let alone to make use of it.

The biggest challenge is to summarize information that by its very nature is complex and unstructured. This is where the latest developments in Computational Intelligence and specifically in Machine Learning come into play. The new data-driven trading paradigm is going to be a big consumer of Computational Intelligence and Machine Learning techniques. By applying these algorithmic methods to the newly expanded financial and alternative data sets, the data-driven paradigm is looking to discover consistently predictive features and potentially useful patterns about the markets beyond what is currently available from traditional financial data sources. This new data-driven trading paradigm will create the conditions for both traders and investors to trade more accurately and informedly.

REFERENCES

Aldridge (2010). *High Frequency Trading: A Practical Guide to Algorithmic Strategies and Trading Systems*. Hoboken, NJ: Wiley, 153–178.

Carver (2015). *Systematic Trading: A Unique New Method for Designing Trading and Investing Systems*. Hampshire, UK: Harriman House, pt. 3.

de Prado (2018). *Advances in Financial Machine Learning*. Hoboken, NJ: Wiley, 23–89.

Hey, Tansley, and Tolle (2009). Jim Gray on eScience: a transformed scientific method. In *The Fourth Paradigm: Data-Intensive Scientific Discovery* (ed. Hey, Tansley, and Tolle). Redmond, WA: Microsoft Research. http://itre.cis.upenn.edu/myl/JimGrayOnE-Science.pdf.

Spicer (2015). Tools of the trade: an historical look at technology and commerce. Computer History Museum. http://www.computerhistory.org/atchm/tools-of-the-trade-an-historical-look-at-technology-and-commerce.

CHAPTER 2

The Role of Data in Trading and Investing

"The secret to being successful from a trading perspective is to have an inde-fatigable, an undying and unquenchable thirst for information and knowledge."

— Paul Tudor Jones, famous investor, hedge fund manager

2.1 THE DATA-DRIVEN DECISION-MAKING PARADIGM

Due to an extraordinary wave of technological innovation our civilization has reached a critical phase in its evolution. Because our ability to collect and analyze massive amounts of data, conditions have been created for the development and implementation of a new paradigm to assist the decision-making process: data-driven decision-making.

This process is driven by several factors:

- **VALUE**: Due to the high costs associated with the process of collecting, cleansing, and hosting data, as well as the potential future business value, organizations are considering their data as a strategic asset.
- **CULTURE**: Global competition forces corporations to adhere to the new *data culture*, where high-quality data, broad access, and data literacy are the baseline requirements.
- **RELIABILITY**: Ultimately, the decision-making process needs to become more transparent, reproducible, and the desired business outcomes need to be more forecast-able. Data as the *single source of truth* is becoming a central theme of this new paradigm.

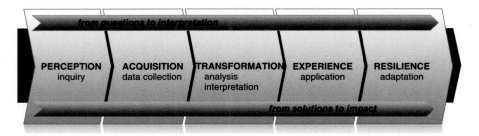

FIGURE 2.1   The data-driven process.

Having access to what one calls a *single source of truth* will lend higher value to the end user of any service or product, as it does for the decision-makers. Efficiency will be enhanced by spending less time in gathering data from across fragmented data stores, yet allocating more time to data analysis and the extraction of actionable knowledge. By providing a richer context about the problem domain, the users will be better positioned to leverage their access to data and find actionable insights.

Traditionally the decision-making process was driven by individuals who could override signals coming from data at any point in time. The so-called HiPPO, or the *highest paid person's opinion*, a term introduced by Avinash Kaushik (n.d.), are usually the *experts* with decades of experience in the problem domain. They may not see data as a relevant part of the decision-making process, especially when this data disagrees with their preconceived notions.

Data-driven decision making is going to require a cultural change in business practice since it will mandate migrating from the current prevailing culture, where intuition is valued more than evidence-based metrics, to a place where data is going to represent the main *source of truth*. The new data-oriented culture will promote data as the main vehicle for objective examination and experimentation. Nevertheless, changing the corporate culture from intuition to evidence-based metrics will require a broad data literacy training of the workforce, from engineers and data scientists to data-trusting managers and decision-makers.

An absolutely necessary intermediary step in creating this culture change is to become *data-informed*. This translates into blending intuition and data to come up with testable hypotheses about a business decision to be made. The qualitative aspects will complement the quantitative ones, and vice versa.

In conclusion:

- Data is at the center of the *data-driven* decision-making paradigm (see Figure 2.1). It is the primary – and sometimes the only – input required. This paradigm relies on data alone to decide the best path forward.
- In *data-informed* decision-making, data is a key input among many other variables. One uses the data to build a deeper understanding of the value one provides to decision-makers.

2.2   THE DATA ECONOMY IS FUELING THE FUTURE

The explosion of technological innovation has created a deluge of new sources of data. The most conspicuous manifestation of this development is reflected in both the immense volume of data produced by the digital economy and the enhanced ability to process it.

Data is quickly becoming the *fuel* of the new digital economy and the algorithms are the engines to burn this *fuel* (Ng 2017). What is truly remarkable is that the data is not merely an output of the fourth industrial revolution, but it is quickly becoming its own fuel. Data has become an asset that could be traded. Implementing a novel methodology to evaluate the commercial value of different types of data is complex and could have far-reaching implications.

Data is representing for the current industrial revolution what oil and steam were for the first one: a driver of growth and change. But data, as the main by-product of the Digital Information age is unlike any of previous resources: it can be extracted, refined, valued, and exchanged in a variety of ways. This ever-changing process adjusts continuously the rules that markets are operating on, and it demands new approaches from the market participants. Today's cloud computing infrastructure is becoming the new refinery of the twenty-first century, where data gets collected, refined, and monetized. In 2016, Amazon, Google, and Microsoft spent together more than \$35 billion in capital expenditure and capital leases to build this new type of refinery according to the *Wall Street Journal*.

The new data economy thrives on analyzing real-time streams of generally unstructured data: either petabytes of information generated by social media users or the flood of data collected from hundreds of sensors in a jet engine. From heavy equipment to consumer accessories, all sorts of devices are becoming sources of data. Because the world is filled with connected sensors, most of the activity will leave a digital trail wherever and whenever it happens. Some of the players in this new space are becoming data *producers*, and they are usually companies that control the data flow; some other ones are becoming *aggregators and custodians* of this data. On the next layer of the data stack there are new entrants that provide the technology platforms; this service layer is supplemented by *insight providers* and *data presenters*, as they leverage their access to data by interfacing with the end consumer and by creating valuable user experiences. And finally there are prospective players who cannot immediately participate in the data economy but who are actively looking for opportunities to play a critical role in the very near future.

As the new data economy grows, rapid changes in both technological advancements and customer expectations will transform the supply chains into very complex ecosystems. Corporate strategies will evolve, and collaboration across ecosystems will create novel open flows of ideas and information. Companies will define their role in this new data economy by evaluating their potential to engage in these ecosystems. As innovation is becoming more and more driven by data, there is a renewed hope that a number of societal challenges could be addressed by this new paradigm:

from tackling traffic congestion and improving water and air quality, to developing novel medical diagnostics, or just to make businesses more productive.

2.2.1 The Value of Data – Data as an Asset

The participants in the first three industrial revolutions had to manage tangible assets such as property, equipment, inventory, or cash – and eventually intellectual property. But in today's digital world, a new type of asset is emerging: the data. Companies are collecting, analyzing, and reporting very large volumes of data. Data is becoming a key metric in whether a company will remain competitive in the digital era. Collecting and analyzing data is increasingly becoming easier and cheaper. More and more data is being exchanged within and among the participants in the new digital economy. This has generated a new economy built upon using data to generate value through both internal and external means. A recent report from the Organization for Economic Cooperation and Development (OECD 2015) estimated that the global volume of data in 2015 was of about 8 zettabytes (8 trillion gigabytes, or 8 followed by 21 zeros), an order of magnitude increase from 2010. The forecast for 2020 points to an increase of up to 40 times over, as new technologies will create vast new data sets.

However, the massive volume of available data is not the only indicator of economic value. As most of the data is unstructured (e.g. text, social media content, pictures and videos, or the exhaust data generated as a by-product of business), its value is very hard to assess. As long as such data is inaccessible for analysis, its potential value will remain unrealized. But the advent of recent advances in data processing (cloud storage and computing) and algorithms will enable new economic actors to unlock new insights from their data assets (e.g. trends, patterns, or associations).

The potential to turn data into useful business insights is the major factor in creating economic value. These insights could be used by decision-makers to optimize the resource allocation of and tackle new business opportunities. Research (Brynjolfsson et al. 2011) has shown that firms adopting data-driven decision-making can have a much higher output and productivity. Data also plays an essential role in the development of automating Machine Intelligence. These cutting-edge R&D domains hold a significant potential for economic growth, with prognosis suggesting that by 2030, they could increase the world GDP by a factor of 10%. The value of data is constantly increasing at this stage of the fourth industrial revolution. Although companies like Facebook and Google initially used the data they collected from users mainly to target better advertising, more recently they discovered that the same data can be turned into any number of *cognitive* services, some of which will generate new sources of revenue (*The Economist* 2017). These services could include translation, visual recognition, or profiling someone's personality by analyzing their purchasing behavior, all of which can be sold to marketers.

The twenty-first-century data refiners are ready to exploit a powerful economic engine called the *data-network effect*. This is the process of using data to attract more users, who then could generate more data, which in turn could help to improve services that will attract more users, and so on. The tech giants are pumping this data from the most bountiful sources. The more users write comments, or otherwise engage via social media channels, the more *the system* learns about those users and the better targeted the ads on newsfeeds could become. *Data-driven* startups are the trailblazers of the new data economy. In their quest for the *digital oil*, they will extract value and turn insights into clever new services. These *digital wells* are becoming attraction points for tech giants. As such, GE developed an *operating system* for the industrial Internet, named Predix, to help customers control their heavy machinery. But Predix is also a data-collection system: it *pumps* data from devices it is connected to, fuses it with other data, and then trains the algorithms that can help improve the operations or help maintain a jet engine before it breaks down.

But there is one aspect of the data economy that would look very atypical to dealers in the oil market: if oil is the world's most traded commodity by value, then data by contrast, is more difficult to be traded or monetized, at least in the current environment. The data economy may infer the existence of thriving digital markets (*The Economist* 2017); but as it stands, it is currently mostly a collection of independent silos. This absence of global markets for data is the result of the same factors that have contributed to the creation of the data firms. All kinds of *transaction costs* (e.g. information search, deal negotiation, and contract enforcing) make it simpler and more efficient to bring these activities in-house. It is often more profitable to generate and use data inside a company than to buy and sell it on an open market.

Even in the era of *Big Data*, data streams are not yet a commodity: each stream of information is different in terms of timeliness and completeness. This lack of *fungibility* makes it difficult for buyers to find a specific set of data and to put a price on it; the valuation process is poorly understood. As such there is a profound lack of incentive to trade, as each side will worry about *mispricing*. As some researchers have begun to develop data pricing methodologies, a new field called *infonomics* has emerged. One of its pioneers is Professor Jim Short (2017) of the University of California in San Diego. The pricing difficulty is an important reason why one firm might find it simpler to acquire another, even if it is mainly interested in its data. In 2015, IBM reportedly spent $2 billion on the Weather Company, just to get its hands on mountains of weather data as well as the infrastructure to collect them. Another field of interest is barter deals: parts of Britain's National Health Service and DeepMind, Alphabet's AI division, have agreed to swap access to anonymous patient data for medical insights extracted from them.

As an added complication in the process of valuation, and unlike oil as a commodity, the digital information can be copied and used by more than one customer (or algorithm) at a time. This means that data can be eventually used for other purposes than those agreed in a contract. And at the end of day, who will own the data? Is it the manufacturer, the user, or the service provider? According to Hal Varian (2006), Google's chief economist, data exhibits decreasing returns to scale, that is, each additional piece of data is somewhat less valuable and at some point collecting more does not add anything. Google's belief is that value is retrieved solely in the quality of the algorithms that process the data and implicitly in the technical talent of the firm that has developed the data. Google's success is about recipes and not ingredients.

2.3   DEFINING DATA AND ITS UTILITY

"Torture the data, and it will confess to anything."
                                             – Ronald Coase, Nobel prize in Economics

Since data is at the core of this chapter, we need to define it. The term *data* is one of the most overused terms in today's culture. What is really the meaning of data? According to some experts, data is a set of "unorganized and unprocessed facts, raw numbers, figures, images, words and sounds derived from observations or measurements." Wikipedia (2019) defines data as "the values of subjects with respect to qualitative and quantitative variables." Very often, yet incorrectly, data and information are used interchangeably. From an information theory perspective, data is a precursor to information as characterized by its Shannon entropy measure: *The information entropy is the average rate at which information is produced by a stochastic source of data.* The word data has been present in the English language since 1640, and it started to shine in the 1940s at the dawn of the computer era. The origin of the word data could be found in the Latin language, where data is the plural of datum, which means a given thing. In today's English language, data is treated as an undifferentiated collection (like "sand" or "rain") and it is generally used in the singular.

Data is a very general concept, and it is used to encode or represent information and knowledge into formats that are suitable for processing. As a vague set of *things* (facts, figures, etc.) data is generally obtained through measurements, and after it is collected, it gets analyzed and eventually reported through visualization tools: graphs, images, and other statistical and summarization tools. Before being *processed*, data is considered to be *raw data*. The data *cleaning* process is often ambiguous and generally domain specific: outliers are removed and instrumentation errors get corrected. Depending on the context in which data was collected (e.g. in an *observational* study or as a result of a *controlled* experiment), causality could be inferred or not from the data.

Data could come in different types, but the two main flavors are:

- **Quantitative** describes objects whose properties could be *measured or valued objectively* (e.g. geometrical dimensions, areas, volumes, prices, or physical properties such as temperature or pressure). This type of data could be continuous or discrete.

- **Qualitative** describes characteristics of objects that are difficult to measure, but that can be observed in a subjective manner (e.g. smells, tastes, textures, or attractiveness).

Another method of classifying data refers to the degree of complexity by which it is organized and structured, and it relates to the ease of searching through it.

There are two main categories (see Figure 2.2):

- **Structured** is represented by repeatable patterns that make data easily searchable by computer algorithms (e.g.. spreadsheets, databases).

Structured data

Unstructured data

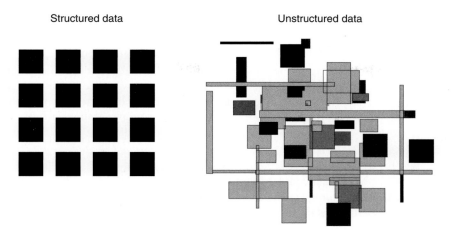

FIGURE 2.2   Structured vs. unstructured data.

- **Unstructured** is represented in a much more complex fashion that is similar in nature to the human language; the searching process becomes extremely challenging, sometimes unfeasible.

By blending these criteria together data could be classified in one of the following four different categories (see Figure 2.3):

1. *Numerical data is of a quantitative flavor, and it could be either discrete or continuous.*
   - Continuous data represents measurable properties of objects, where their possible values cannot be counted, but they can only be described using real number intervals.
   - Discrete data represents items that can be counted, and they could take on possible values that can be listed in a discrete manner. The list of possible values may be finite or infinite. When data is represented in a numeric format, it is usually used for a quantitative representation of the object studied.

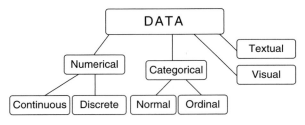

FIGURE 2.3   Types of data.

With numerical data one could represent:

○ Distributions on different scales (e.g. linear, log-linear, or curve-linear)

○ Graphics (e.g. histograms, kernel densities, fitted distributions)

○ Regression and apply methods (e.g. regularization, ridge, lasso, or boosting).

Since numerical data could be very sensitive to variance, a feature that could come from either the measurement process or the generative process, it is very important to ensure that one uses the proper scaling in order to extract the optimal amount of information from the data.

2. *Categorical data is a form of data describing categorical variables or data that has been converted into that form, like binned data.*

Categorical data could be derived from observations made of qualitative data that are summarized as counts or cross-tabulations, or from observations of quantitative data grouped within given intervals. Purely categorical data could be summarized in the form of a contingency table. Generally, in the data analytics parlance one uses the term *categorical data* to any data sets that, while containing some categorical variables, may also contain non-categorical variables. A categorical variable that can take on just two values is termed a binary variable or *dichotomous* variable. Some categorical variables could take on more than two possible values and they are called *polytomous* variables. Categorical variables are generally assumed to be *polytomous* unless otherwise specified. Categorical data could also be classified into:

○ Normal (regular) data – where observations could be assigned labels that cannot be ordered.

○ Ordinal data – where labeled observations could be ranked (put in order). These observations could be both counted and ordered.

By using discretization one can transform continuous data into a categorical form. On the other hand, techniques like regression analysis could sometimes transform categorical variables into one or more quantitative dummy variables.

The main utility of categorical data is to encode categorical features that are used for the Representation, Classification, and Evaluation of Machine Learning algorithms:

○ *Representation* – used for ordering ranks, visualizing data *missingness*, re-binning, or for model selection;

○ *Classification* – used in combination with methods such as trees, boosting, Support Vector Machines, or Neighbor-based classifiers;

○ *Evaluation* – used for assessing a classifier accuracy, precision, or recall, as well as for any other parameters of the ROC-AUC (Receiver Operating Characteristic–Area Under the Curve) or Confusion matrix.

3. *Textual or Linguistic data is an unstructured type of data, and it comprises speech and text databases, lexicons, text corpora, and other metadata-added textual resources used for language and linguistic research.* Given the unstructured nature of textual data, its analysis is very complex.

Extracting knowledge from textual data requires special text analytics tools such as Natural Language Processing or Computational Linguistics. These analytics tools could be used to assess the *mood* of a tweet or the *truthfulness* of a product review. In a clinical setting, text analysis can add context to test results and other forms of quantitative medical data.

Typical applications of this kind of unstructured data are:

○ Analyzing clinical notes from a healthcare records database
○ Sentiment analysis using social media data feeds
○ Quantitative and qualitative analysis of financial markets based on newsfeed information

The process of textual data analysis includes Extraction and Normalization of linguistic features, from orthographic features, to semantic and lexical ones. Through a technique called *vectorization*, linguistic features could be transformed into either numerical or categorical features, therefore structuring data that is unstructured in nature.

4. ***Visual** data is a structured type of data, and it encodes features such as color, intensity, texture, or shape.* Visual data is generally collected from light sensors, including cameras, scanners, and devices such as the Microsoft Kinect.

According to numerous medical studies, the human brain responds to and processes visual data much better than any other type of data. The human brain processes images 60,000 times faster than text, and more than 90 percent of information transmitted to the brain is visual. Since humans are visual by nature, one could use this skill to enhance data processing and organizational effectiveness. Visual data analysis is becoming a large field of research and development, and it includes techniques such as segmentation, convolution, smoothing, or pattern matching.

Visual analytics has become an integrative approach by combining visualization, psychology, and data analysis. Besides visualization and data analysis, areas of cognition and perception play an important role in the communication between the human and the computer, as well as in the decision-making process.

This goal of this section is to define data in the context of knowledge extraction and to define its main categories. Finding one definition for data that fits all its possible uses is not practical, and therefore the idea is to define data in the context of its use.

I will define data as the artifact employed to *encode* the surrounding reality. It is an orthogonal dimension to the concept of Algorithm, which is the complementary device used to *decode* or understand the world around us.

From a physicist's perspective, data is nothing more than a *messenger* of the surrounding reality and a reflection of its phenomena. From a computer scientist's perspective, data is an *encoding* for the properties of the objects that one studies.

The next step in our journey to understand the utility of data is to seek the ultimate reward – extracting actionable Intelligence from data via a process that is quite often misunderstood and very opaque. On its own, data is nothing more than meaningless noise that needs to be captured, filtered, and analyzed in order to decipher from it the true meaning of the process that generates it. More often than not the generative process is hiding behind the scenes and can be brought to light.

2.4 THE JOURNEY FROM DATA TO INTELLIGENCE

The ability to extract actionable insights from data is absolutely critical to the discovery and innovation process. The last decade has seen the emergence of a new interdisciplinary field labeled *Data Science* (see Figure 2.4).

This relatively new discipline, according to Wikipedia, uses "scientific methods, processes, algorithms and systems to extract knowledge and insights from structured and unstructured data." From a practical perspective Data Science studies the processes and systems that could enable the extraction of actionable insights from data. Data Science has evolved as an interdisciplinary field that integrates approaches from statistics (e.g. data mining and predictive analytics) with advances in scalable computing and data management. As a discipline, Data Science is only in its infancy.

The *raison d'être* for Data Science is to accomplish a very lofty goal: *extracting actionable Intelligence from Data in order to drive better business decisions!*

For this goal to become a reality, a lot of effort has to be directed toward understanding the process of how data could lead to business intelligence (see Figure 2.5). Modeling this very complex transformation involves distilling Data into meaningful Information and encoding it into Knowledge to eventually achieve the desired outcome: actionable Intelligence.

The journey from raw Data to Intelligence (see Figure 2.6) is the subject of this section. This evolutionary process was studied for some time and there are several frameworks that have been proposed. From Kenneth Boulding (1955) in the 1950s, to Russell Ackoff (1989) in the 1980s, many researchers attempted to model the transformation of Data into a superior form, Intelligence (Schoech et al. 2002).

- This metamorphosis starts with the capturing of signals from the environment in its rawest and most unfiltered form: the **Data**. This *digital ore* could be a set of symbols, a signal, or just a collection of facts. The output of the initial distillation process, coupled with the contextualization of the Data, will identify patterns that in turn will be structured into Information.

FIGURE 2.4   Data science.

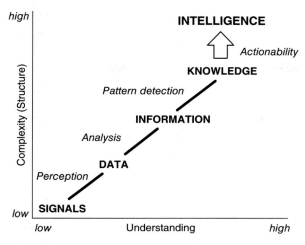

FIGURE 2.5   From perception to intelligence.

- *Information* is the output of the *distillation* process that aims at the structure of the Data and its functionality. Once Data is contextualized and structured into Information, a set of rules could be devised, and models could be inferred. This will engender predictability and the informational patterns will be encoded into Knowledge.

- The study of ***Knowledge*** is a very old branch of Sciences, called Epistemology. An even more modern discipline called Epistemetrics was recently developed; it deals with the theory of Knowledge from a quantitative perspective. Professor Nicholas Rescher (2006) is one of its main promoters.

- Once Knowledge (or the *know-how*) is devised, the ability to apply it to real-world problems becomes the ultimate goal – thus achieving ***Intelligence***. Knowledge is a very valuable asset, but its value degrades as technologies get obsolete and are replaced by newer ones. Intelligence needs to be sustainable and extend beyond temporal barriers. Although Einstein once said that "the true sign of Intelligence is not Knowledge but imagination," there is a very powerful causality relationship between Knowledge and Intelligence.

- Intelligence is defined as the ability to use Knowledge to solve problems, to be creative, to adapt to new situations, and to learn from past experiences. It is a purely human trait and the main goal of Data Science is to create the tool set to achieve it (see Figure 2.6).

- Achieving Intelligence creates the conditions to eventually crystalize everything into the highest form of human ability: **Wisdom**. Wisdom is also known as the *know-why* factor, or the ability to achieve progress. Wisdom implies the availability of sound judgment that in turn will drive the decision-making process.

The term Business Intelligence has been around for some time, and it was defined as "a set of theories, methodologies, architectures, and technologies that

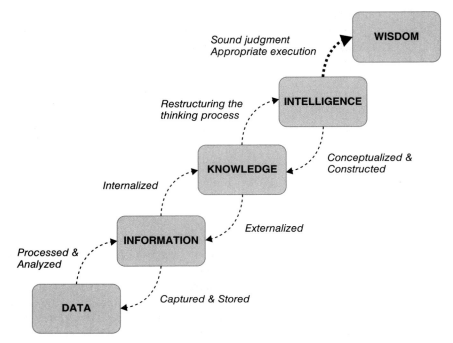

FIGURE 2.6   Journey from data to intelligence. **Source:** Anthony Liew (2013), DIKIW: data, information, knowledge, intelligence, wisdom, and their interrelationships. *Business Management Dynamics* 2 (10): 49–62. Licensed under CC-BY-3.0.

transform raw data into meaningful and useful information for business analysis purposes." Figure 2.6 summarizes the transformation process from Data to its most refined form, Wisdom:

- *Data*

  Probably the most challenging element to define in this transformation process is the starting layer, the Data. Data is sometimes considered as the *know-nothing* element, because the usability of this *un-refined* form is pretty limited. Rowley described Data as being "a discrete, objective set of observations, which are unorganized and unprocessed and therefore have no meaning or value because of lack of context and interpretation" (Rowley and Hartle 2006). Although most of the definitions relate to the abstract nature of Data, different categories of abstractions could be used based on the data type:

  ○ **Symbols** are placed at the highest level of abstraction in this layer, and they represent properties of objects that are encoded as numbers, graphs, images, or words. These symbols are the building blocks of the communication process and they have to be captured and stored with the purpose of modeling and understanding the processes that are responsible for their generation.

o **Signals** are situated more in the *subjective domain* because they are generated either by sensors or perceived through our senses (i.e. light, sound, smell, taste, or touch). This type of subjective data is related with a special type of knowledge, Experiential Knowledge, or knowledge by acquaintance that is based on direct experience of stimuli, and less on *factual* data (Zins and Chaim 2007).

o **Facts** are a special type of data that is considered to be *factually true* because it reflects an objective reality and it can be verified. This would eliminate any false, meaningless, or nonsensical data, and as such the principle of garbage in–garbage out would not be accounted for.

No matter the category of data abstraction, the *distillation* process will result in a superior form which will be structured, organized, and useful: the Information.

- *Information*

The distillation process is driven by interrogative questions, of which the first one is the *what?* question. Answering this question will reveal relationships and it will detect patterns in very descriptive forms. Once Data is endowed with meaning and purpose it becomes Information.

According to Rowley, Information is the outcome of "organized or structured data, which has been processed in such a way that the information now has relevance for a specific purpose or context, and is therefore meaningful, valuable, useful and relevant" (Rowley and Hartle 2006). As such, the relationship between Data and Information could be seen either as functional or just structural, depending on whether one is interested in the dynamics of the process. Depending on the data abstraction used (e.g. symbolic, factual, or subjective), the generated Information could be of a symbolic or of a subjective type, or a combination of the two. Sometimes Information is also equated to *know-what*.

- *Knowledge*

Knowledge is a much more abstract and complex concept than Information. Let's just think about how to measure it. Probably the simplest definition is that Knowledge is like a map of the world imprinted in the human brain. This map helps one to know where Information is located. It also contains one's beliefs and expectations (e.g. "If I do this, I will probably get that"). The brain links all the information together into a giant network of ideas, memories, predictions, and beliefs.

The decision-making process is usually grounded on this *map* and not on factual realities. The human brain is constantly updating this map from the signals coming from the sensorial receptors. The most natural place to store Knowledge is in the brain, because the brain connects all acquired information together. Comparatively, computers do not *understand* what they are processing, and they cannot make independent decisions based on the inputs – therefore computers do not exhibit "*consciousness*" in the human sense.

Although humans have studied Knowledge since ancient times (Plato's dialogues) through Epistemology, the modern definition is grounded on the concept of Information. Some definitions refer to Knowledge as Information that was processed or organized such that it could be applied or put into action. Answering the *why?* question is going to reveal the patterns that will synthetize the contextualized data (a.k.a. Information). But probably the most quoted definition of Knowledge is a "mixture of experience, values, contextual information, expert insight and grounded intuition that provides an environment and framework for evaluating and incorporating new experiences and information." Wallace (2007) notes that Knowledge "becomes embedded not only in documents and repositories but also in organizational routines, processes, practices and norms." Internalized Information is becoming Knowledge and as such it could be seen as the "synthesis of multiple sources of information over time, and the organization and the processing necessary to convey understanding, experience and accumulated learning" (Rowley and Hartle 2006).

Knowledge could be procedural, i.e. *know-how*, *know-who*, or *know-when*, but also propositional, which relates more to the subjective realm, or belief structuring. According to ancient Greek philosophers, Knowledge is characterized by an "individual's justifiable belief that it is considered to be true." The distinction here between subjective Knowledge and subjective Information is that the former is characterized by justifiable belief while the latter is a description for the meaning of data.

- *Intelligence* as a concept is usually defined in a very loosely fashion. American Psychologist R.J. Sternberg once said that "there seem to be almost as many definitions of intelligence as there were experts asked to define it" (Sternberg 1998). Despite a long history of research and debate, there is still no standard definition of intelligence. There are some experts who believe that intelligence may be approximately described but cannot be fully defined.

  Let's explore some of the most commonly accepted definitions of Intelligence:

  ○ "The ability to use memory, knowledge, experience, understanding, reasoning, imagination and judgement in order to solve problems and adapt to new situations" – *AllWords Dictionary* (2006).

  ○ "The capacity to acquire and apply knowledge" – *American Heritage Dictionary*, 4th ed. (2000).

  ○ "The ability to learn, understand and make judgments or have opinions that are based on reason" – *Cambridge Advance Learner's Dictionary* (2006).

  ○ "The ability to adapt effectively to the environment, either by making a change in oneself or by changing the environment or finding a new one ... Intelligence is not a single mental process, but rather a combination of many mental processes directed toward effective adaptation to the environment" – *Encyclopedia Britannica* (2006).

○ "Intelligence is a very general mental capability that, among other things, involves the ability to reason, plan, solve problems, think abstractly, comprehend complex ideas, learn quickly and learn from experience" – common statement with 52 expert signatories (Gottfredson 1997).

There are also more specialized definitions coming from either psychologists or Artificial Intelligence experts (Legg and Hutter 2007). In layman terms, Intelligence is generally defined as "the ability to achieve complex goals." This definition comes down to two important concepts: understanding and complexity.

A typical example is solving a puzzle game. The individual pieces are simple units, very easy to define and manipulate. What makes the problem highly complex is the understanding of how the pieces are related to each other. Therefore a more accurate definition for Intelligence would be "the ability to achieve difficult goals by understanding the parts that form the main goal." Examples of complex goals:

○ Sensorial: seeing, hearing, touching

○ Actions: moving

○ Cognitive: learning, understanding

- **Wisdom or Understanding** could be formulated as the "ability to transform complexity into simple useful information."

  This process involves the decoding of the relationships between the constituent parts that form the complex unitary item that represents the *complex goal* to be achieved. And this process is called modeling. The process of understanding the surrounding reality consists of creating a higher-level representation that will describe the things one is seeing, hearing, or feeling, but not the actual real thing.

Human Intelligence could be summarized as follows:

- Modeling the surrounding *reality* and understanding its parts.
- Transforming the raw Data into useful and simple Information.
- Understanding how these parts form more complex relationships, accomplishing at the outset the *difficult* goals.

Generating intelligent decisions from Data is the ultimate goal of Data Science. From a business point of view, this comes down to solving problems, or to Actionability. The tool set that Data Science employs covers a large array of domains, from Mathematics to Computer Science and Scientific methods. It involves the generation of hypotheses, the design of experiments and tests through the analysis of data, and the development of predictive models. Once enough value is generated from Data, its associated Information, and the acquired Knowledge, one could employ the degree of Intelligence achieved to answer more questions such as *What is best?* and *How to optimize?* (see Figure 2.7).

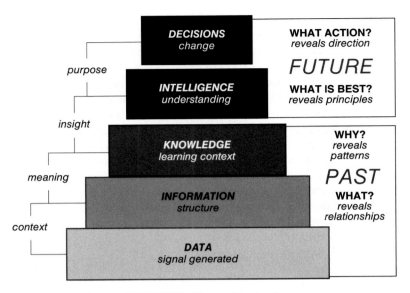

FIGURE 2.7   The questions to ask.

2.5   THE UTILITY OF DATA IN TRADING AND INVESTING

The impact that Big Data is making in the financial world today has the proportions of a tsunami. Technology is developing at an exponential rate and the consequences are far-reaching. Solving problems of increasing complexity demands more high-quality data and better algorithms for processing. These new trends are positioning the financial industry in a new *post-digital revolution* era.

Human activity worldwide is creating several quintillions bytes of data daily, and this represents a unique opportunity for processing, analyzing, and leveraging the information in ways that were not available until very recently. Machine intelligence and algorithmic techniques are increasingly being used in financial trading and investing to process vast amounts of data and generate predictions and decisions that humans may not have the capacity for.

As many other human endeavors, financial trading and investment rely on accurate inputs being fed into business decision-making models. Traditionally, the decision-making process was driven by numbers handled by humans and decisions were made based on inferences drawn from perceived risks and trends. Nowadays, this functionality is provided by informatics systems that could compute at massive scale and draw Intelligence from a multitude of sources to arrive at more accurate conclusions practically instantaneously.

In recent years, both Data Science and Machine Learning have become the main directions in which the financial industry is betting its future. According to Bacoyannis and collaborators (Bacoyannis et al. 2018), there are three distinct cultures of data-centric applications in quantitative finance:

- Data modeling culture
- Machine Learning culture
- Algorithmic decision-making culture

The **Data modeling culture** is characterized by the fact that the financial markets could be described as a black boxes employing relatively simple models that are fed by observational market data. The task of the data modeling practice is to find an approximate functional approximation for this data-generating process (a quantitative model) and to extract its parameters from the data. The model output is then fed into a decision-making process. Although the approach may look straightforward, the complexity of the financial markets and the collective behavior of market participants pose very serious challenges to the data modeling culture. Such simple models are prone to serious failures because they do not properly capture the essential properties of the environment and may often give a false sense of certainty.

The **Machine Learning culture** takes an agnostic approach to the question whether financial markets are simple. From an empirical perspective, the world of finance looks more Darwinian than Newtonian since it is constantly evolving. From this perspective the processes that are responsible for generating the observed market data could be described as emerging behaviors rather than just data-generating machines. In this approach "complex and sometimes opaque functions are used to model the observations" (Bacoyannis et al. 2018). The functions inferred by the ML techniques do not generally reveal the nature of the underlying processes. As in the Data modeling culture, Machine Learning models are built and their outputs are fed into decision-making processes. Complex ML models are prone to failures that are due to the phenomenon of *over-fitting*; thus, the risk of the model failure increases with its complexity.

In the **Algorithmic decision-making culture** the focus is on decision-making rather than on model-building. By bypassing the stage of learning how the world works, this technique proceeds directly to training agents to distinguish *good* decisions from *bad* decisions. This approach presents its own challenges due to the general inability to understand and explain the decisions that the algorithmic agent takes. In this approach the agent learns that certain actions are to be avoided because they lead to negative outcomes. The users of this technique still have to impose constraints that will steer the agent away from taking actions which may be viewed as prohibited but which the agent cannot learn from its environment or its history.

There is a large variety of use cases that could have a high impact on the adoption of these methodologies by the industry as a whole:

- **The use of Big Data analytics to feed financial models**

  Financial analytics is no longer just the narrow exploration of prices and their dynamics, but it incorporates the fundamentals that affect prices, the political and societal trends, as well as any available *signals* that could augment the understanding of the problem space. The use of *Big Data* in the context of financial analytics could be accomplished by predictive models that estimate the rates of return and probably outcomes on investments. Expanding the access to big data will provide more accurate predictions and therefore the ability to mitigate more effectively the inherent risks associated with financial trading. This ongoing data revolution will expand the realm of applicability for machine trading beyond the current limited range of high frequency trading, where ultra-short time processing is of the essence. In general *Big Data* requires much longer processing times, and as a result a new automated trading paradigm is developing: market participants will take advantage of accurate *extrapolations* made possible by models fed by very large amounts of data.

- **The use of real-time analytics**

  Algorithmic trading is about executing trades at speeds and frequencies that humans cannot operate on. This trading paradigm utilizes the best possible prices, generates trades on very specific timelines, and mitigates the risk of manual errors that could emerge due to behavioral mishaps. The advent of *real-time* analytics has the potential to improve the applicability of algorithmic techniques at time frames that are a lot longer than the usual microsecond level of the HFT. It will also affect the markets by leveling the playing field and providing all market participants with access to powerful information. The advent of *real-time* analytics could provide algorithmic trading with almost limitless capabilities. A variety of data could be employed to drive trading decisions, from the traditional structured data (prices and volumes), to a more unstructured one such as social media content, consumer data, or satellite imagery.

- **The use of Machine Learning**

  The use of the term Machine Learning is becoming ubiquitous in today's financial industry landscape. But as far as realizing a deep and long-lasting impact on the financial sector, Machine Learning has a long way to go. Its full potential has not yet been realized, although the prospects for its applicability are immeasurable. Machine Learning is supposed to enable computing systems to effectively learn from data and make decisions based on the newly acquired information. The data-driven decision-making paradigm will mitigate the human emotional response from trading models and will generate decisions based on information without bias.

- **Automated Risk Management**

  Risk management is a mission critical area for all financial institutions, since it is responsible for company's security, trustworthiness, and strategic decisions. Since the last financial crisis, the approaches to handling risk management have changed significantly, transforming the finance sector in a fundamental fashion. Risk could arise from many sources, such as competitors, investors, regulators, or company's customers. Also, risk could be stratified by its importance and its potential for losses.

  The reliance on Data Science as the main toolset to take advantage of the Big Data equates to identifying, prioritizing, and monitoring the risk factors. Training ML models on large amounts of customer data, financial lending, or insurance results could improve the risk-scoring models but are also expected to enhance cost efficiency and sustainability. Probably one of the most important applications of Data Science and Machine Learning in Risk Management is identifying the creditworthiness of potential customers. To establish the appropriate credit amount for a particular customer, ML algorithms are used to analyze past spending behavior and detect behavioral patterns. The process of digitalization and automatization of Risk Management workflows is in the early stages, but the potential is considerable. The financial industry will need to undergo structural changes in order to prepare for the large-scale automation of its core financial processes. This will require improving the analytical skills of its workforce and making strategic technology investments.

- **Data Management**

  For many financial firms, data is arguably the most important resource after its human and financial capital. Therefore, efficient data management is as important as human capital or financial capital management. Financial firms are spending a lot on improving their data management infrastructure and on educating their workforce to use it efficiently.

- **Consumer Analytics**

  For financial firms that are interacting with clients on a regular basis, *real-time* analytics will facilitate a better understanding of their customers and allow for effective personalization. Complex ML algorithms and customer sentiment analysis techniques could generate insights from clients' behavior, social media interaction, their feedback and opinions, and improve personalization and ultimately enhance the bottom line.

- **Fraud Detection**

  Guaranteeing the highest level of security to its users is today a very strict legal requirement for any business in the financial sector. Fraud detection systems are tools for the detection or the prevention of any anomalies in user behavior. Examples could be generating alerts for unusual financial purchases or for large cash withdrawals that will lead to blocking those actions, until the customer confirms them. In the financial trading sector, ML tools could identify patterns in trading data that might indicate manipulations and alert enforcement agencies to investigate.

The trading industry is a very competitive field of endeavor, and it will always continue to be. Maintaining a competitive advance in this landscape is the principal tool to survive, and as such this new era of *Big Data* is considered to be another lifesaver. If a couple of decades ago digitalization was the name of the game, today the buzzwords *du jour* are *Big Data* and *AI*. In reality the financial industry is looking for novel ways to increase productivity by generating better returns through automation and cost reductions. In 2015, Thomson Reuters reported that their data customers were mostly machines, and therefore they were providing more information to be fed directly into algorithms than to humans to make their own informed decisions. This trend will likely continue at an increasing rate.

The reliance on *Big Data* is also evident in the world of Asset Management and investment in general. Investors, both high-net-worth individuals as well as firms, are focused on creating data-driven investment models that can objectively evaluate public companies globally through the use of both classic and *alternative* financial data. Historically these investment models have utilized large sets of company-specific data like publicly available financial statements, as well as market data like prices, returns, and volumes. But the availability of nontraditional data sources such as Internet web traffic, consumer data, patent filings, social media content, and satellite imagery has created the conditions to use more specialized data to gain an informational edge and make more informed investment decisions.

The new era of *Big Data* has created tremendous business opportunities not just for financial firms, but especially for technology solution vendors. *Big Data* does not refer to just the data itself but also to a set of technologies that capture, store, manage, and analyze large and variable collections of data to solve complex problems. The proliferation of real-time and historical data from sources such as the web, connected devices, sensors, social media, and transactional applications has generated a *Big Data* boom that is aggressively promoted by a diverse range of vertical sectors. Market research studies (Research and Markets 2018) estimate that Big Data investments in the financial services industry accounted for about $9 billion just in 2018 alone. This demand was driven by a variety of business opportunities for banks, insurers, credit card and payment processing specialists, asset and wealth management firms, lenders, and other stakeholders. These investments are expected to grow at a compound annual growth rate (CAGR) of approximately 17% over the next three years.

The mainstream of traditional financial services are more attuned to the idea of adopting cloud-based platforms in an attempt to alleviate the technical and scalability challenges associated with the *on premise* Big Data environments. At the same time, *Big Data* technologies are playing a very important role in the success of innovative FinTech startups, most notably in the alterative insurance and money transfer sectors. In addition to utilizing traditional data sources, the financial industry is increasingly becoming reliant on alternative sources of data – ranging from social media to satellite imagery – that can provide previously hidden insights for multiple application areas including data-driven trading and investments, or credit scoring.

2.6 THE ALTERNATIVE DATA AND ITS USE IN TRADING AND INVESTING

Alternative data refers to a wide variety of data used to obtain insight into the *investment process*. Alternative data sets contain information about a particular business that is published by sources outside of the company and which can provide unique and timely insights into investment opportunities. Alternative data sets are generally classified as *Big Data*, since they may be very large and complex and often cannot be handled by traditional databases.

The alternative data sets could be compiled from a variety of sources, but they are generally by-products of individual business operations, which are often less readily accessible and less structured than traditional sources of data. They are also known as *exhaust data*. In recent years many data brokers and aggregators, together with other intermediaries, began specializing in providing alternative data to investors and analysts. Alternative data has become today a very fashionable tool for investment management firms seeking alpha. Although this field is still in its early phases of development, investment managers participate more and more in this new paradigm.

The process of extracting benefits from alternative data could be very challenging. The technologies employed for processing such data are relatively new and most institutional investors do not have the capabilities to integrate alternative data into their investment decision process. However, by choosing the appropriate set of tools and strategies, investment managers could alleviate costs while creating a solid competitive advantage.

Examples of alternative data sets:

- Geolocation (business traffic)
- Financial transactions: credit card, point of sales, websites
- Social media content: images, videos, posts
- Satellite imagery: parking lots, store traffic, weather, shipping container traffic
- News outlets
- Product reviews and customer feedback
- Web traffic
- Public records: SEC filings, press releases, the Internet
- Private information: presentations, internal reports, consumer data, etc.

All these alternative data sets could be acquired through different methods:

- Raw data acquisition
- Web scrapping
- Third-party licensing

The main factors that are taken into account when analyzing alternative data are:

- Structure or lack thereof: CSV, JSON vs. text or images
- History, in a time-series form
- Granularity, or the level of aggregation detail (usually time)
- Coverage: local vs. global
- Scarcity or the frequency of overloading with financial-specific information

When it comes to investing, the name of the game is Information. Keeping up with the competition or outperforming in an increasingly competitive market requires that both institutional and retail investors alike are always on the lookout for crucial information that will give them the desired edge. Information could come in a variety of forms: from traditional financial data, to the rapidly expanding offering available in the form of *alternative data*. Unlike the traditional data sources, alternative data is information collected and utilized in an investment strategy that does not come directly from the company in question.

According to Deloitte (2017), "The lure of alternative data sets is largely the potential for an information advantage over the market with regard to investment decisions. True information advantage has occurred at various times in the history of securities markets, and alternative data seem to be just the most recent manifestation ... Speed and knowledge are advancing with the use of advanced analytics, and there will be no waiting for laggards, no turning back."

A recent study by Greenwich Associates (Johnson 2018) found that more than 60% of traditional asset managers and nearly 75% of hedge funds are already using social media – a rich source of alternative data – as part of their investment process. One major driver is represented by the transition of multifactor analysis from statistical models to Machine Learning. Gaining new insights into the alternative data may represent a competitive advantage in harvesting more alpha.

REFERENCES

Ackoff (1989). From data to wisdom. *Journal of Applied Systems Analysis* 16: 3–9.

Avinash (n.d.). Occam's razor. https://www.kaushik.net/avinash/seven-steps-to-creating-a-data-driven-decision-making-culture/ .

Bacoyannis, Glukhov, Jin et al. (2018). Idiosyncrasies and challenges of data driven learning in electronic trading. https://arxiv.org/pdf/1811.09549.pdf.

Boulding (1955). Notes on the information concept. *Exploration* 6: 103–112.

Brynjolfsson et al. (2011). Strength in numbers: How does data-driven decision making affect firm performance? Research paper. SSRN. https://pdfs.semanticscholar.org/3393/315f1685c801c545990070026a2d3fbe2811.pdf?_ga=2.150823925.278839993.1558036766-790121169.1558036766.

Deloitte (2017). Alternative data for investment decisions: Today's innovation could be tomorrow's requirement. Deloitte Center for Financial Services. https://www2.deloitte.com/content/dam/Deloitte/us/Documents/financial-services/us-fsi-dcfs-alternative-data-for-investment-decisions.pdf.

Economist (2017). Fuel of the future: The data economy. *Economist* 423 (9038): 22.

Gottfredson (1997). Mainstream science on intelligence: An editorial with 52 signatories, history, and bibliography. *Intelligence* 24 (1): 13–23.

Johnson (2018). A buyer's guide to alternative data. Greenwich Associates. https://www.greenwich.com/equities/buyers-guide-alternative-data.

Legg and Hutter (2007). A collection of definitions of intelligence. *Frontiers in Artificial Intelligence and Applications* 157: 17–24.

Ng (2017). Fueling the deep learning rocket with data. The Artificial Intelligence Channel. https://youtu.be/UZbwFw4wB2w.

OECD (2015). Data-driven innovation: Big data for growth and well-being. https://www.oecd-ilibrary.org/science-and-technology/data-driven-innovation_9789264229358-en, 20.

Rescher (2006). *Epistemetrics*. Cambridge University Press, 9–14.

Research and Markets (2018). https://www.researchandmarkets.com/reports/4585631/big-data-in-the-financial-services-industry-2018#pos-0.

Rowley and Hartle (2006). *Organizing Knowledge: An Introduction to Managing Access to Information*. Ashgate Publishing.

Schoech et al. (2002). From data to intelligence: Introducing the intelligent organization. *Administration in Social Work Journal* 26 (1): 1–21.

Short (2017). What is your data worth? Sloan Management Review. https://sloanreview.mit.edu/article/whats-your-data-worth/.

Sternberg (1998). Intelligence. In *The Oxford Companion to the Mind* (ed. Gregory). Oxford, UK: Oxford University Press, 472.

Varian (2006). *Intermediate Microeconomics*, 7th ed. New York: Norton, 359.

Wallace (2007). *Knowledge Management: Historical and Cross-Disciplinary Themes*. Libraries Unlimited, 123–140.

Wikipedia (2019). Entropy (information theory). https://en.wikipedia.org/wiki/Entropy_(information _theory).

Zins and Chaim (2007). Conceptual approaches for defining data, information, and knowledge. *Journal of the American Society for Information Science and Technology* 58 (4): 479–493.

CHAPTER 3

Artificial Intelligence – Between Myth and Reality

"If people do not believe that Mathematics is simple, it is only because they do not realize how complicated life is."

– John von Neumann, polymath, computer scientist

3.1 INTRODUCTION

We are witnessing today the onset of a new technological revolution that is driven by what one calls the fourth paradigm of scientific discovery. This new development is going to change forever many industries and the structure of the workforce for generations to come. Dr. James Gray, one of the greatest American computer scientists of the twentieth century and recipient of the Turing award in 1998, has predicted this development more than two decades ago. He has labeled this new era as *eScience* or the *Data exploration* era. Dr. Gray has predicted that this will be a time when theory, experimentation, and simulation will come together to solve some of the most important problems of our civilization.

The accelerated pace of technological progress of the past decades has contributed to the generation of vast amounts of data, and the birth of what one calls the *Big Data* age. Recent advances in High Performance Computing (HPC) and hardware acceleration (GPUs and FPGAs), coupled with new discoveries in algorithmic processing, has created the conditions to train and utilize very complex Machine Learning algorithms at an unprecedented speed. All these new technological developments are going to have a revolutionary impact on many industries, and the financial industry is expected to be at the forefront of the adoption process. A new concept is already making its way in today's financial world: *data-driven decision-making*, which we have explored in the previous chapter. Nowadays, both trading and investing are more and more driven by large-scale data analysis, and the new concept of alternative data is becoming more ubiquitous.

This brave new world will require a new breed of quantitative workforce – one combining classical quant skills with deep knowledge of computer science and hands-on knowledge of modern HPC technologies. Not so long ago, our world stepped into the fourth industrial revolution era, where the name of the game is Innovation. As Innovation is mainly driven by technology, achieving technology fluency is a hard-core prerequisite that requires life-long education. The life cycle of modern technologies is averaging less than two and a half years today and it will get even shorter. This new breed of quants is going to be present in a variety of industries, way beyond the realm of the finance. Fields like Computational Medicine, Healthcare, and the Internet-of-Things and Education are going to be big consumers of this modern profession. Since the whole society is so immersed and dependent on data and the methods to extract actionable information from it, the twenty-first-century quants will position themselves at the core of the system that drives the most important business decisions.

The fabric of Data Exploration is essentially composed of two fundamental threads:

- Data, which is the *what-to-operate-on* element, and the
- Algorithmic tool set, or the *how-to-do-it* component, which is used to extract the actionable knowledge from data.

The previous chapter projected a comprehensive picture for the role of data in today's financial industry. From defining terminology, to classifying its different types, the previous chapter advocated for a principled use of data in the decision-making process. This process was illustrated as the fascinating journey that starts with raw Data being distilled into structured Information, which is leading to Knowledge extraction and then eventually to the desired outcome, which is Intelligence gathering. Data was interpreted as *the agent that encodes and relays to the astute observer a quantitative measure of the surrounding reality*. As such, Data is becoming nowadays the fuel of the modern digital economy and one of its most important assets. Its utility exceeds that of classical commodities, specifically because it fuels the generation of Knowledge and thus makes possible to extract actionable Intelligence.

This chapter is dedicated to the second thread of the data exploration fabric, namely the understanding of the *how-to* mechanism that is used to extract actionable knowledge that is needed in the decision-making process. As I have mentioned in the Introduction, one of the main goals of this book is to provide an adequate level of engineering and scientific rigor and clarity to the usage of the term *Artificial Intelligence*, especially as it relates to its use in the financial industry. This chapter will attempt to uncover some of the hype surrounding the so-called *Artificial Intelligence revolution*.

The AI tag has become one of the most exploited labels in today's tech parlance, and I contend that its use should be carefully aligned with scientific facts and not just with marketing needs. I also think that the expectations generated by this hype should be appropriately calibrated with the current status of the progress achieved in this field. Technologists, business leaders, and investors must not fall into the trap of the *hype curve of inflated expectations*. When novel yet untested technologies are moving from research labs into the real economy, a significant amount of hype is usually baked in. Hence the main goal of this chapter is to clarify the terminology surrounding the term AI and to adjust the expectations for the reader in regard to its use in quantitative finance.

3.2 THE EVOLUTION OF AI

Although *Artificial Intelligence* has been a well-established field of research for many decades, the term is still one of the most ambiguously defined topics in Computer Science and other related fields. This is largely due to an ambigous characterization of the term AI. This elusiveness eventually led to the birth of a new mantra (i.e. the AI logo), which has become an intellectual wildcard in today's tech vernacular.

One of the funniest yet most sobering illustration of this phenomenon was coming from Baron Schwartz, one of the creators of MySQL, who tweeted:

"When you're fundraising, it is AI,

When you're hiring, it is ML,

When you're implementing, it is linear Regression,

When you're debugging, it is printf ()"

– Baron Schwartz, @xaprb

The goal of this chapter is to *de-noise* the hype surrounding AI. This ambitious goal could be achieved only by understanding the scientific and technical complexity of this topic. Let's start by diving into the history of an ancient human undertaking – understanding what Intelligence is and how it works. Although the term Artificial Intelligence was first coined by John McCarthy more than six decades ago, the concept of *intelligent machines* has a much longer and more complex history. Many of the fundamental ideas of AI have an ancient origin. Let's review some of the most important milestones on this journey.

3.2.1 Early History

- The intellectual roots of AI, and the concept of *intelligent machines*, could be tracked deep into the Greek mythology (AAAI n.d.). Mythological figures like Hephaestus, or the *god of blacksmiths*, was depicted as having manufactured mechanical servants. The account of the bronze man named Talos is one of the first mentions of the idea of *intelligent robots*. Human-like artifacts have been the subjects of many other myths in antiquity. According to historical accounts, several mechanical models were actually constructed by skillful craftsmen and artists like Hero, Daedalus, or Archytas of Tarentum.

- Logic, as a formal theory of reasoning, was first mentioned in the fourth century BC in Aristotle's *Prior Analytics*. The syllogistic logic is considered to be the first formal deductive reasoning system – one of the stepping-stones of modern AI.

- An important milestone in the history of conceptual development of *intelligent machines* originated in the thirteenth century. At that time Ramon Lull, a Spanish poet and theologian (1232–1316), published *Ars generalis ultima* or *The Ultimate General Art*, where he described a machine for discovering non-mathematical truths through combinatorics (Glymour, Ford, and Hayes 1998). His original idea was that thinking is a computational process, which involves combining symbols, and that computation could be *mechanized* via the use of mathematical tools involving combinatorics.

- The second half of the second millennium was a very fertile ground for new inventions like the printing press (Gutenberg 1456), the first clocks (fifteenth to sixteenth centuries), as well as new attempts to build robots: DaVinci's walking Lion (1515) or Golem – the *walking clay-man* (Rabi Loew 1580).

- The debut of the Renaissance coincided with the creation of new theories:

  - In 1646, the French philosopher, mathematician, and scientist Descartes suggested that the bodies of animals could be modeled as complex machines.

  - In 1642, the French mathematician, physicist, inventor, and writer Pascal created the first mechanical digital calculating machine.

  - Thomas Hobbes published in 1651 *The Leviathan*, where he was describing a mechanistic and combinatorial theory of thinking.

  - In 1666, the German mathematician and philosopher Leibniz improved on Pascal's machine to do multiplication and division with a machine called the Step Reckoner (1673). He also envisioned a universal way of reasoning by which arguments could be decided mechanically.

  - In 1763, English statistician and philosopher Thomas Bayes developed a framework for reasoning about the probability of events. Machine learning will adopt later Bayesian inference as one of its main tools.

- The nineteenth century was a very progressive period in this journey:

  - In 1801, the French weaver and merchant Joseph-Marie Jacquard invented the first programmable machine, with instructions on punched cards.

  - In 1832, the English polymath Charles Babbage and Ada Byron (Lady Lovelace, the daughter of Lord Byron) designed a programmable mechanical calculating machine, called the Analytical Engine.

  - The English mathematician, philosopher, and logician George Boole developed in 1854 a binary algebra representing the *laws of thought*.

- At the beginning of the twentieth century, the British mathematicians Bertrand Russell and Alfred North Whitehead published *Principia Mathematica*, which revolutionized formal logic. Two other very important milestones happened in quick succession:

  - In 1936, Alan Turing, the famous British scientist, who pioneered the mathematical possibility of Artificial intelligence, proposed the ground-breaking Universal Turing Machine concept (Turing 1937) – laying the foundations of modern AI.

  - In 1943, Warren McCulloch and Walter Pitts published A Logical Calculus of the Ideas Immanent in Nervous Activity (McCulloch and Pitts 1943), laying foundations for neural networks.

- The interest in this field exploded after modern computers became available, following World War II. The advent of modern computers made possible the creation of programs that perform difficult intellectual tasks. As such:

  - An American inventor, Vannevar Bush, proposed a system which amplifies people's own knowledge and understanding, by publishing his seminal work As We May Think (Bush 1945).

  - In 1949, Alan Turing wrote a paper on the notion of machines being able to simulate human beings and the ability to do intelligent things, such as to play the game of chess. One year later, he published the paper Computing Machinery and Intelligence (Turing 1950) – an introduction of the Turing Test as a way of operationalizing a test of intelligent behavior. This seminal work originated during the World War II, when Turing worked on cracking the *Enigma* code used by Germans by developing what was called the *Bombe* machine. This work laid the foundations for Machine Learning and later inspired the idea of an *imitation game*, or the Turing Test.

3.2.2   The Modern AI Era

In the first half of the twentieth century, science fiction familiarized the world with the concept of artificially intelligent robots: be it the *heartless* Tin Man from *The Wizard of Oz* or the humanoid robot that impersonated Maria in *Metropolis*. By the mid-1950s, a new generation of scientists, mathematicians, and philosophers was created having the concept of AI culturally baked-in. One of the brightest and the most prominent figures of this generation was Alan Turing. He suggested that if humans could readily use information and reasoning in order to solve problems and make decisions, computers could just mimic this process as well. This idea was representing the logical framework of Computing Machinery and Intelligence in which he discussed how to build intelligent machines and how to test their intelligence.

Unfortunately, the first generation of computers lacked a key prerequisite for achieving intelligence; that is, they could not store commands, they could only execute them. In addition computing was extremely expensive at that time. The cost of leasing a computer ran up to $200,000 a month in the late 1950s. Only prestigious universities and big technology companies could afford to use them. The year 1956 represents the beginning of the modern AI era. A first proof of concept – *Logic Theorist* – was brought to life by Allen Newell, J.C. Shaw, and Herbert Simon. This program was designed to mimic the problem-solving skills of a human and was funded by the RAND Corporation. It's considered by many to be the first artificial intelligence program and it was presented at the Dartmouth Summer Research Project on Artificial Intelligence hosted by John McCarthy and Marvin Minsky.

At this historic conference, McCarthy brought together top researchers from various fields for an open-ended discussion on Artificial Intelligence. Unfortunately, the conference fell short of McCarthy's expectations since the participants failed to agree on standard methods for the field. In spite of this, the general sentiment was that AI was within the realm of the achievable, and this helped create the catalyst for the next twenty years of AI research. AI has encountered a wide variety of obstacles, the biggest one being the lack of computational power to do anything substantial: computers simply could not store enough information or process it fast enough.

In its first stage of development, AI was represented by the vision of emulating human intelligence. This *human-imitative* view later evolved toward the development of a more applicable engineering discipline in which algorithms and data are brought together to solve a variety of pattern recognition, learning, and decision-making problems. More and more, the AI research started to intersect with other engineering and scientific disciplines. A different approach was adopted, where the *human-imitative* perspective was replaced by a more practical one – *intelligence-augmentation*. The systems needed not to be intelligent themselves, but to reveal patterns that humans could use. Examples are search engines, recommender systems of natural language translation.

3.2.3   Important Milestones in the Development of AI

1956

- John McCarthy came up with the term *Artificial Intelligence* as the topic of the Dartmouth Conference, the first conference devoted to the subject. The goal of the project was to "proceed on the basis of the conjecture that every aspect of learning or any other feature of intelligence can be precisely described that a machine can be made to simulate it" (McCarthy et al. 2006).

- Demonstration of the first running AI program, the Logic Theorist (LT) written by Newell, Shaw, and Simon (Carnegie Mellon).

- Arthur Samuel (IBM) wrote the first game-playing program, for checkers, to achieve sufficient skill to challenge a world champion.

1958

- John McCarthy (MIT) invented the Lisp language.

1963

- Edward A. Feigenbaum and Julian Feldman published *Computers and Thought*, the first collection of articles about artificial intelligence.

1965

- Joseph Weizenbaum (MIT) built ELIZA, an interactive program that carries on a dialogue in English on any topic.

1974

- Ted Shortliffe's PhD dissertation on MYCIN (Stanford) demonstrated the power of rule-based systems for knowledge representation and inference in the domain of medical diagnosis and therapy – called the first expert system.

1981

- Danny Hillis designs the connection machine, a massively parallel architecture that brings new power to AI and to computation in general (later founds Thinking Machines, Inc.).

Mid-1980s

- Neural networks become widely used with the Backpropagation algorithm (first described by Werbos in 1974).

1987

- Marvin Minsky publishes *The Society of Mind*, a theoretical description of the mind as a collection of cooperating agents.

1989

- Dean Pomerleau at CMU creates the Autonomous Land Vehicle in a Neural Network, which became the system that drove a car coast-to-coast under computer control for all but about 50 of the 2,850 miles.

1990s

- Major advances in all areas of AI, with significant demonstrations in machine learning (especially SVM), intelligent tutoring, case-based reasoning, multi-agent planning, scheduling, uncertain reasoning, data mining, natural language understanding and translation, vision, virtual reality, games, and other topics.
- The Deep Blue chess program beats the current world chess champion, Garry Kasparov, in a widely followed match and rematch (May 11, 1997).

The new millennium

- A.k.a. the era of Deep Learning (Hinton – 2006 and 2012 – CNN, Univ. of Toronto).
- Google driverless car project (2009).
- IBM Watson system (2011).
- AI finds new applications in smartphones: Siri, Cortana, Alexa, Bixby.
- DeepMind and its quest to board games solving (2016, Go game).

Exaggerated levels of optimism had raised the expectations impossibly high, and when the promised results failed to materialize, the necessary funding for AI research disappeared (see Figure 3.1). The AI research has known two long periods of stagnation, or the so-called AI-winters: 1974–1980 and 1987–1993. During these periods of time AI was subject to critiques and financial setbacks. From the very beginning a large majority of AI researchers had failed to appreciate the difficulty of the problems they faced. Just two of the earliest examples:

> *"Machines will be capable, within twenty years, of doing any work what man can do."*
> *– Herbert A. Simon (CMU)*

> *"Within a generation … the problem of creating Artificial Intelligence will substantially be solved."*
> *– Marvin Minsky (MIT)*

The second AI wave started in the 1980s and it was reignited by two sources: an expansion of the algorithmic tool kit, and a substantial increase in funding. Alexey Ivakhnenko and David Rumelhart popularized Deep Learning techniques which allowed computers to learn using experience.

The third wave of AI (see Figure 3.2) was marked by events like the one when IBM's *Deep Blue* computer system defeated the reigning world chess champion and

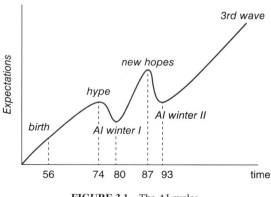

FIGURE 3.1   The AI cycles.

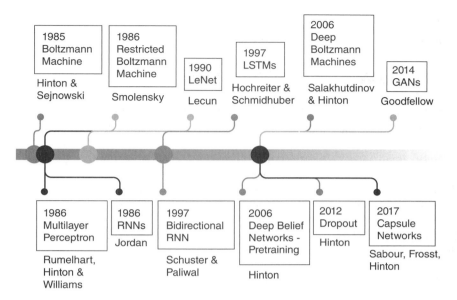

FIGURE 3.2 Recent milestones in machine learning.

grand master Gary Kasparov. This highly publicized match was the first time a reigning world chess champion lost to a computer and served as a huge step toward an "artificially intelligent" decision-making program. In 1997 Deep Blue was the 259th most powerful supercomputer with 11.4 GFLOPS.

The most powerful supercomputer then had 1,068 GFLOPS or as today's the most powerful supercomputer is 100 times more powerful. In 2011 IBM's Watson system defeated the two greatest *Jeopardy* champions. This was the beginning of a new era where huge amounts of data were used in connection with massive computational power.

To the surprise of many researchers the combination of massive amounts of data and great computational power, aided by new innovations in the field of hardware acceleration, managed to rapidly catapult a new field of research – *Deep Learning*. The use of this novel approach yielded surprising outcomes, particularly in speech and image recognition, as well as for most classification tasks. Impressive progress has also been achieved in the field of board games; in 2016 Google's *Alpha Go* was able to defeat the world's Go champion.

The big question that remains is "Have we gotten any smarter about the way we understand and implement Artificial Intelligence nowadays?" Do we fully understand the concept and grasp the current technological limitations? The fundamental limitations – storage and compute power – that were holding AI back 40 years ago are no longer a concern. Moore's Law was quite correct for some time in the fact that the memory and speed of computers doubles every year, and in many cases this expectation is surpassing our needs. Looking back at the first 60 years of AI research one could find a quite plausible explanation for the AI *roller-coaster* effect. Given the level of technological progress achieved on a specific time period (e.g. computer storage and processing speed), the AI research was able to reach a plateau of progress, and then it entered a new winter period in which it waited for Moore's Law to catch up again. The reality is that being able to emulate human Intelligence demands a lot more than just very large amounts of data and compute power – it requires the encoding of cognitive functions into computer code and this is just not available yet!

One can understand very well computer's ability to process data in logical, programmed fashion. But can machines *think*? A well-known example is the *Chinese room* argument (Searle 1980). Let's imagine someone trying to make sense and answer to information passed in Chinese. By using an entire library of knowledge-based rules the individual would be able to produce valid responses in Chinese, but would she be really able to understand the language? This argument is highly debated, and it is at the core of modern AI. What is the state-of-the-art in AI today? In the age of Big Data, which is a time when one has the capacity of collecting extremely large volumes of diverse information that is unpractical and sometimes impossible for a human to process, the most conspicuous applicability of AI comes in the form of *automation*.

The application of AI in this regard has already been quite successful in several industries such as banking, marketing, or entertainment. Even with quite simplistic algorithms, the availability of large amounts of data and massive computing power provides the ability to learn through *brute force*. Even if there is enough evidence that Moore's law is plateauing, the increased access to data could keep the momentum for a brief period of time until the next technological revolution will trigger the next AI burst. Breakthroughs in computer science, mathematics, and neuroscience will all serve as potential outs through the ceiling of Moore's Law. The most notable successes achieved by AI systems so far relate to very specialized areas, such as games (chess, *Jeopardy*, or Go) or visual and voice recognition.

3.2.4   Projections for the Immediate Future

In the immediate future, AI will continue to oversell its potential and be depicted as the next *big thing*. Although it is indisputable that AI research and related technology have achieved a discernable amount of success in areas related to automation, like call centers, chat bots, real-time translation, and recommender systems, there are still unfulfilled promises related to the availability of expert systems that could maintain an *intelligent* human-like conversation in areas that are more cognitive in nature, as opposed to just automation. One of the biggest promises of AI is to see self-driving cars on a large scale in the next decade. But the long-term goal is to understand and program *General Intelligence*; that is, to design and implement a machine that meets or surpasses human cognitive abilities in a variety of tasks. This very ambitious task is extremely unlikely to be accomplished in the foreseeable future. But even if the goal will be attained, a series of very strong ethical barriers will be erected against the use of these technologies at scale. Personalities like Elon Musk, Stephen Hawking, and Bill Gates have expressed serious concerns about the use of AI at scale, especially before we understand very well the implications of such a transfer of decision powers to machines.

3.2.5 Meta-Learning – An Exciting New Development

Meta-Learning is an exciting new trend in ML research which tackles the problem of *learning to learn*. The traditional paradigm in ML research is to get a huge data set on a specific task and train a model from scratch using this data set. Evidently this manner of learning is quite limiting, and it is very inefficient when compared with how humans leverage past experiences in order to learn very quickly a new task from only a limited set of examples.

Current ML-based systems implemented as *artificial* agents could master complex skills from scratch, using large amounts of experience (data) and time for training. But in order to add the *intelligent* attribute to the label, the *artificial* agent needs to be able to acquire many skills and adapt to a variety of environments, as opposed to train each skill in each setting from scratch. The *artificial* agents need to learn how to learn new tasks faster by reusing previous experience, rather than considering each new task in isolation. This approach of learning to learn, also called *meta-learning*, is an important step toward implementing versatile agents that could continually learn a variety of tasks throughout their lifetimes.

The goal of Meta-Learning is to train a model on a variety of learning tasks, such that it can solve new learning tasks using only a small number of training samples. Fast learning is a hallmark of human intelligence. Recognizing objects from a limited number of observations or rapidly learning new skills after a limited practice is something that a human could do *by default*. The next generation of *artificial* agents should be able to learn and adapt quickly after being exposed to only a few examples and continuing to adapt as more data becomes available. A fundamental component of Intelligence is versatility, which is the capability of performing many different tasks. Currently, ML-based systems are mastering very well on-off skills, like games, for example (Go, *Jeopardy*). But, when asked to perform a variety of apparently simple tasks, they will struggle. For example, the AlphaGo program that beat the Go world's champion cannot hold a simple conversation about the game of Go, for which it was not trained. By contrast, a human can adapt and act *intelligently* to a wide range of new, unseen situations. Enabling the *artificial* agents to acquire such versatility will be the next big revolution in Computational Intelligence!

The ability to learn fast and in a flexible manner is very challenging for *artificial* agents, because they must integrate all prior experience with a small amount of new information while avoiding overfitting to the new data. Moreover, the encoding of prior experience and new data is very much task-dependent. As such, the mechanism of learning to learn (or Meta-Learning) should be very generic and independent of the task or the form of computation required to complete that task. Meta-Learning systems are trained by being exposed to a wide range of tasks, and then their ability to learn new tasks is tested. Let's take the example of classifying a new object within 100 possible classes, given one example of each class, or learning to efficiently play a new board game with only one practice. This approach is very different as compared to standard ML techniques, where training is performed just on a single task and testing on held-out examples from that task. During the process of Meta-Learning, a model is trained to learn tasks from the meta-training set. Two kinds of optimizations are performed: one for the learner, which learns new tasks, and the other for the meta-learner, which trains the learner.

Meta-Learning methods can be classified in one of three categories:

- *Recurrent models* are ingesting the data set sequentially, and then it processes new inputs from the task set. While the meta-learner is using Gradient Descent for optimization, the learner simply rolls out the recurrent network.
- *Metric learning* involves learning a metric space in which learning is particularly efficient. The Meta-Learning optimization is performed using Gradient Descent while the learner optimization comes down to a comparison scheme (like Nearest Neighbors), in the meta-learned metric space.
- *Learning optimizers*, where one network (the meta-learner) learns to update another network (the learner) so that the learner effectively learns the task. The meta-learner is typically a Recurrent Network so that it can remember how it previously updated the learner model. The meta-learner can be trained with either Reinforcement Learning or Supervised Learning.

A more recent meta-learning algorithm called MAML (Model Agnostic Meta-Learning) was developed at Berkeley Artificial Intelligence Research lab (Finn, Abbeel, and Levine 2017). This model could be directly applied to any learning problem and model that is trained with a gradient descent procedure. The central idea underlying this new method was to "train the model's initial parameters such that the model has maximal performance on a new task after the parameters have been updated through one or more gradient steps computed with a small amount of data from that new task." The MAML task-agnostic algorithm is training the parameters of a model in such a way that a small number of gradient updates could lead to fast learning on a new task. The MAML algorithm was tested on different model types, including both fully connected and convolutional networks, and in several distinct domains, including few-shot regression, image classification, and Reinforcement Learning.

The success of Machine Learning could be attributed in large part to its *data-driven* philosophy that favors automatic discovery of patterns from data over the manual design of *expert* systems. But there is a far-reaching paradox that is deep-rooted in the current paradigm, the fact that the algorithms that power ML are still *manually designed*. A natural question is whether one could *learn* these algorithms instead. It is very likely that one could devise new algorithms that perform much better than the manually designed ones, thus opening the possibility of improving the learning process.

From a practical perspective, there are some serious obstacles that need to be overcome. The most critical issue is how to parameterize the space of algorithms such that it is both expressive and efficiently searchable. The expressivity and *search-ability* of the algorithmic space are acting in opposition, and therefore a trade-off has to be made. A small algorithmic space would allow for efficient searching (i.e. via simple enumeration of algorithms in the set), but because the representation is so sparse, the space would most likely not contain the best possible algorithm. Conversely, if the algorithmic space is represented by a large set containing the best possible algorithm, the searching process could be very inefficient (as an example, enumeration would take exponential time).

3.3 THE MEANING OF AI – A CRITICAL VIEW

"There's no sense in being precise when you don't even know what you're talking about."

– *John von Neumann*

Artificial Intelligence is becoming the *tech-mantra* of our time. This term is overused by academicians and technologists alike, as well as by journalists, venture capitalists, and others who do not have a solid understanding of the scientific and technological complexity of this topic.

What is particularly worrisome about the overuse of the tag AI is the fact that even a large category of scientists are often as confused as the general public when it comes to properly using this term. When the verbal rampage is coming from solution vendors, the justification may be purely business related; but when it is perpetuated by scientists and engineers it is becoming worrisome. The mere idea that the current AI tool set is emulating human intelligence *in silico* is indeed far-fetched and could lead to some very dangerous consequences. Let's just consider situations involving computers taking life-or-death decisions in a healthcare setting.

This *in silico* Intelligence fantasy was very quickly and carelessly extrapolated to a "planetary-scale inference-and-decision-making system" (Jordan, 2018) by an army of self-proclaimed AI pundits who are aggressively preaching the blending of Computer Science with Statistics in order to better serve humanity.

According to Professor Jordan, "Whether or not we come to understand Intelligence any time soon, we do have a major challenge on our hands in bringing together computers and humans in ways that enhance human life." This new challenge will have to be encoded into a new branch of engineering, one that will be built on ideas that are a century old, like *information*, *algorithm*, *data*, *uncertainty*, *computing*, *inference*, or *optimization*. We witness today the existence of a very powerful current within the technology and business media that is forcefully using AI as an intellectual wildcard, one that makes it difficult to reason about the scope and consequences of this emerging technology.

The first level of confusion comes from the fact that *most of what is being called AI today is what has been called Machine Learning (ML) for the past several decades.* ML is an interdisciplinary field that blends ideas from Statistics, Computer Science, and other disciplines to design and implement algorithms that process data in order to make predictions and help with decision-making. ML has already generated a profound impact on the real world by helping businesses in solving mission-critical problems such as fraud detection, supply-chain prediction, and building innovative recommendation systems for their customers. As data sets and computing resources have grown at a sustained pace, Machine Learning has become an essential tool for enterprises where decision-making could be related to large-scale data.

"All of machine learning is about error correction."
– Yann LeCun, chief AI scientist, Facebook

But the idea that the current generation of AI is imitating human intelligence is just aspirational at best at this point in time. Prior to the debut of the modern AI era, there were many other academic fields that were inspired by human intelligence. But the majority of these fields have been focused mostly on *low-level* primitives such as signals or decisions. Scientific disciplines such as Statistics, Pattern Recognition, Information Theory, Operations Research, and Control Theory are just a few examples.

The central idea of AI is to focus on understanding and encoding into software the high-level cognitive capability of humans, such as the ability to *reason* and to *think*. More than 60 years later after the start of the modern AI era, the aspiration of coding *in silico* high-level human reasoning remains a distant goal. The technological developments that are currently labeled emerged mostly from engineering fields associated with *low-level* pattern recognition and statistics, and they were focused on finding patterns in data and on making well-founded predictions that could generate efficient business decisions. R&D conducted in fields such as text classification and document retrieval, fraud detection, recommendation systems, personalized search, and social network analysis have been a major success and have powered companies such as Google, Netflix, Facebook, and Amazon.

The current generation of AI could be characterized as *Weak AI*. It is fundamentally an *optimization algorithm* that could learn from data that is *very domain specific* and that could perform extremely well on a test set of the same *kind* of data. AI performs reasonably well a *vertical single task* and has become a very useful tool that could add value through automation of mundane tasks. The current AI algorithms cannot learn behaviors such as *common sense*, *emotion*, or *self-awareness*, and therefore they could not offer any understanding on what it means to be *human*. The current algorithms also cannot learn creativity, one of the most valuable human traits, which involves inventing things, curing diseases, creating art works, etc.

But beyond mislabeling, a more critical issue is that the use of this ill-defined acronym may prevent a correct understanding of the range of intellectual and commercial issues at play. The last two decades have seen a concerted effort to redefine the initial scope of AI. A more recent concept referred to as *Intelligence Augmentation* (IA) addresses the use of data and computation for the development of services that could augment human intelligence and creativity (Jordan, 2018). A search engine could be viewed as an example of IA because it augments human memory and factual knowledge. By the same token *natural language processing* could augment the ability of humans to communicate.

Another emerging discipline labeled as *Intelligent Infrastructure* (II) studies the synergy between data, computation, and physical infrastructure side-by-side in order to make human environments safer and more accommodating. This type of

Intelligent Infrastructure is becoming present in industries such as transportation, commerce, medicine, and finance. This vast area of R&D is sometimes referred to as the *Internet of Things*.

AI research has made the imitation of human intelligence its main goal from its inception. But Psychology research has decisively shown that humans are not always flawless when it comes to reasoning; their behavior shows biases and limitations, and modeling these traits from a quantitative perspective could be extremely challenging. The biggest limitation of the *human-imitative* AI is related to this challenge. Practical implementations of *intelligent* systems have shown empirically that it is neither necessary nor sufficient to make each component of the system be intelligent. Instead the focus should be on the development of intelligent *building blocks* or components that work well with each other and with the human operator. During their biological and cultural evolution, humans have not been empowered with the necessary abilities to perform *large-scale* decision-making tasks, such as the ones that modern AI systems are designed to implement. Humans were not built to face or to handle the types of uncertainty that could arise in these new contexts. Professor Jordan (2018) argues that "an AI system should not only imitate human intelligence, but they should also correct it and scale it to arbitrarily large problems." According to him there are many algorithmic and infrastructural challenges that are not addressed by the *human-imitative* AI research. Just a few examples:

- Designing systems that can find abstractions quickly
- Designing systems that can explain their decisions
- Performing causal reasoning
- Robustness when facing unexpected situations or adversaries
- Protecting privacy and data ownership

While the digital economy will continue to drive technological development, the academic research will maintain its essential role in providing fresh scientific ideas. While the contributions from humanities and cognitive-social sciences are going to be essential for the success of this enterprise, the engineering effort required will be of a gigantic scale and scope. Visionaries like Professor Jordan believe that we are going to witness the birth of a new engineering discipline – *a human-centric engineering discipline* – that will be at the same time data-focused and learning-focused. Until one finds a better nomenclature for this new engineering discipline, we will continue to use the acronym AI as a placeholder. But let's be aware of the very real limitations that come with its use!

It took about 200,000 years for the human brain to evolve from a primitive state to where it is today, and merely 80 years since Konrad Zuse created Z1, the first programmable computer. The umbrella of *Computationally Intelligent* techniques has developed at a very rapid pace in the last 60 years, and it offers the promise of building the bridge between the awesome mystery of Human Intelligence and the aspirational world of AI (see Figure 3.3).

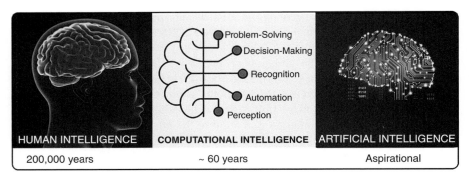

Problem-Solving		
Decision-Making		
Recognition		
Automation		
Perception		
HUMAN INTELLIGENCE	COMPUTATIONAL INTELLIGENCE	ARTIFICIAL INTELLIGENCE
200,000 years	~ 60 years	Aspirational

FIGURE 3.3   The place of computational intelligence.

3.4   ON THE APPLICABILITY OF AI TO FINANCE

Now that the reader has been exposed to a more comprehensive picture for the origins of AI, its historical development, and the controversy surrounding its name, it will be quite useful to apply this knowledge to our domain of interest – Trading and Investing. Since AI is generally used as an *umbrella* term for the different branches of Machine Learning, this section is going to concentrate on evaluating the applicability of ML techniques to the field Quantitative Finance. Machine learning is defined as a set of computational tools that aim to create a mapping between the *feature* space and the *outcome* space with the purpose of classification or of generating predictions about the dynamics of the feature space. While traditional statistical modeling relies on linear measures or linear estimators, Machine Learning is essentially a tool set designed to find nonlinear relationships in large data sets. In the statistical parlance, ML algorithms are designed and implemented as a system of *factors* and their respective *weights*. The main objective of any ML algorithm is to discover hidden relationships between the feature space and the outcome space.

ML algorithms have an implicit problem space where they could be extremely effective – examples are speech and image recognition. The main question that we will address in this section is whether ML algorithms could be successfully applied to financial market data. This exercise will require a solid understanding of the nature of the problem space. What is really special about the financial markets? How are the characteristics of this particular problem space going to impact the applicability of general-purpose ML algorithms? In order to answer all these important questions, one needs to carefully consider the nature of several important mechanisms that are responsible for the uniqueness of financial market data, that being:

- Data *generation* process – Is the generative process *stationary* such as to ensure that training and testing could be performed on the same *kind* of data?
- Data *quality* – Is the financial market data associated with *manageable* noise-to-signal ratio such that overfitting will be kept under control?

- *Dimensionality* of the feature space – Could one engineer a feature space of enough dimensions such that the *measurable* properties of the financial markets could be properly learned by the ML algorithms?

Let's start by defining the *Problem*: given an experimental data set and a specific task to be carried out (e.g. Classification, Regression, Clustering, or Dimensionality Reduction), the goal is to come up with the proper feature set and the most proficient model that will map the feature space to the outcomes.

The process that maps the feature space to measurable outcomes starts with processing the data set and culminates with the inference of the *best* model (by determining its functional form) that could be applied to *unseen* data of the same *kind*.

Let's call this process the *Machine Learning pipeline* (see Figure 3.4).

- The ML pipeline starts with the ingestion of a certain amount of raw data that usually requires some kind of pre-processing. The effectiveness of machine learning techniques is very dependent on the quality of the data they consume. Therefore ensuring a high standard of quality for the input data is a hard requirement.
- After the data is *cleansed* it proceeds to the *Feature engineering* stage. Depending on the type of data and the ML algorithm utilized, the process of Feature engineering could be manual or it could be automated.
- Once the features are extracted, and the feature space is fixed, the data is split into several sets: training, testing, and *hold-out*.
- A complex iterative process is started whereby the selected ML algorithms are used on these three different data sets to build the *candidate* data model.
- Complex validation procedures are used to ensure that the model produced by the pipeline will be useable in *real-world* settings.

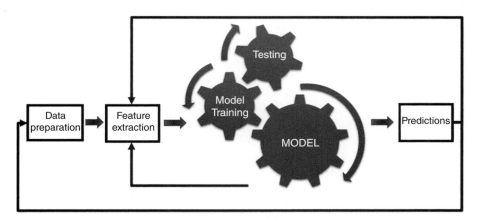

FIGURE 3.4   Machine learning pipeline.

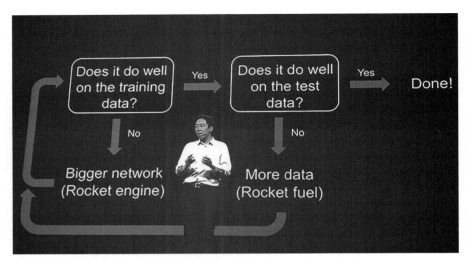

FIGURE 3.5   Professor Ng on the rocket analogy.

- In many situations there is a combination of ML models that are produced by the pipeline – what one calls the *Ensemble* methodology that usually offers the best results.

One of the most distinguished Deep-Learning researchers, Professor Andrew Ng from Stanford, co-founder of Coursera and key member of the Deep-Learning teams at Google and Baidu, likes to use the *rocket-fuel* analogy to describe the Machine Learning pipeline (Pitney 2015):

> *"A rocket ship is a giant engine together with a ton of fuel. Both need to be really big. If you have a lot of fuel and a tiny engine, you won't get off the ground. If you have a huge engine and a tiny amount of fuel, you can lift up, but you probably won't make it to orbit. So you need a big engine and a lot of fuel. We finally have the tools to build the big rocket engine – that is giant computers, that's our rocket engine. And the fuel is the data. We finally are getting the data that we need."*
>
> *– Andrew Ng (see Figure 3.5)*

How can we judge the applicability of ML techniques to the world of financial data? As mentioned in Chapter 2, data is nothing else but a vector-carrier of information about the nature of the process generating this data. Acquiring, modeling, and interpreting data will shed light into the nature of the process generating this data.

The applicability of Machine Learning methodologies to financial data depends on:

- Ability to determine the *nature* of the process that generates the data – stationary vs. nonstationary

- Capacity to assure a *high-quality standard* for the data sets used for training and testing
- Competence to select an *informative, independent, and descriptive* feature space that must be an accurate representation of the process that generates the data

3.4.1 Data Stationarity

The most commonly used Machine Learning techniques in Quantitative Finance are Classification, Regression, and Dimensionality Reduction. If the *Representation* phase of the ML-pipeline is well understood, what about the *Evaluation* step: How *well* are these ML techniques working when applied to financial market data? The majority of ML models assume that the data generation process is *stationary* and *Independent and Identically Distributed* (iid). But what if by the time the ML algorithm has *learned the data*, conditions may have changed significantly? Using ML techniques to learn from market data may work well in one regime (training data) but may be completely ineffective in another regime (test data, out-of-sample). Is there any guarantee?

Predictive modeling of financial time-series is very different in nature from more traditional predictive modeling tasks. And this is due to the temporal structure of the data that has higher than usual dimensionality. In statistical modeling one assumes that time-series are being generated by stationary processes. In general Statistics makes quite strong assumptions about the data. Classical statistical time-series analysis and forecasting methods are concerned with transforming nonstationary time series data into stationary ones. This is generally done by both identifying and removing the trends or by removing the seasonal effects. Stationarity tests use summary statistics like mean and variance for a change over a period of time and then check the statistical significance to identify if a time series is stationary or not. There are several families of stationarity tests, but the Augmented Dickey-Fuller test (ADF) is one of the most utilized statistical tests, also known as the *unit root test*. The intuition behind the ADF test is to determine how strongly a time series is defined by a trend. It uses an autoregressive model and optimizes an information criterion across multiple lag values.

Now the question is how well general-purpose ML techniques could work on financial market data given the very nature of it. This type of data is quite special in the sense that it describes a very complex *herd behavior* that is highly nonlinear and nonstationary in its nature. Dealing with nonstationarity is one of modern Machine Learning's greatest challenges. As such, the ability to detect transitions from stationarity to nonstationarity and vice versa is an absolutely necessary tool in ensuring that the ML algorithms are properly extracting actionable information from the market data. There are several forms of stationarity that have been studied:

- Weak stationarity – shift-invariance in terms of mean, and
- Strong stationarity – shift-invariance in terms of all moments of the distribution.

It is generally accepted that the financial market data finds itself most of the time in a weak stationarity regime. This implies the fact that even though the price levels are nonstationary, the use of price returns allows for a quite accurate approximation of weak stationarity. There is a proven fact that for the majority of traded financial securities, price returns during time intervals smaller than 15 minutes are dominated by the bid-ask bounce, and therefore after filtration of this kind of noise, the time-series stays in a weak stationarity regime for most of the trading day. The state-of-the-art research in this field is very well summarized by Sugiyama and Kawanabe (2012) in *Machine Learning in Non-Stationary Environments: Introduction to Covariate Shift Adaptation.*

3.4.2   Data Quality

Financial market data is a very special kind of data not just because the process that generates it could transition unexpectedly into a nonstationary regime, but also because it is associated with a high noise-to-signal ratio. It is widely accepted that the algorithms that power Machine Learning engines need high-quality data in order to validate the conclusions they draw from it.

Bad Data + Good Models = Bad Results

The principal ingredients of any ML technique are the data consumed for the learning process and the algorithms used to actuate that. So is there a preference for one or the other? Do we need more data or just better algorithms? According to Peter Norvig, director of Engineering at Google, "We don't have better algorithms. We just have more data … We should stop acting as if our main goal is to author extremely elegant theories … Instead use the best ally we have: the unreasonable effectiveness of data" (Norvig and Pereira 2009).

The factors that are affecting the data quality are:

- Completeness of data set
- Consistency of data types
- Accuracy
- Validity – whether the data measures what it is intended to measure – noisiness
- Timeliness – real-time vs. historical

Noise is probably the principal factor that affects the quality of the data used by Machine Learning applications in Quantitative Finance. There are two types of noise:

- *Class* or label noise occurs when an example is incorrectly labeled. This could come in two flavors: contradictory examples and misclassifications.
- *Attribute* noise refers to corruptions in the values of one or more attributes. These attributes could be erroneous attribute values, missing or unknown attribute values, and incomplete attributes or *do not care* values. This type of noise is more harmful than the class noise, especially for attributes highly correlated with class labels.

There are several useful de-noising techniques:

- Filters
- The use of Ensemble learning methods for eliminating systematic noise: combining Bagging, Boosting, and Stacking
- Dimensionality Reduction – PCA
- The use sampling and x-fold cross-validation
- Selecting features that are less prone to noise

One of the most employed filtering techniques for noise reduction in financial market data is the Kalman filter. The Kalman filter is an algorithm used to find a good state estimation of stochastic time series data. The Kalman filter is the optimal linear filter also known as the Best Linear Unbiased Estimator. It assumes that the noise is Gaussian, and it minimizes the mean squared error of the estimated state parameters.

Other useful techniques are the Ensemble learning ones:

- Bagging (Bootstrap Aggregating) is a way to decrease the variance of prediction by generating additional data for training from your original data set using combinations with repetitions to produce multisets of the same cardinality/size as your original data.
- Boosting is a two-step approach; in a first step, one uses subsets of the original data to produce a series of averagely performing models. Then in a second step, performance could be boosted by combining the average models together using a majority vote cost function.

Training an ML model on noisy market data will likely produce an *overfitted* model due to the presence of noise. When this overfitted model will be used for predictions it may generate very costly false signals. The use of Regularization techniques and/or Bagging could alleviate this problem.

3.4.3   Data Dimensionality

As the term *feature* is defined as a measurable property of a phenomenon, an essential step in the ML-pipeline is the engineering of the optimal set of features. The goal of Feature engineering is to select informative, independent, and descriptive features such that the ML pipeline will generate models with a specified degree of predictability. The feature space refers to the numbers of attributes that a data set possesses and it must preserve the most relevant aspects of the data. Mapping feature space to the input data space requires having a *weight* for each of the distinct feature that could determine the classes of the inputs. There are problem domains such as Genomics or Astronomy where constructing a feature space is quite laborious given the high dimensionality of that space. High dimensionality makes the learning process *easy yet prone to overfitting*.

There are some fundamental differences in the way that one could map the Feature space in Machine Learning as opposed to Probability theory, where one deals with the Sample space. While the Feature space in ML could be further increased by extracting new features, the dimensionality of the Sample space in Probability theory cannot be increased. The Sample space is exhaustive while the Feature space in ML is expandable. The ML pipeline derives a model from the raw data. After the raw data is pre-processed and *cleansed*, it is subjected to Feature engineering. The features are then passed onto algorithms to train a candidate model, which represents nothing but a mathematical *summary* of features.

There are many Feature engineering approaches, but the most utilized ones are:

- Filters are using the most promising N features according to rankings from a proxy measure.
- Wrappers are searching through the space of data subsets and are training and evaluating a model using a greedy search.
- Embedded methods – feature selection is part of the model construction process.

In the special case of financial time-series, Feature engineering could be done by:

- Discretization – construct bins for continuous features.
- Delta method – taking the difference between two features.
- Windowing.
- Standardization – zero mean and unit standard deviation.
- Normalization – feature vectors with unit norm.

From a feature dimensionality perspective, the financial market data is very special. The fundamental two features of market data are price and volume. Is it even possible to play piano on just two strings? Fortunately given the time-varying nature of this kind of data, one is able to *fabricate* quite easily more dimensions via splitting the time series into small fragments and constructing a multidimensional vector that represents each fragment. In addition one may be able to synthesize new time series from the initial one via derivation, integration, or filtering, and build a truly multidimensional time series.

3.5 PERSPECTIVES AND FUTURE DIRECTIONS

The concept of Artificial Intelligence is very well anchored in today's pop culture. It is a term that is used so frequently and so liberally that it very soon could become a verb or an adjective, à la "Let's google that." Beyond all one could say about the intellectual honesty of promoting a term that is not factually correct, it is also fair to mention that the development of the many scientific disciplines that one could group under the *AI umbrella* is creating a lot of value to the society on several levels, by:

- Providing insights and foresights via the use of Statistical Learning techniques, such as data mining and predictive analytics
- Augmenting human decision-making via the use of Machine Learning methods (supervised or unsupervised)
- Providing adaptive learning techniques such as Reinforcement Learning that could learn and adapt within continuously changing environments (robots and autonomous vehicles).

The penetration of AI into the world of finance is not as easy as one may think. Although the AI keyword is widely utilized, the real use of the concept is still in its infancy. Switching the AI label to ML may bring us a bit closer to real-world applications. What makes financial market data very unique from an ML applicability perspective is mainly related to the very complex nonlinear and nonstationary nature of the processes that drive the financial markets. Therefore characteristics such as stationarity, noise-to-signal-ratio, and dimensionality are very important considerations to be taken into account when one attempts to use ML techniques on this type of data.

To these specific characteristics of the financial market data one could add the contribution of the very fine granularity of *tick-data*. This very special type of data is the messenger of the market microstructure processes that are fundamental in the understanding of price dynamics at very short time scales. This market microstructure data is captured at the resolution of individual orders (therefore is very noisy and nonstationary), but it encodes extremely useful information about factors like hidden liquidity, or operations like cancellations and executions.

Time is an absolutely critical factor in trading, especially in the field of High-Frequency trading. From this perspective applying a *plain-vanilla* ML-pipeline in a trading setting is a very challenging, but not to say a practically impossible task. For real-time decision-making, a typical ML pipeline could be a non-starter since it creates a critical bottleneck for the trading-decision pipeline. Therefore ML algorithms need extremely fast offloads.

New techniques have been recently developed whereby the learning is done *online* from streaming real-time data, as opposed to historical data. These state-of-the-art methods are looking to eliminate the need for lengthy lookups and complex calculations, by allowing fast memory access and hash-function lookups. These online learning techniques (Shalev-Shwartz 2012) are sometimes described as *data in motion* analysis because it treats data as a running stream, and it learns as the stream flows. Classical offline learning or batch learning treats data as a *static pool*, assuming that all data is available at the time of training.

Given a financial market data set, the traditional offline learning produces only one final model, with all the data being considered simultaneously. Online learning algorithms look at a limited (usually quite small) data set at a time. With each *read*, online learning makes a small incremental update to the model it built with past data. The model gradually improves as it receives more data in real-time from the available stream.

But probably the most important challenge in applying ML techniques to HFT data is the profound lack of understanding of how such low-level data could be related to actionable circumstances, such as optimally executing large orders, or alpha generation. The case studies presented in Chapters 6 through 11 will bring to the reader the latest research published in this field.

REFERENCES

AAAI (n.d.). "A Brief History of AI." https://aitopics.org/misc/brief-history.

Bush (1945). As we may think. *Atlantic Monthly* (July).

Finn, Abbeel, and Levine (2017). Model-agnostic meta-learning for fast adaptation of deep networks. https://arxiv.org/abs/1703.03400.

Glymour, Ford, and Hayes (1998). Ramón Lull and the infidels. *AI Magazine* 19 (2).

Jordan (2018). Artificial intelligence – the revolution hasn't happened yet. Medium. https://medium.com/@mijordan3/artificial-intelligence-the-revolution-hasnt-happened-yet-5e1d5812e1e7.

McCarthy, Minsky, Rochester et al. (2006). A Proposal for the Dartmouth Summer Research Project on Artificial Intelligence. *AI Magazine* 27 (4): 12.

McCulloch and Pitts (1943). A logical calculus of the ideas immanent in nervous activity. *Bulletin of Mathematical Biophysics* 5: 115–133, 1943.

Norvig and Pereira (2009). The unreasonable effectiveness of data. *IEEE Intelligent Systems* 24 (2): 8–12.

Pitney (2015). Inside the mind that built google brain. *HuffPost* (13 May). https://www.huffpost.com/entry/andrew-ng_n_7267682.

Searle (1980). Minds, brains, and programs. *Behavioral and Brain Sciences* 3 (3): 417–424.

Shalev-Shwartz (2012). Online learning and online convex optimization. *Foundations and Trends in Machine Learning* 4 (2): 107–194.

Sugiyama and Kawanabe (2012). *Machine Learning in Non-Stationary Environments: Introduction to Covariate Shift Adaptation.* MIT Press, 137–174.

Turing (1937). On computable numbers, with an application to the *Entscheidungsproblem. Proceedings of the London Mathematical Society* s2-42 (1): 230–265.

Turing (1950). Computing machinery and intelligence. *Mind* 59 (236): 433–460.

CHAPTER 4

Computational Intelligence – A Principled Approach for the Era of Data Exploration

"The science of learning explores how a computationally limited entity can succeed in a world that is too complex for it to model."

– Leslie Valiant, Turing Award winner

4.1 INTRODUCTION TO COMPUTATIONAL INTELLIGENCE

The debate over the legitimacy of the term *Artificial Intelligence* is not going to settle anytime soon. There is a continuous display of pros and cons, and both sides rely on powerful advocacy groups. Whether or not one side will win the argument over the other one is absolutely irrelevant. What matters more is the achievement of some palpable progress that will advance the understanding of human intelligence and hopefully pave the way for machines to emulate it in a way that will be beneficial for the society as a whole.

4.1.1 Defining Intelligence

Since the concept of *intelligence* is fundamental to any human endeavor, and especially because it makes up *half* of the term *Artificial Intelligence*, it is both wise and fair to build upon its foundation any scientific endeavor that may claim to emulate it. Intellectual honesty requires that any reference to AI should take into consideration a clear definition of the term *intelligence*. So let's attempt to define this very complex concept. *Webster's* definition, which is one of the most commonly used, states that Intelligence is "the ability to learn, or to understand, or to deal with new or trying situations," or alternatively "the ability to apply knowledge in order to manipulate one's environment, or to think abstractly as measured by objective criteria (tests)." David Fogel (1995), one of the pioneers of evolutionary computing, defined Intelligence as "the capability of a system to adapt its behavior to meet its goals in a range of environments. It is a property of all purpose-driven decision-makers." This definition of Intelligence is perhaps more relevant to the subject matter of this book, so we will keep it as a reference.

We have recently witnessed the development of a large variety of analytic and computational tools that made possible solutions to problems that were previously considered difficult or impossible to solve. Many of these new tools have been grouped under the umbrella of yet another composite term that includes the word Intelligence, namely Computational Intelligence. The concept of Computational Intelligence refers to the ability of an algorithm to learn through computational means a specific task from experimental observation from data. What is specific to Computational Intelligence is the fact that it represents a set of nature-inspired computational techniques that are applicable to complex real-world problems for which traditional mathematical modeling does not work. The two main sets of problems addressed by Computational Intelligence relate to modeling of processes that might be either too complex for mathematical reasoning or could be considered as stochastic in nature. Although both Computational Intelligence and Artificial Intelligence may seek similar goals, there's a clear distinction between them and this will be the subject of this chapter.

An important note to the reader: *there will be many references to* Computational Intelligence *throughout this book. In many instances, the meaning of Computational Intelligence is not going to be necessarily the one used in Computer Science (CS) circles. My interpretation and use of the term CI is a lot more flexible and refers specifically to any computational methodologies that could be used in the process of learning from data with the purpose of driving decisions in the realm of trading and investing. In the vast majority of cases, especially in the chapters that will introduce the case studies, my definition of CI refers mainly to Machine Learning techniques that are currently used in Quantitative and Computational Finance. But I also added references to other methods, like the Probably Approximately Correct framework, which promises to bring us closer to achieving true Intelligence via evolutionary techniques (ecorithms) that are more akin to human behavior than to machines. I will try to be consistent in the use of the term, by using the acronym CI for the more narrow interpretation related to data-intensive computations, and Computational Intelligence for the umbrella term that is used in computer science.*

4.1.2   What Is Computational Intelligence?

From a pure computer science perspective, Computational Intelligence is focusing on problems that only humans can solve, problems requiring Intelligence. The methods used by Computational Intelligence are close to the human way of reasoning that is using inexact and incomplete information, with the declared scope of generating controlled actions in an adaptive way.

Computational Intelligence encompasses a multidisciplinary framework that includes well-established research fields such as:

- *Artificial Neural Networks*, which allow a system to learn from data in an experiential way, by operating like a biological neural system
- *Fuzzy logic*, which enables a computer to understand natural languages
- *Evolutionary computing*, which is based on natural selection criteria
- *Swarm intelligence*, which studies the collective behavior of decentralized and self-organized systems
- *Statistical analysis*, which helps dealing with uncertainty imprecision

Computational Intelligence is closely related to the field called *soft* computing. According to Lofti Zadeh (1998), the inventor of fuzzy logic, "Soft computing is not a single methodology. Rather, it is a consortium of computing methodologies which collectively provide a foundation for the conception, design and deployment of intelligent systems." When compared with the traditional hard computing methodology, soft computing is more permissive of imprecision, uncertainty, and partial truth. The guiding principle of soft computing is to "exploit the tolerance for imprecision, uncertainty and partial truth to achieve tractability, robustness, low solution cost and better rapport with reality." Zadeh believed that the philosophy of soft computing is foundational to the emerging field of Computational Intelligence. He describes AI as a discipline relying on hard computing techniques, whereas Computational Intelligence is based on soft computing methods.

It is quite common that scientific disciplines are not statically defined, but they slowly evolve in scope and coverage by sharing and clustering of common interests with other related fields. When the AI community started to develop in the late 1950s, the main objective was to encode human intelligence into a format that computers could operate on (by developing *in silico* agents). The evolution of AI's initial goal was summarized in the twenty-fifth anniversary issue of *AI Magazine* by Mackworth (2005): "In AI's youth, we worked hard to establish our paradigm by vigorously attacking and excluding apparent pretenders to the throne of intelligence, pretenders such as pattern recognition, behaviorism, neural networks, and even probability theory. Now that we are established, such ideological purity is no longer a concern. We are more catholic, focusing on problems, not on hammers. Given that we do have a comprehensive toolbox, issues of architecture and integration emerge as central."

The idea of Computational Intelligence was crystalized into an impressive number of societies and scientific journals. The most active group is the IEEE Computational Intelligence Society, which defines its subjects of interest as Neural Networks, Fuzzy Systems and Evolutionary Computation, including Swarm intelligence. The approach taken by both journals and by book authors was to treat Computational Intelligence as an umbrella under which more and more methods could be added.

Computational Intelligence is a computing methodology that provides a system with an ability to learn and deal with new situations. The system is required to possess reasoning attributes such as generalization, discovery, association, and abstraction. Computational Intelligence systems usually incorporate a mixture of paradigms such as Artificial Neural Networks, Fuzzy Systems, and Evolutionary Computation, augmented with specific domain knowledge. They are often designed to mimic one or more aspects of biological intelligence. The concept of Computational Intelligence is also closely related to concepts such as adaptation and evolution; this could facilitate the appropriate actions (via intelligent behavior) necessary for systems to survive in complex and changing environments.

For many Computational Intelligence advocates, the field exhibits a series of obvious biological inspirations:

- ANNs use neurons as their building blocks.
- Fuzzy logic is founded on the idea of uncertainty and vagueness, and it draws its roots from the behavioral expression of organisms and their interaction with the environment.
- Evolutionary computing is using genetics and evolution at its core.

But there are also other categories of Computational Intelligence tools that have no biological connections, such as Bayesian learning, probabilistic and possibilistic reasoning, alternative approaches to handle uncertainty, kernel methods, or search algorithms.

4.1.3 Mapping the Field of Study

Computer Science focuses on the study on computable processes and the design of processing systems. Computational Intelligence studies a different set of problems for which there are no adequate practical implementations of algorithms. This impracticality arises when either the problem formulation is not possible in a codable form or when the problem is NP-hard and therefore a practical implementation does not exist. I will define Computational Intelligence as a "branch of computer science studying problems for which there are no effective computational algorithms" (Duch 2013). The implementation of truly intelligent *in silico* agents, which was the initial goal of AI, is one of these problems.

Biological organisms deal with such hard problems every day: extracting meaning from information that was acquired through perception, communicating, and understanding via the use of languages, solving all kind of ill-defined problems. These problem-solving skills have been acquired by living organisms as a result of their ability to adapt to their environment. Biological organisms are facing a great variety of problems, and they have acquired the capacity to survive by learning how to solve these problems in a multitude of ways. Being inspired by nature's ability to adapt in order to survive and thrive, the *Computational Intelligence's field of study is defined by the problems it tries to solve rather than by the methods and tools used in the problem-solving process.*

The vast majority of Computational Intelligence research concentrates on low-level cognitive functions, such as perception (e.g. object recognition and signal analysis), pattern discovery, object association, and system control. By comparison, the stated goal of AI was from the beginning to focus on problems that require higher cognition. Higher-level cognitive functions are required to solve non-algorithmizable problems involving systemic thinking, reasoning, planning, and understanding of symbolic knowledge. These problems are currently addressed by the AI community using methods based on search, symbolic knowledge representation, and Natural Language Processing methods. The overlap between the low-level approach used in Computational Intelligence and the high-level cognitive AI-style could be found in both Machine Learning (e.g. Sequence Learning and Reinforcement Learning) as well as Distributed Multi-Agent systems. All applications that require reasoning based on perceptions, such as robotics or self-driving cars, require methods for solving both low and high-level cognitive problems, and they represent a common area of interest for both AI and Computational Intelligence experts.

The concepts of Learning and Adaptation are deeply grounded on evolutionary biology, and they are becoming nowadays the conceptual foundation upon which Computational Intelligence is developing (Eberhart and Shi 2007). While the Learning applies globally to the entire intelligent system, Adaptation is applicable just to the portion of the system where Computational Intelligence is relevant. The three main Adaptation paradigms are:

- Supervised Adaptation that uses a teacher paradigm
- Reinforcement Adaptation that uses a critic paradigm
- Unsupervised Adaptation that employs an algorithm operating on the data set with no feedback (no labeling)

In Supervised Adaptation, a teacher has access to detailed input/output information involving a number of specific examples. The more examples that are available, the better the system will be able to adapt to model the structure underlying them, given that the distribution from which they were drawn is known and stationary.

In the case of Reinforcement Adaptation, a critic agent has access to a metric (and not a quantitatively defined cost function!) that determines whether a solution is qualitatively better than another one in spite of the fact that it cannot calculate a fitness measure for that problem. As such, the critic (see Figure 4.1) does not know about the location of an optimum solution or even if one exists. By comparison, the teacher from the supervised case may be able to discover the optimum solution for the problem space. When there is neither fitness information nor any labeled feedback available, the Adaptation process is becoming *Unsupervised*. This type of Adaptation process will be used to find features (clusters) in the data. There are situations when in spite of having labeling information available one still prefers to use Unsupervised Adaptation to reduce the problem's dimensionality and facilitate the use of Supervised Adaptation for later stages.

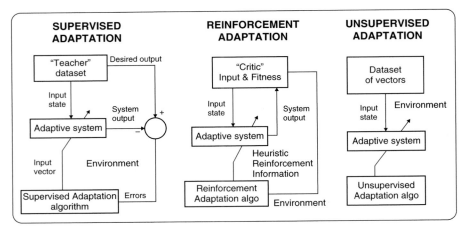

FIGURE 4.1   Different types of adaptation mechanisms.

All these types of adaptation are using similar principles with methods from the field of Machine Learning. No matter what kind of Adaptation is implemented, there are three different spaces that are used for any implementation choice:

- The *Input Parameter (Problem)* space is defined by the range of the input variables. These ranges are generally specified, but sometimes just sample patterns are available.
- The *System Output (Function)* space is defined by the range of the outputs. These ranges could be specified either by using hard or soft constraints. A hard constraint is one that cannot be violated, as opposed to a soft constraint that could be violated while applying a penalty to the Cost function.
- The *Fitness* space is the space used to define the goodness of the solutions in the output space generated by the adaptive system.

One needs to emphasize the fact that AI is intrinsically connected with the concept of hard computing. Important properties of systems such as the ability to generalize, to deal with partial truths and uncertainty, to allow for some tolerance for errors and noise, but mostly to perform well in changing and complex environments, are not easily implemented (if at all) by using the hard computing paradigm.

Since most systems in real life are characterized by imprecision, uncertainty, partial truths, and nonlinearity, Computational Intelligence becomes a more convincing candidate for implementing optimization and diagnostics algorithms in complex and changing environments.

4.1.4   Problems vs. Tools

Another defining characteristic of Computational Intelligence is represented by its *problem-solving* focus. This multidisciplinary field is viewed more as an approach to solving problems than just another set of tools. And one should not confound the field's purpose with its methodology. The purpose is to understand how intelligent behavior is possible, but the ultimate goal is to design, implement, and experiment with computational systems that perform tasks commonly viewed as intelligent. Creating these artifacts is an essential goal for Computational Intelligence that, after all, is a truly empirical science.

The concept of Computational Intelligence was created initially with the desire to avoid the use of the adjective *artificial*, which hints at *simulated* rather than *natural* intelligence. But during its evolution Computational Intelligence's goal shifted to the understanding of both natural and synthetic intelligent systems by means of implementing them. Let's consider as an example the simulation of an intergalactic flight mission. Computers could be seen as the archetype of a formal symbol-manipulation system, and as such they are the tool carrying out most of the simulations nowadays. But a computer simulation will not amount to a real intergalactic flight. The goal of Computational Intelligence is to actually create the intelligence that could make the practical implementation of this flight possible.

One has to realize that there is a healthy competition between the science of Computational Intelligence, which is attempting to understand the principles of reasoning, and the engineering of Computational Intelligence, which focuses on coding the programs required to solve particular problems. This duality is one of the main drivers of this new discipline. As a scientific discipline Computational Intelligence is aiming at the creation and testing of debatable theories, specifically looking at how hard practical problems could be represented and solved by a computer. These theories should have empirical support in real-world implementations, whose quality should be judged by traditional Computer Science principles. The main purpose of Computational Intelligence is to bridge the duality of specifying theories and building implementations.

4.1.5 Current Challenges

From its inception, the world of AI has been accustomed to a number of grand challenges, and it started with the famous Turing test for machine intelligence. This test is still unsolved today mainly because it requires a very-large knowledge base and a super-efficient system for retrieval of information.

What could be today's greatest challenge for Computational Intelligence? Naturally the answer should align with the declared scope of Computational Intelligence, which is dealing with low-level cognitive functions. The nature and the complexity of dealing with Intelligence are not very different for low- or high-level representations of cognition. Therefore the challenges are gravitating around the same themes, which are represented by more efficient *knowledge representation* and *retrieval structures*. Most of the Computational Intelligence research attempted to come up with candidate models for knowledge representations by looking for inspiration in the associative memory of the brain. Current forms of knowledge representation used in Machine Learning such as *vector-* and *similarity*-based models cannot replace the complexity of the reasoning processes. Semantic networks are representing alternatives that could provide efficient association and inference mechanisms, but they have never been used on large-scale practical implementations. But the ultimate challenge for Computational Intelligence would be to build an intelligent agent that for example could be able to survive in a hostile environment. Several intermediary steps will be required to achieve the ultimate solution, specifically being able to understand and model:

- Perception – e.g. object recognition, auditory and visual analysis, spatial orientation
- Memory organization and retrieval
- Learning process
- Behavioral control
- Reasoning and planning

This survival test may be a necessary prerequisite required to pass the Turing test.

4.1.6   The Future of Computational Intelligence

What Computational Intelligence intends to achieve is a form of Intelligence based on computational power. Many questions remain unanswered. Is Intelligence even computable, and if it is, could it be learned? Humans are natively able to draw general lessons from life experiences. Can this be coded? Once our intelligent agent will be able to learn how to survive simple situations, would it be able to evolve and adapt to more complex scenarios?

Similarly to AI, Computational Intelligence will not escape the scrutiny of societal utility and safety, as its main objective should be human-centered. Because of its emphasis on solving problems, Computational Intelligence should become an important tool in the decision-making process by generating scenarios that are presenting the users with choices and their possible consequences. A long-term goal for Computational Intelligence is to create cognitive systems that could compete with humans in a variety of areas. Nowadays this is possible only in restricted domains, such as pattern recognition, automation of the processing of a large amount of numerical information, high-precision control for a limited number of degrees of freedom, and reasoning in board games.

Despite a great deal of progress achieved by Computational Intelligence research, systems designed to solve lower-level cognitive functions are still far behind the natural ones. The situation is even worse when higher-level cognitive functions (AI) like language understanding, reasoning, problem solving, and planning are considered. The reality is that AI is a far cry from what the meaning of Intelligence will infer. The ability of humans to apply semantic and episodic memory is vastly superior to the most sophisticated artificial systems, storing complex memory patterns and rapidly accessing them in an associative way. As a majority of academics and technologists agree, Computational Intelligence is defined as the science of solving non-algorithmizable problems. Therefore this new domain is firmly anchored in the field of Computer Science. Focusing on problems instead of just tools will allow for a greater cooperation with the AI community, and it will enable a productive competition between these two fields, facilitating real progress toward more difficult problems.

4.1.7 Examples in Finance

As mentioned in the previous section, Computational Intelligence is a multidisciplinary field of research that aims at developing machine intelligence by incorporating foundational concepts from biological intelligence, such as Learning and Adaptation. This methodology represents a bottom-up approach.

One of the realities that quantitative finance practitioners have to deal with on a daily basis is the fact that many of the problems they face have no closed form solutions but require trade-offs and optimizations instead. A typical example is the Optimal Execution problem that will be addressed in Chapter 6. From a high-level decision-making perspective, it is obvious that for every order there is an optimal execution rate or execution schedule. But reaching an optimal rate of execution or an optimal execution schedule depends very much on preferences and tolerances assigned by market participants. These parameters depend on market impact and appetite for risk. This is an example of high-level decision-making under uncertainty informed by low-level granular data and quantitative models.

But during the process of Learning and Adaptation to the state of the market, the agent has to deal with a system of variable and high dimensionality. And this will require a low-level decision-making capability. Every observed market state can potentially evolve into an almost infinite number of other market states. In such an environment the set of possible actionable parameters (e.g. order time, price, size, and duration) is very large and dense. In addition, for this type of problem local optimality does not necessarily translate into a global optimality; what could be considered as a bad decision (trade) now could turn out to be an excellent one later. This is referred to as *non-local optimality*. The usual Machine Learning techniques are not going to be efficient for these kinds of problems! In the second part of the book we will explore the applicability of Computational Intelligence methodologies to these very domain specific problems.

As mentioned before, the field of Computational Intelligence is built on well-established research areas such as Artificial Neutral Networks, Fuzzy Logic, or Evolutionary Computing. The last few decades have seen these disciplines find interesting applications in the financial industry. Financial applications are usually aiming to predict the outcome of future events based on historical data.

Some of the areas where Artificial Neural Networks (Bishop 1995) have been effectively used:

- Predicting equities market price direction
- Forecasting term structure of interest rates
- Loan application evaluation and underwriting
- Credit scoring

Fuzzy logic has also been applied to a variety of applications in Finance in Narayana (2017). Using historical data fuzzy, logic systems could be used to analyze and predict future market price trends. Some examples are:

- Stock ranking, by evaluating corporations based on fundamental indicators, such as: profitability, management performance, capital structure, volume of transactions, and a variety of technical indicators;
- Stock selection, by using fuzzy rules and decision trees;
- Trading rule generation using fuzzification and de-fuzzification of technical indicators.

There were also attempts to apply Evolutionary Computing in Financial Engineering (Iba and Aranha 2012), most of them related to the generation of trading strategies, trend analysis, price forecasting, and portfolio optimization.

Although these techniques have been used for several decades, what Computational Intelligence brings new to Quantitative Finance and Financial Engineering is the centrality of the learning process. Dealing with the ever-increasing complexity of the financial markets will require a fresh new approach to cope with real-world situations for which hard computing techniques are not effective any longer. The ability to adapt dynamically to rapidly changing environments, such as the financial markets, requires the use of different methodologies, more akin to the principle of soft computing. Brand new algorithms need to be developed. What is specific to this new family of algorithms is the fact that they do not run on environments already known to the designer, but they need to learn from the environment they run on and cope with unknown scenarios.

4.2 THE PAC THEORY

Since the beginning of the AI era, a considerable amount of time and effort was spent by the Computer Science community studying the theory of Computational Complexity. One of the most fundament questions was referring to which aspect of Intelligence could be modeled as a quantitative theory. The vast majority of researchers in this field agreed that the answer must be *Learning*.

Unfortunately there was a general lack of consensus on how to define the process of Learning. For a long period of time Learning was not regarded as a field that would qualify as a scientific discipline. Until relatively recently Learning was considered as an extension of Education Psychology and other related non-quantitative disciplines. In spite of the fact that Learning is a very reproducible process, a rigorous quantitative modeling is still not available.

Last decade has seen a resurgence of interest in modeling the process of Learning. Pioneering work in this area was published in 2012 by Koedinger and collaborators at Carnegie Mellon (Koedinger, Corbett, and Perfetti 2012). They introduced the *Knowledge-Learning-Instruction* framework that was used to identify a broad range of learning events and influencing factors such as memory, induction, understanding, and sense-making processes. Other researchers believe that Learning must be modeled from both a statistical and a computational perspective. Since Learning is a central component to Computational Intelligence, this section is dedicated to understanding the relationship between Learning, Evolution, and Intelligence.

Dr. Leslie Valiant is one of the most prestigious computational theorists and computer scientists of our time. Professor Valiant was the recipient of the Turing award in 2010 for his "transformative contributions to the theory of computation, including the theory of probably approximately correct (PAC) learning, the complexity of enumeration and of algebraic computation, and the theory of parallel and distributed computing." He is the T. Jefferson Coolidge Professor of Computer Science and Applied Mathematics at Harvard and also the author of the *Probably Approximately Correct* (PAC) learning model (Valiant 1984, 2013) that I am going to use in this section as the framework upon which to build the case for the use of CI in Quantitative Finance. Professor Valiant is well known for avoiding the use of the term AI. At the beginning of his scientific career, while talking to the famous Edsger Dijkstra (one of the most influential computer scientists of the twentieth century, inventor of Dijkstra's algorithm), he was asked about the subject of research that he worked on at that time. After proudly responding AI, Dijkstra said: "Why don't you work first on the 'Intelligence' part?" That was a WOW moment for Dr. Valiant that prompted him to dedicate most of his scientific career to studying the mechanisms of Learning and Intelligence.

This section will introduce the PAC framework, which is a revolutionary way of studying and emulating Intelligence. The PAC theory was introduced by Leslie Valiant in 1984 and for this contribution he was given the Turing award in 2010. Prof. Valiant is one of the pioneers of formalizing the fundamental equivalence between the capabilities of brains and computers. Several decades of research in this field allowed him to come up with the *Probably Approximately Correct* model, which defines mathematically the conditions under which a mechanistic system could be said to learn information.

4.2.1 The Probably Approximately Correct Framework

Algorithms are defined in classical computing as step-by-step instructions needed to achieve an expected outcome, similar to recipes in cooking. The designer of the recipe has full knowledge and is in full control of the environment utilized for achieving the desired goal.

PAC theory introduced a novel algorithmic concept called the ecorithm. The ecorithms are a special category of algorithms. Unlike classical algorithms, they run in environments that are initially unknown to the designer. The ecorithms learn new information that was not available at the design time by interacting with the environment without being programmed to do so. After sufficient interaction with the unknown environment, the ecorithms will gain new knowledge that was not provided by the designer but extracted from the environment instead.

The Probably Approximately Correct model provides a mathematical framework by which algorithmic designers could evaluate the expertise achieved through the Learning process (the Representation step) and devise the Cost function associated with it (the Estimation step). The performance of an ecorithm is evaluated against input information collected from a rather uncontrolled and unpredictable environment and its goal is to perform well enough to ensure survivability.

Another novelty introduced by the PAC theory is that ecorithms are not merely characteristics of computers. Dr. Valiant generalizes the ecorithms as computational concepts that could be used to explore fundamental mysteries related to the evolution of life on Earth. Evolutionary Biology explains how evolution was shaped by living organisms interacting with and adapting to their environments. According to PAC the combination of bio-inheritance and the new knowledge acquired through learning from the environment are the major factors on determining the dynamics of a system or bio entity. The PAC theory suggests a unified way of studying the mechanisms of learning, evolution, and intelligence using computer science methods.

If algorithms are currently implemented in *in silico* systems, ecorithms could be applied to a much broader category of systems, from simple organisms to entire biological species. The PAC framework illustrates a computational equivalence between the way that individuals learn and the way that entire biological systems could evolve. For both cases, ecorithms are describing adaptive behavior in a mechanistic way. PAC's declared goal is to find "mathematical definitions of learning and evolution which can address all ways in which information can get into systems." (Valiant 1984, 2013) A possible outcome will result in integrating life and computer sciences in novel ways never attempted before. The notions of Learning and Intelligence could then be expanded to include non-biological entities.

Chapter 2 illustrates in great detail the transformative journey of data from Information into Knowledge and eventually Intelligence. The PAC theory defines as theoryful the mathematical rules for predicting the process of transforming Information into Knowledge. Everything else is termed as theoryless. Theoryless processes, including evolution in biological systems or decision-making in cognitive systems, are considered as innovative applications of the ecorithm concept.

The computational features of the Learning process as modeled by the PAC theory have the following important properties:

- The learning process should take place in a *relatively limited number of steps* (in polynomial time).
- The *number of interactions* with the environment from which the entity is learning should be *limited*.
- The *probability of making errors* in applying the knowledge acquired by learning should be *sufficiently small*.

One of the main assumptions of AI has been that one could eventually emulate in software the computations that our brains are performing by identifying their algorithms. This claim asserts that Artificial Intelligence and General Intelligence are practically one and the same. The biggest failure of AI so far lies in its inability to precisely determine what these computations should be and what the algorithms responsible are. Fortunately Machine Learning has been proven to be a quite effective mechanism of bypassing this deadlock. One of the biggest challenges for achieving the AI dream is the ability to implement computations that model evolutionary behavior.

A typical example of this problem is the toddler learning to walk problem. What is the process by which a small child is learning to walk by crawling, touching, and sensing the surrounding environment? This is a process of learning that involves acquiring knowledge that is not described in a *user manual*, could not be coded in the classical sense of hard computing, and is very domain and individual specific.

Although this problem is clearly not of a hard computing type, a certain level of computational activity is performed by the learner while the Learning process is unfolding. Until very recently the general assumption was that Learning could take place exclusively in biological systems. The novelty of the PAC theory is that Intelligence is made up of tangible, mechanical, and ultimately understandable processes. According to Professor Valiant, "We will understand the intelligence we put into machines in the same way we understand the physics of explosives – that is, well enough to be able to render their behavior predictable enough that in general they don't cause unintended damage." (Valiant 2013)

4.2.2 Why AI Is a Very Lofty Goal to Achieve

The central idea of PAC's theory is that the successful Learning of any concept of unknown nature should involve the determination of a high-probability hypothesis that represents a good approximation of it. This will assert that most decisions, either conscious or evolutionary, could be represented in terms of PAC learning.

The field of Machine Learning has convincingly demonstrated that the notion of Learning is central to Intelligence. Unfortunately the Learning algorithms responsible for human intelligence are yet to be identified. Although the current ML algorithms are detecting regularities or patterns that are learned from data, trying to understand and emulate Intelligence, especially human Intelligence, requires a lot more than that. The mere fact that one could detect regularities in data does not make a problem simpler to solve. It has been experimentally proven that even the most complex and theoryless data could exhibit predictable patterns. Functional MRI analysis has shown that predictable patterns of blood flow in the brain could be detected when the experimental subject is reading a text. This problem pertains undoubtedly to the theoryless realm since the understanding of how knowledge is represented in the brain is almost nonexistent.

How is computer science currently dealing with problems when using the hard computing paradigm? For any given problem, a computer:

- Could be programmed to solve it via a predefined algorithm, or
- Could be instructed to learn how to solve it by giving it access to lots of data, or
- Could use a combination of these two approaches.

Because the process of learning is statistical in nature, it cannot be made error-free. If developing a flawless program is an achievable goal, the learning alternative will always be exposed to the risk of not being sufficiently accurate. For problems where the desired outcome could be explicitly specified, programming would be the best solution, assuming that one is able to do so. For a variety of reasons there are situations where one may not be able to program a solution. As a consequence, the learning solution becomes vital whenever one cannot specify explicitly the outcome or one cannot get direct programming access to the system. When the learner is a human agent, all these conditions may apply, and there is no alternative to learning. When the learner is a computer system, some or all of these conditions could be present and then the learning solution is the only possibility.

The inability to explicitly specify outcomes is the most common use of general-purpose ML applications. E-mail spam detection is a typical example. As new sources of spam are rapidly developing, the task of manually incorporating ways of detecting it into e-mail systems would be prohibitive. Instead ML algorithms learn specific patterns from e-mail data that enable them to distinguish between e-mails that users label as spam from e-mail that they do not.

The success of Machine Learning is due in large part to the effectiveness of several learning algorithms, such as boosting or ensemble learners. One of the most remarkable innovations in ML is the boosting methodology, which is used currently as a generic technique for improving the performance of almost any basic learning algorithm. The building block is represented by a weak learner that is using a learning style in which the hypothesis employed predicts just marginally better than random guessing. Then the Boosting algorithm will translate the weak learning algorithm into a strong learning algorithm. The idea is to use the weak learning method several times to get a succession of hypotheses and keep the focus on the examples that previous hypotheses found difficult to classify. Because weak learning works for any distribution, modifying the distribution at each stage will enable the learner to achieve better results by this repeated refocusing. Boosting has proved to be a very robust method for improving the predictive accuracy of a wide variety of simple learning methods.

Besides the choice of what learning algorithm to use, the selection of features to represent the problem is another important aspect in Machine Learning. It was empirically proven that good choices yield to more accurate predictions. But how can one gauge what a better choice of features is? The process of feature engineering is computational in nature but not quite well understood. Biological systems for example are using *high-level* features. These features are acquired most likely through the evolution process and were passed from generation to generation in a genetically encoded fashion. Learning these high level features from scratch individually every time one needs to use them would make the evolution a lot less efficient. ML has benefited greatly not only from the development of better algorithms and from the access to large volumes of data but also from the development of hardware accelerators like GPUs or FPGAs. The success of ML on a broad variety of problems is powerful evidence for the effectiveness of learning in areas related to human information processing.

Undoubtedly Machine Learning is the most successful branch of AI to date. One of the most sobering questions about the use of this methodology is how can one predict for which problems one expects ML to succeed, and for which to fail. This question is especially important in Quantitative Finance. A strong requirement would be that the distribution on which the system needs to perform well must be identifiable. The distribution does not need to be described explicitly, but just unambiguously. This means that one should have the assurance that algorithms trained on labeled data sets of typical examples will perform at least as well when used out in the wild on unseen data of the *same kind*. But even when this data distribution consistency is present, the ML approaches may fail because the patterns that one searches are either inherently hard to learn or because the information in the data set is not sufficient for the task at hand.

What really makes AI so difficult to achieve?

The short answer is the inability of machines to handle common sense knowledge in a way that is similar to humans. According to Professor Valiant, the human cognitive system is the outcome of a very long period of evolution coupled with a lifetime of learnable target pursuit since birth. Alan Turing's dream was to educate a computer as one would educate a child. That would entail endowing the computer with human-like cognitive capabilities. But because human cognitive abilities are the result of complex evolutionary ecorithms, and because of our very limited understanding of how our brain is hardwired, this process is absolutely theoryless. There have been attempts to describe the algorithms of evolution, but the experimental results (the data) are no doubt, theoryless.

Let's suppose that one may have access to a powerful super-theory that will allow the computation of the atomic features of the human nervous system at birth. This encoded information could be used to educate a computer in a similar way humans are educating their offspring. But what to do about the knowledge encoded in the human DNA by the evolutionary processes? The only alternative will be to start from the beginning of life on Earth and simulate all evolution stages. Quite an unfeasible task, not just computationally but also because the inputs and parameters that accompanied evolution are just impossible to determine. According to Professor Valiant, the most important barrier to meaningful advances in AI is related to the lack of understanding of how humans acquire knowledge through learning after birth. There are several means of communication through language, vision, smell, taste, and touch. But encoding this knowledge into a computer-ready format is beyond our current capabilities. One empirical observation is that the more common sense the knowledge is, the more difficult is to encode it into a computer-ready format. And this is just a reflection of our inability to identify how humans acquire and process common sense information.

Alan Turing realized that some areas of human activities such as game playing, language translation, cryptography, and mathematics were well suited to automation by machines mainly because these tasks require little contact with the outside world (Copeland 2004). What makes it really difficult for AI to succeed is the fact that the system one attempts to emulate (i.e. human intelligence) is the outcome of the learning process that occurred throughout human evolution and whose explicit traces have been erased a long time ago. As long as a fundamentally new approach for understanding and modeling the human intelligence is not discovered the AI research is going to be limited in its success. AI is not artificial because its computational processes are different from the ones used in nature. As physicists know very well, there is no impediment to emulating natural processes by using computer simulations. If there is something fundamentally different between real intelligence and artificial intelligence, then it must be in the way Knowledge is extracted from the environment.

The vast majority of AI techniques may be construed as attempts to emulate the human knowledge acquisition process by using computerized means. There are problem domains where these techniques are more effective than their natural counterparts. In board games, computers could proceed to massive searches of game trees exploring billions of times faster than a human could. It is an *artificial* technique that happens to be a lot more effective than its natural, human counterpart.

The most fundamental impediment in emulating natural intelligence is represented by the immensity (and the practical impossibility) of the task for recreating the conditions responsible for the natural evolution. The fundamental way that humans are extracting knowledge from the environment is through a yet unknown learning process that has evolved over billions of years of evolution. Even if the emulation of all algorithmic processes involved in natural intelligence would be possible, emulating the outcomes of these processes will be impossible because the environments from which those algorithms learned are not available anymore.

The PAC theory provides the guidelines for the development of intelligent systems. The task could be divided into several components:

- Providing generic Learning and Reasoning algorithms.
- Providing some architecture that describes how to use these algorithms.
- Producing appropriate teaching materials – the examples from which to learn.

Although the last issue is a fundamental component of human education, it is rarely discussed in AI. As AI will become more *learning centered*, preparing a computer's curriculum should be done with no less care than a student's. Placing learning at the center of AI makes a lot of sense because it creates the interface between the current state of knowledge of the learner and the invariably complex state of the environment that one has to learn from.

4.2.3   Examples of Ecorithms in Finance

Ecorithms are a special type of algorithms that are meant to run in environments unknown to the designer. They learn by interacting with the environment as opposed to being programmed to deal with it. After interacting with the environment, the Ecorithms will acquire the expertise (knowledge) that could not have been provided by the designer ex-ante. The Probably Approximately Correct framework provides a quantitative framework for Ecorithms in which designers can evaluate the expertise achieved and the cost of achieving it. Drawing inspiration from evolutionary Biology, the Ecorithms could be seen as generic learning mechanisms that could eventually explain how learning from data (the environment) coupled with evolution could be conducive of Intelligence.

Let's try to find examples of Ecorithms in the world of Trading and Investing. In general trading algorithms are classic algorithms, where the rules are programmed by the designer up-front. I would suggest considering a class of trading strategies called *Volatility Pumping*. Volatility Pumping or the Optimal Growth strategy is based on the Kelly Criterion and it was used for some time to calculate the *optimal* size of your capital at risk. Volatility Pumping is based on concepts from information theory and entropy. In 1956 – by a strange coincidence also the beginning of the modern AI era – two Bell Labs scientists claimed to have discovered the *scientific formula* for getting rich. One of them was the father of the Information theory, the mathematician Claude Shannon, the other was John Kelly Jr., a Texas-born physicist. The two of them have applied concepts of information theory to the very general problem of portfolio theory.

Later Shannon and Ed Thorp, an MIT mathematician, took the Kelly Criterion and tried to apply it to the Las Vegas casinos. And it worked, at least for a while. In the process they realized that there were even more opportunities in the financial markets. Ed Thorp used the Kelly Criterion for his very successful hedge fund, named Princeton-Newport Partners. Shannon became a successful investor as well, topping even Warren Buffett's rate of return. In the 1960s, Shannon gave a lecture in a packed MIT hall, on the topic of maximizing the growth rate of wealth. He detailed his method on how one can grow an investment portfolio by rebalancing a fund between equities and cash while the stock component stays within a random ranging market. The general idea of Optimal Growth was further explored by Prof. Thomas Cover (1991), with his Universal Portfolios concept. Prof. Cover had left academia at one point to work on a hedge fund. All these interesting developments were at the origin of the Volatility Pumping family of strategies.

Much research has been done since in the field of portfolio rebalancing, with the belief that this could be a source of additional performance – the rebalancing premium (Maeso and Martellini 2017). This is sometimes referred to as the Volatility-Pumping effect or the diversification bonus, since volatility and diversification turn out to be key components of the rebalancing premium. Most of the research was concentrated on the numerical and empirical analysis of the Volatility-Pumping effect in the equity markets in order to determine the conditions under which the effect could be maximized. A completely different approach would be to consider an Ecorithm that will learn all the information necessary directly from the markets without any *a priori* programming of the rule set.

Figure 4.2 depicts the behavior in time of a Volatility Pumping strategy for a portfolio of 10-year notes and cash. Please note the PNL growth profile obtained by just *following* the realized variance of the security without any additional constraints imposed by the algorithm's designer. At the core of the Volatility-Pumping strategy

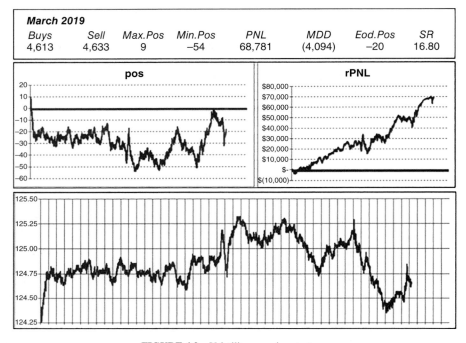

FIGURE 4.2 Volatility-pumping strategy.

there is a very simple *adaptation* rule, whereby using the cash component one buys more when the security price goes lower, or sells more when security price goes higher, keeping an allocation of 50%–50% value at each interval. This very simple *adaptation* rule allows for efficient learning without any pre-programmed rules. For as long as the security price stays within a range (keeps its quasi-stationarity), the strategy is going to produce a profit that is optimal among all different possibilities to rebalance (Cover 1991).

Other examples of ecorithms in the financial world could be found in the use of evolutionary algorithms, or Genetic programming. By using methods inspired from Genetics, like crossovers, mutations, and selections, these algorithms could optimize the PNL and the risk profile of a portfolio. Some of the steps of the Genetic programming workflow include:

- Initializing a random population of parameters
- Selecting the parameters that presumably would increase the net profit
- Applying mutation or crossover operators to the selected parents and generating an offspring set
- Recombining the offspring and the current population to form a new population with the selection operator
- Repeating the steps until the optimization criterion is achieved

4.3   TECHNOLOGY DRIVERS BEHIND THE ML SURGE

This section will consider the principal factors responsible for the recent progress made in Machine Learning, as well as the surge in interest to apply it to a variety of domains. Although Machine Learning has been an active field of research for many decades, why are we hearing so much about it now?

According to a majority of researchers and practitioners working in this field, there are three major factors at play:

- *Data* – A massive amount has become readily available.
- *Algorithms* – Significant progress has been achieved: Deep Learning, Boosting.
- *Computation* – Substantially more-powerful hardware acceleration platforms.

According to Erik Brynjolfsson and Andrew McAfee (2017) the availability of data has increased by a factor of 1,000 over the last two decades, the efficiency of key algorithms has improved by two orders of magnitude, and the ability of hardware to accelerate computations has improved by at least 100-fold (see Figure 4.3). The combination of these three factors could explain improvements for up to a million-fold in applications such as image and sound recognition, self-driving cars, and others. Researchers and academics have been excited about the promises of ML since the beginning of the AI era. But for that vision to become reality a lot of history had to be made and many industry giants had to rise and fall. Companies like Intel had to build the microprocessor, Microsoft had to put a computer on every desk, Cisco had to build the hardware to power global networks, AOL had to bring the Internet to

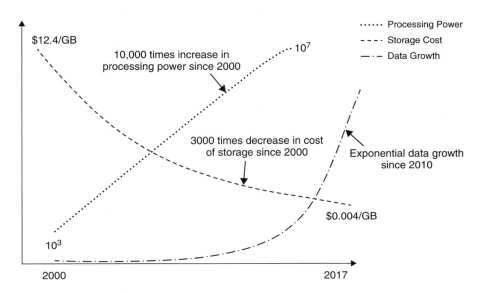

FIGURE 4.3   The major factors of progress. **Source:** Adapted from Quindazzi (2018).

the masses, Netscape had to invent the web browser, Amazon had to bring commerce online, Google had to organize the world's information, and Facebook had to digitize human relationships.

4.3.1   Data

One of the greatest unintended consequences of the shift from desktop to web technologies is represented by the possibility to collect and analyze vast amounts of data on just about everything. Companies like Google that have instant access to vast repositories of search queries, clicks, page views, web pages, or links, were among the first ones to apply ML to huge amounts of data, which is why technologies like MapReduce and BigTable were invented there. Every day the world creates about 2.5 quintillion (10^{18}) bytes of data. This huge amount of data comes from digital footprints left on social media platforms, digital photos and videos, IoT sensors, wearables, and e-commerce transactions to name just a few. Ninety percent of the digital data in the world today has been created in the past two years alone. So far only about 1% of data collected is ever analyzed. To put it into perspective, all that innovation and insights driven by analytics are from analyzing just 1% of the data collected globally.

4.3.2   Algorithms

The data deluge was a crucial moment in the development of modern ML not only because it made already-existing algorithms more effective, but also because it has encouraged, supported, and accelerated the development of better algorithms.

Because great progress has been made in Optimization theory, many problems that could not have been solved some years ago have nowadays found solutions. The two families of algorithms that now dominate the field of ML such as Deep Learning and Reinforcement Learning share a common trait – their results improve dramatically as the amount of training data they're given increases.

The performance of numerical algorithms as a function of the amount of data ingested levels off at some point. After the *saturation* point was reached, feeding it more data has little or no effect.

But this *saturation* point, which relates to the data absorption capacity of the algorithm, seems to shift more and more toward higher values for many of the ML algorithms used today (see Figure 4.4). At the same time the ability to pre-train and to transfer the learning ability from one algorithm to another makes it easier to learn from fewer and fewer examples.

4.3.3   Hardware Accelerators

Nowadays computation is becoming inexpensive and readily available. The beginning of the twenty-first century has witnessed the rebirth of neural networks. The Backpropagation algorithm has not changed fundamentally since it was invented in 1974. But because today one has a million times more compute power available, new

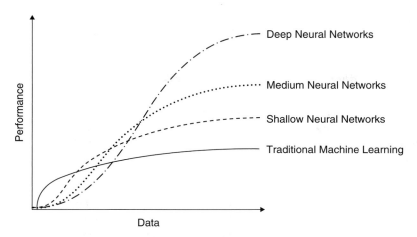

FIGURE 4.4 – Depth vs. performance in neural networks. **Source:** Adapted from Cyxtera (2017).

technologies based on Deep Neural nets are not just possible, but they are becoming quite ubiquitous.

Moore's Law stated for more than 50 years that integrated circuit capability steadily doubles every 18 to 24 months. Many have argued for some time that this scaling law should be running up against the limits of physics and as such it will slow down in the near future. Sure enough the clock speed for standard microprocessors has leveled off.

But by a fortunate coincidence, another type of computer chip, called a Graphic Processing Unit, or GPU, has been developed just in the last decade. It turns out to be very effective when applied to the types of calculations needed for Artificial Neural Networks. Speedups of 20 to 50 times are very common when neural nets are moved from traditional CPUs to GPUs. As neural net applications become commonplace, several companies have developed specialized chips optimized for this application, including Google's tensor processing unit, or the TPU.

GPUs have been critical to the growth of the ML industry, driving training and inference in a data center environment. However, in the field, applications of all types have different needs and there are so many possible use cases. There is a definite need that chips have to be optimized for different types of application, and that could be very expensive. That's especially true for highly customized needs that don't provide enough of a market for economies of scale.

But there is another family of chips, called Field Programmable Gate Arrays or FPGAs. They have been around since the 1980s and the main idea is that they can be reconfigured on demand. The FPGA is a chip that helps companies and researchers work around the problem of customization and economies of scale. The FPGA is an integrated circuit that can be programmed for multiple uses. It has an array of *programmable logic blocks* and a way to program the blocks and the relationship between the blocks. It is a generic tool that can be customized for multiple uses. Since

FPGAs can be reprogrammed, that makes them valuable for the nascent ML industry. Algorithms are constantly being added and fine-tuned for different algorithms by reprogramming the blocks. In addition, low-power FPGAs running lower-precision computations could be a solution for remote sensors and the IoT domain. Whether they are used in factories, on the roads and pipelines, or on drones for remote inspection, the FPGA allows system designers to use one piece of hardware flexibly, for multiple purposes, allowing for a simpler physical design that can be more readily hardened for field applications.

All these hardware acceleration developments have had a synergistic effect on related components of the Machine Learning workflow. Faster hardware makes it possible for engineers to test and develop better algorithms while enabling machines to process bigger data sets in reasonable short time periods. Some of the most utilized applications of ML, such as automated voice translation, would take literally centuries to run on hardware from a decade ago. A natural consequence of these well-advertised tech success stories should be that more researchers and engineers are motivated to go into this field and more investors and executives are persuaded to fund R&D work. But is this really the case? The decrease of storage costs coupled with a tremendous increase in compute power has contributed to an explosion in ML Research and Development. These great technological advances have been further amplified by two additional technologies: global networking and the cloud infrastructure. The mobile Internet can now deliver digital technologies virtually anywhere on the planet, connecting billions of potential customers to the latest ML breakthroughs.

With the advent of cloud computing there is a great potential for cloud-based ML and robotics to accelerate learning and the diffusion of information and knowledge in this field. Imagine an ML-based application that struggles with a task, such as recognizing an object. Once it has mastered that task, it will be able to upload that knowledge to the cloud and share it with other systems that use a compatible knowledge-representation system. The cloud-based ML paradigm could effectively help gather data from hundreds, thousands, and eventually millions of data sensors. By combining all this information in a single system, they can learn vastly more rapidly and share their insights almost instantaneously.

REFERENCES

Bishop (1995). *Neural Networks for Pattern Recognition*. Oxford Press, 2–28.

Brynjolfsson and McAfee (2017). What's driving the machine learning explosion? *Harvard Business Review* (18 July). https://hbr.org/2017/07/whats-driving-the-machine-learning-explosion .

Copeland (2004) *The Essential Turing: Seminal Writings in Computing, Logic, Philosophy, Artificial Intelligence and Artificial Life: Plus the Secrets of Enigma*. Oxford Press, 421.

Cover (1991). Universal portfolios. Mathematical Finance 1 (1): 1–29. http://web.mit.edu/6.454/www/www_fall_2001/shaas/universal_portfolios.pdf.

Cyxtera (2017). Building AI applications using deep learning. https://blog.easysol.net/building-ai-applications/ .

Duch (2003). What is computational intelligence and what could it become? *Computational Intelligence, Methods and Applications Lecture Notes*. Nanyang Technological University, Singapore.

Eberhart and Shi (2007). *Computational Intelligence – Concepts and Implementations*. Elsevier, 17–38.

Fogel (1995). *Evolutionary Computation: Toward a New Philosophy of Machine Intelligence*. IEEE Press, 24.

Iba and Aranha (2012). *Practical Applications of Evolutionary Computation to Financial Engineering*. Springer, 61–84.

Koedinger, Corbett, and Perfetti (2012). The knowledge-learning-instruction framework: bridging the science-practice chasm to enhance robust student learning. *Cognitive Science* 36 (5): 757–798.

Mackworth (2005). The coevolution of AI and AAAI. *AI Magazine* 26 (4): 51–52.

Maeso and Martellini (2017). Measuring volatility pumping benefits in equity markets. EDHEC-Risk Institute. https://risk.edhec.edu/publications/measuring-volatility-pumping-benefits-equity-markets .

Narayana (2017). Application of fuzzy logic in financial markets for decision making. *International Journal of Advanced Research in Computer Science* 8 (3): 382–386.

Quindazzi (2018). 3 emerging tech megatrends leading the rise of #deeplearning. Infographic. Twitter. https://twitter.com/MikeQuindazzi/status/1037551977415233542/photo/1.

Valiant (1984). A theory of the learnable. *Communications of the ACM* 27 (11): 1134–1142.

Valiant (2013). *Probably Approximately Correct*. New York: Basic Books, 57–136.

Zadeh (1998). Some reflections on soft computing, granular computing and their roles in the conception, design and utilization of information/intelligent systems. *Soft Computing Journal* 2 (1): 23–25.

CHAPTER 5

How to Apply the Principles of Computational Intelligence in Quantitative Finance

"Beating the wisdom of the crowds is harder than recognizing faces or driving cars."

– Marcos Lopes de Prado

5.1 THE VIABILITY OF COMPUTATIONAL INTELLIGENCE

The second chapter of this book is dedicated to understanding the importance of knowledge extraction from data and its role in data-driven decision-making. Information is a particularly invaluable asset for the financial markets. However, with the digitization of the financial industry and the pervasiveness of information systems, the sheer amount of information available for decision-makers (traders and investors) could become a great obstacle in the quantitative analysis of financial assets.

The last decades have seen a resurgence of interest in developing computationally intelligent methods and algorithms to support decision-making in different market segments. The ultimate goal for the field of Computational Intelligence is to create cognitive systems that could compete with or at least complement humans in a variety of areas. Traders and investors have currently at their disposal a wide variety of tools for automating the processing of large amounts of information, which will expedite data analysis and pattern recognition. The globalization of asset trading coupled with the emergence of ultrafast information and compute technology have created an insurmountable handicap for humans to efficiently compete with machines specifically in the low-granularity decision-making process. Currently most microstructure-level trading decisions in equities and electronic futures markets are made by algorithms that decide what and where to trade, as well as in what quantity and at what price.

Research in neurosciences has shown that humans have a limited ability in handling large amounts of information at once. When the number of factors involved in a decision-making process increases above a certain threshold, the modeling of the decision-making process and its outcomes become both time-consuming and imprecise. If a typical chess algorithm is just about 40 steps long in average, and one for the game of Go is approximately 200 steps long, a medium frequency electronic trading algorithm could account for up to 3,600 steps (Bacoyannis et al. 2018). And the complexity does not come just computationally, but is also rooted in the complexity of the state space for the problem. The space of possible states for the games of Chess or Go is well known and fully contained, as opposed to the case of electronic trading, where the resulting action space is extremely large and could exponentially increase with the number of features that one considers in the modeling process. Trading algorithms developed by humans are in general very complex. According to Bacoyannis and co-authors, they are "a blend of scientific, quantitative models which expressed quantitative views of how the world works." They contain "rules and heuristics which expressed practical experience, observations and preferences of human traders and users of algorithms." Encoding all this very *human* kind of information could be extremely complex. Most human-compiled algorithms are "tens of thousands lines of hand-written, hard to maintain and modify code." Over time, they could "accumulate many layers of logic, parameters, and tweaks to handle special cases." This is the hard programming concept that was described in some detail in the previous chapter.

One of the most important objectives of this book is to persuade the reader about the merits of Computational Intelligence in dealing with the complexity and the non-linearity of problems on Quantitative Finance (Cavalcante et al. 2016). As a trained physicist I am constantly asking this question: Is randomness truly a natural phenomenon? Or maybe randomness is just simply a byproduct of simulations done by deterministic programs run *in silico*? One needs to accept the possibility that natural observations that one labels as random or stochastic could be actually the reflection of nonlinear dynamics exhibited by complex systems. These questions are very germane to the field of Quantitative and Computational Finance and they are still waiting for answers. In the meantime one should note one of Albert Einstein's quotes: "God does not play dice with the universe."

Chapter 4 introduced Computational Intelligence as a collection of computing methodologies that exhibit the ability to learn from, or at least *deal* with new situations in a way that was not envisioned or *programmed* by the designer of the algorithm. As a result, a system built on the premises offered by Computational Intelligence is expected to possess one or more attributes of reason, such as generalization, discovery, association, and abstraction. Computational Intelligence offers principles and methods for practical adaptation and self-organization and allows for implementations that enable or facilitate the *appropriate* actions (intelligent behavior) in complex and changing environments.

In silico–based Computational Intelligence systems include crossbreeds of different paradigms, from Artificial Neural Networks and Fuzzy Systems, to Evolutionary algorithms, that are augmented with expert knowledge, and often designed to mimic one or more aspects of the *carbon-based* biological intelligence. As such Computational Intelligence refers to the ability of natural and potentially artificial agents to behave intelligently. Computational Intelligence is often used together with the concepts of soft computing, which is a consortium of computing methodologies that collectively provide a foundation for the design, development, and deployment of intelligent systems. In contrast to the more traditional hard computing, soft computing is tolerant of imprecision, uncertainty, and partial truth. According to one of the pioneers of this field, Lofti Zadeh (1997), the guiding principle of soft computing is: "Exploit the tolerance for imprecision, uncertainty and partial truth to achieve tractability, robustness, low solution cost and better rapport with reality."

The section on the Probably Approximately Correct framework introduced in Chapter 4 underlined the centrality of Learning and Adaptation in the process of understanding and modeling Intelligence. Learning is defined as the process of acquiring knowledge and skills by instruction or experience. The necessary complement is Adaptation, defined as the process of adjusting to environmental conditions such that it makes the learner more fit for survival under the conditions of its environment. Professor John Henry Holland (1992), one of the pioneers in the field of Evolutionary (genetic) algorithms, once said that "adaptation is any process whereby a structure is progressively modified to give better performance in its environment." Adaptation overcomes the barriers of nonlinearity and local optima. It involves the progressive modification of some structures and uses a set of operators acting on the structures that evolve over time. But there are also barriers to Adaptation:

- Large problem spaces, and large numbers of features
- Complex and nonlinear cost functions
- Cost functions that change over time and over the problem space
- Complex and changing environments

What makes Computational Intelligence particularly useful for these situations is the *Law of Sufficiency*, which states that if a solution to a problem is good enough (by meeting the specs), fast enough, and cheap enough, then it is deemed to be sufficient. From a computational perspective there are several paradigms used to achieve Adaptation:

- Supervised adaptation is the process of adjusting the parameters of a system such that it generates specified outputs in response to a set of given inputs – implemented by Supervised Learning. Example: backpropagation for ANNs.
- Unsupervised adaptation is the process of adjusting to regularities in data according to rules implicit in its design. The *design* is a substitute for the *teacher* and there is no indication of fitness. Offline evaluation occurs only after

the algorithm stops running. Examples: Clustering, Dimensionality Reduction (PCA).

- Reinforcement adaptation is closely related to biological systems and its implementation is rooted in Dynamic Programming. The Cost function only looks at outcomes and not at individual error measures. Example: Particle swarm optimization.

As a result of the Adaptation process, systems could behave in different ways: they could converge to stability, or they could exhibit a Cyclical, Chaotic, or Complex behavior. A system is considered to be *computationally intelligent* when it:

- Deals only with numerical low-level data
- Has a pattern recognition component
- Exhibits computational adaptability, computational fault tolerance, speed approaching human-like turnaround, and error rates that approximate human performance

Let's conclude this section by considering again the dividing line between Computational and Artificial Intelligence. In the 1992 *Dictionary of Science and Technology* published by Academic Press, Professor Gordon S. Novak defined AI as "the study of the computation required for intelligent behavior and the attempt to duplicate such computation using computers. Intelligent behavior connects perception of the environment to action appropriate for the goals of the actor. Intelligence, biologically costly in energy, pays for itself by enhancing survival. It isn't necessary to understand perfectly, but only to understand well enough to act appropriately in real time."

There are several Computational Intelligence attributes that do not hold for AI and hard computing techniques:

- Ability to generalize
- Ability to deal with partial truths and uncertainty
- Graceful degradation of system performance
- Ability to perform well (survive) in complex and changing environments

One of the main goals of Learning is the ability to generalize already acquired knowledge. Learning representation allows for the generation of a function $y = f(x)$ that is used to map each input x to an output y in the problem space, under the assumption that the data set represents only a small part of the problem space. Generalizing this representation involves building a model $F(x)$ such that other values of x could be mapped into the problem space Y in a way that $F(x) \sim f(x)$ for x not present in the data set. Since the data set is split into training and test sets, one usually measures the generalization capability on the test set. On the other hand, hard computing attributes like Precision and Certainty do not hold for Computational Intelligence systems.

In the quest to achieve *Artificial* Intelligence, Machine Learning is one of the very few means currently available to give artificial agents (like computer programs) the ability to behave intelligently. Machine Learning refers to the ability of a computer program to learn from a set of inputs either in a supervised (by being actively trained) or unsupervised (by exploring the characteristics of raw data on its own) fashion, in order to provide answers to questions that it wasn't specifically designed to know the answer to. The field of Machine Learning strives to mimic natural occurring processes associated with Computational Intelligence such as Neural Networks or Genetic optimization algorithms. From this perspective Machine Learning is a foundational element of Computational Intelligence.

5.2 ON THE APPLICABILITY OF CI TO QUANTITATIVE FINANCE

A brief review of the literature (Cavalcante et al. 2016) has revealed that a considerable volume of scientific work has been done to investigate the utility of Computational Intelligence in solving financial market problems. However most of the published research has been limited in scope, focusing on either a specific financial market application or just a family of Computational Intelligence algorithms. Achieving success in the financial markets depends greatly on the quality of the information that one uses to support the decision-making process, but also on how fast the decision-making process is. The fields of Quantitative and Computational Finance have been developing at a rapid pace and they have drawn inspiration from more established domains like Engineering and Mathematics (Yoo, Kim, and Jan 2005).

Both Statistical and Hard computing methodologies have been used for many decades to provide support to decision-makers in different financial market segments. Financial time-series prediction could be considered as one of the main challenges in the Quantitative Finance literature. The two main classes of methods that are currently in use to forecast financial time series are Statistical models and Machine Learning techniques. The traditional Statistical methods are based on the simplifying assumption that financial time series are generated by linear processes and they model them as such in order to make predictions about the future values of the series. However, since financial time series are fundamentally nonlinear, nonstationary, and stochastic in nature, the linearity assumptions are not realistic. On the other hand, ML techniques have been applied with some degree of success in modeling and predicting financial time series. These ML techniques intend to capture nonlinear relationships between relevant factors with no prior knowledge about the input data. Among these techniques, Artificial Neural Networks have been used more frequently in time-series forecasting. Because ANNs are both data-driven and self-adaptive methods, they are able to capture nonlinear behaviors of time series without any statistical assumptions about the data.

More recently techniques such as Natural Language Processing (NLP) have been used to predict future market movements by mining information in textual format. Textual data sources such as financial news, financial reports, or even professional blogs are considered as relevant sources of information for predicting future market behavior. NLP techniques have been used to extract important features from textual data in order to identify market sentiment and improve the forecasting of financial assets.

The nonlinearity and non-stationarity of such dynamic systems as the financial markets require the use of different kinds of modeling techniques in order to improve the accuracy of financial forecast (Huang and Tsai 2009). Several Computational Intelligence methods have been suggested recently as tools to be used in forecasting financial markets (Lin, Chiu, and Lin 2009). Soft computing techniques, such as ANNs and fuzzy systems, have been applied to the modeling and forecast of financial time series (Lee et al. 2009). The main goal of soft computing techniques is to gain the ability to capture nonlinear relations among relevant market factors without making any statistical assumptions about the nature of the input data (Atsalakis and Valavanis 2009). Soft computing algorithms present several advantages when compared with traditional statistical methods. These methods usually exhibit higher tolerance to imprecision and perform well in noisy data environments. And because they are data-driven, nonparametric, and self-adaptive mechanisms, they will require less data to be trained on (Cheng and Wel 2014). It was reported (Liang et al. 2009) that nonparametric methods outperform the parametric one in the accuracy of predicting future behavior.

As mentioned in Chapter 3, Bacoyannis and co-authors (2018) have described the three paradigms associated with the use of data when developing trading algorithms:

- Data modeling
- Machine Learning
- Algorithmic decision-making

The *Data modeling culture* is based on the belief that financial markets act like overly simplified black box models that are employed to generate the observational data. The goal is to find a plausible functional approximation for the data-generating process (the quantitative model) and to extract its parameters from the data by using a fitting procedure. The output of the model is then used by the decision-making processes. Unfortunately the complexity of the markets and the collective behavior of its participants raise an unsurmountable challenge to the data modeling culture. Simple models are just not able to capture the complexity of the environment. Moreover, critics of this approach argue that simple models offer "a false sense of certainty and for this reason is prone to abject failures" (Bacoyannis et al. 2018).

The *Machine Learning culture* uses a set of more *opaque* functions to model observations. This modeling paradigm does not claim that its functional representation reveals the nature of the underlying processes. From this perspective the world of finance looks more stochastic than deterministic because it is constantly evolving, and the observed trading processes are better described as emerging behaviors rather than data generating devices. Once the outputs of the ML models are generated they are fed into the decision-making processes. At the same time, complex ML models are more prone to failure and are much harder to interpret.

The *Algorithmic decision-making* culture is about making decisions rather than building models. Instead of trying to build a map about how the world works, this paradigm attempts to train electronic agents (or algorithms) to distinguish between good and bad decisions. What makes this approach very challenging is the ability to understand and explain the decisions made by the algorithmic agent, to make sense of its policies, and to be able to ensure that the agent will proceed with sensible actions in all situations and environments. In the Algorithmic decision-making paradigm the agent learns that certain actions are bad because they lead to negative consequences (outcomes). But the agent still has to come up with the values, the rules, and the constraints that steer the algorithm away from taking actions which could be deemed as *counterproductive* and that could not be learned from its environment or its history. The interplay between the algorithm's constraints and its rewards makes possible some practical applications for the financial markets.

Quantitative Finance represents a very rich area of research and development connected to practical problems that could be precisely encoded in terms of objectives and constraints. The last decade has seen a surge of interest in the application of Machine Learning methodologies to problems in High Frequency Trading and Market Microstructure data. The primary focus of this kind of research is on developing computationally and informationally efficient algorithms for devising good predictive models from large data sets. The main problems arising in HFT are natural candidates for ML applications both for trade execution and the generation of alpha. The goal to create predictive models based on historical data is not new in the field of Quantitative Finance. It started decades ago with the CAPM model, the Fama and French factors, and similar approaches. The attempt to use ML in HFT brings on new challenges, mainly related to the very fine granularity of the data – an example is the market microstructure data at the resolution of individual orders, partial executions, cancellations, and hidden liquidity. There is an incomplete understanding of how such low-level granular data could relate to actionable circumstances (e.g. buying or selling shares or optimally executing large orders) (Kerns and Nevmyvaka 2013). Models such as CAPM have already prescribed the relevant *features* used for prediction and modeling (excess returns, book-to-market ratios, etc.). However, in the HFT context one may not have any prior intuitions about these relevant features necessary to build a predictive model. Thus the process of feature selection or feature engineering becomes a crucial aspect in the use of Machine Learning in the HFT world.

A special class of HFT problems that is of a particular interest and could be a good candidate for the use of ML techniques is represented by the algorithmic approaches to execution problems via the use of optimality. And here a specific ML paradigm could be of great use – the Reinforcement Learning (RL) method. Given the specificity of the dynamics of financial markets, the problem could be framed in terms of what is called a Markov Decision process. When a model to describe the probabilities of transition between different states is available, the solution comes down to the use of *Dynamic Programming*. When this model is not available or just impractical to use, Reinforcement Learning is the technique to use. The applicability of RL algorithms to HFT problems penalizes the algorithm for making a wrong decision while rewarding it for making a profitable one. In general one could apply Reinforcement Learning whenever a problem could be framed as an agent acting within a given Environment, where it can be informed of the State and a goal-driven Reward function. More formally, Reinforcement Learning theory is based upon solutions to a Markov Decision Process. Reinforcement Learning has been used quite successfully in the field of gaming. This is due to the fact that game environments can be coded efficiently and could run fast on generic hardware where one emulates very accurately both the environment and the agent. For classic board games, such as backgammon, checkers, chess, or Go, human experts could be used to compare the results with.

Gordon Ritter (2017), a senior portfolio manager at GSA Capital Partners in New York, recently published an interesting study on the applicability of Reinforcement Learning to trading. When the results obtained within the training environment meet a certain criteria, the algorithm could be used for live trading because it has acquired an optimal course of action. The task given to the RL algorithm is to maximize the expected utility of a trade, that is, the value of trade less all associated costs, and adjusted for the risk of the trade. According to Ritter, "What has always restricted traditional optimal execution algorithms is the number of factors that can be used in the models." The larger this number, the more difficult the problem is to solve. RL algorithms learn by way of trial and error by being in different states and figuring out the optimal path of execution on its own. An extremely large number of scenarios (in the millions) could be run during the training process. Once the training is complete, the technique can be used in real time to trade. Trading firms such as JP Morgan and Portware are using RL techniques to optimize their trading schedule.

5.3 A BRIEF INTRODUCTION TO REINFORCEMENT LEARNING

Reinforcement Learning (Sutton and Barto, 1998) is the process of mapping the states of the environment to the actions that need to be taken by the learner in order to maximize a scalar Reward function or the Reinforcement signal. Informally, Reinforcement Learning (RL) is seen as learning by *trial and error* from performance feedback coming from the environment or from an external evaluator. The learner has absolutely no prior knowledge of the actions to be taken, and it has to discover through exploration which actions will be conducive of the highest reward.

A typical RL problem could be depicted by the diagram in the Figure 5.1:

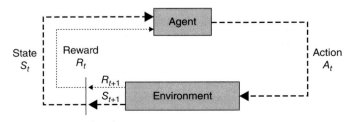

FIGURE 5.1 The reinforcement learning concept. **Source:** Adapted from https://i.stack.imgur.com/eoeSq.png.

The *learner* or the *agent* receives inputs from its environment in a *descriptive* form that is encoding the current state of the environment. Based on the inputs received from the environment, an action is performed, and then a reinforcement signal or reward is received by the agent. This reward can be a positive or negative, depending on the utility of the action. A negative reward has the effect of punishing the agent for a detrimental action. It is important to note that the agent's action may cause a change in the environment, thereby affecting the future options and actions of the agent. The consequences of actions on the environment and the evolution of future states cannot always be predicted. Therefore it becomes necessary that the agent frequently monitors its environment.

What differentiates Reinforcement Learning from other Machine Learning paradigms is the fact that in RL there is no *supervisor*, but the feedback comes only from a *reward* signal that tells the agent how beneficial was the action taken. The feedback coming from the environment is not necessarily instantaneous, but it may be delayed over several time steps. In some cases the feedback may be obtained just at the end when the agent reaches its goal. By contrast, in supervised Machine Learning the training data set describes the environment to the algorithm by providing the right answers or actions to be taken when faced with a specific situation, and the algorithm tries to generalize from that data to new situations. One of the most notable differences between supervised ML and RL is that in Reinforcement Learning the data is not assumed to be Independent and Identically Distributed (iid). As a result of this generalization the agent may spend a considerable amount of time in specific regions of the environment and not spend enough time in other ones which could be potentially interesting to learn the optimal behavior. Therefore the agent is generally influencing the environment through its actions which in turn affects the subsequent data it receives from the environment. From this perspective, RL models are representing more realistic active learning processes.

A typical Reinforcement Learning process is composed of two phases:

- A trial and error search to find the most beneficial actions, which forms the *exploration* component of RL.
- A memorization step that keeps track of which actions worked well and under which conditions. This is the *exploitation* component of RL.

One of the most important aspects in understanding how Reinforcement Learning works is the *trade-off between exploration and exploitation*. On one hand it is crucial that the agent exploits what it has already learned, such that a reward can be secured. On the other hand the *trial and error* search ensures that the agent must do an exhaustive exploration to improve action selections in the future. In the phase of Exploration the learner (agent) takes a new action with unknown consequences, and by that one gets a more accurate model for the environment while discovering higher-reward states than the ones found so far. At the same time by exploring the environment the utility is not maximized. During the phase of Exploitation the agent proceeds with the best strategy found so far by maximizing the current utility estimate. This phase could impose some limitations on the state space search and slow down the process of finding the optimal strategy.

5.3.1   Defining the Agent

A Reinforcement Learning Agent could be characterized by the following components:

- A **Policy** – π is the decision-making function of the agent.

  A Policy is used to specify which action to execute in each of the situations that the agent may encounter during the learning process. The policy is basically a mapping between actions and states, or alternatively, a set of stimulus-response rules. The Policy is a probability distribution over the actions given the states.

  A Policy could be either deterministically learned from experience $action = \pi(state)$ or it could be a stochastic function $\pi(action|state) = P[A_t = action|S_t = state]$.

- A **Reward** – r_t is a scalar feedback signal that indicates how well the agent is performing at a given time step t and it defines the goal of the agent.

  The reward function defines the beneficial and the detrimental actions for the agent in any possible situations. The reward is immediate and is representative of the current state only. The goal of the agent is to maximize the total reward that it receives over the long run. RL is based on the Reward Hypothesis which states that "All goals can be described by the maximization of expected cumulative rewards." (Sutton and Barto, 1998) Although the agent's goal is to select the actions that maximize future rewards, there could be actions that might have long-term negative consequences. Since some rewards could be delayed, the agent cannot be greedy at all times. This translates into the fact that the agent cannot take an action associated with maximum reward at the current time but instead it has to plan ahead. Sometimes it may be preferable to sacrifice an immediate reward to gain a more consistent long-term one.

- A **Value** function, which specifies the goal in the long run. The value function is used to predict a future reward, and is used as a metric to indicate what the benefit should be in the long run. For the value function, an important aspect is how the future should be taken into account.

Several models are in use:

(a) The **finite-horizon** model, in which the agent optimizes its expected reward for the next n_t steps, where $r(t)$ is the reward for time-step t:

$$ E\left[\sum_{t=1}^{n_t} r(t)\right] $$

(b) The **infinite-horizon discounted** model, which takes the entire long-run reward of the agent into consideration. However, each reward received in future is geometrically discounted according to a discount factor, $\gamma \in [0, 1)$:

$$E\left[\sum_{t=0}^{\infty} \gamma^t r(t)\right]$$

The discount factor enforces a bound on the infinite sum.

(c) The **average reward** model, which prefers actions that optimize the agent's long-run average reward:

$$\lim_{n_t \to \infty} E\left[\frac{1}{n_t}\sum_{t=0}^{n_t} r(t)\right]$$

Let's take the example of training a dog. While teaching the dog a new skill, the trainer will reward any *positive attitude* toward the learning process. The dog represents the Agent for the RL algorithm. The reward system and the training process represent the Environment. The training phases are representing the States in which the agent is found at any point during the process. The training process is usually an optimization procedure: in the long run the dog will behave in such a way that she will maximize the rewards. This is equivalent to implementing a decision-making process by which the evaluation of a Value-function will ensure the maximization of the rewards. Every time the dog moves from one state to another in the training process she will get a Reward. The methods used to complete the training program will generate the Policy.

A very important aspect in implementing any RL methodology is how one models the Environment. The environmental model mimics the behavior of the environment. This can be done by transition functions that describe transitions between different states. The environment state S_t is the internal representation of the environment or the data that the environment uses for the next state and reward. The environment state is generally not visible to the agent. The state of the agent captures what happened to the agent so far, summarizes it, and then the agent is using this information to pick the next action.

Reinforcement Learning uses a Markov representation for the agent's state:

$$P[S_{t+1}|S_t] = [S_{t+1}|S_1, S_2, \ldots, S_t]$$

This means the agent state could be represented as a *Markov* state if that state contains all the useful information the agent has encountered so far, which in turn means that one can discard all the previous states and retain just the agent's current state. This also means that *the future is independent of the past given the present*. Once the current state is known, the history may be discarded, and the current state becomes a good metric to characterize the future at least as good as the whole state history.

In order to find an optimal policy, π, it is necessary to find an optimal value function. A candidate optimal value function could be:

$$V^*(s) = \max_{a \in A} \left\{ R(s, a) + \gamma \Sigma_{s' \in S} T(s, a, s') V^*(s') \right\}, s \in S,$$

where

A is the set of all possible actions,
S is the set of environmental states,
$R(s, a)$ is the reward function, and
$T(s, a, s')$ is the transition function.

The equation above states that the value of a state s is the expected instantaneous reward, $R(s, a)$, for action a plus the expected discounted value of the next state, using the best possible action. As such a clear definition of the model in terms of the transition function T and the reward function R is therefore required. A number of algorithms have been developed for such RL problems.

There are several types of Reinforcement Learning agents:

- **Value-Based** – The agent evaluates all the states in the state space, and the policy will be implicit. The Value function is used by the agent to choose the best policy.
- **Policy-Based** – Instead of using a Value function representation, the policy will be represented explicitly. The agent searches for the optimal action-value function which in turn enables it to act optimally.
- **Actor-Critic** is a combined value-based and policy-based agent. This type of agent stores both the policy as well as how much reward it is getting from each state.
- **Model-Based** – The agent builds a model for the environment, and then searches for the best possible behavior.
- **Model-Free** – The agent is agnostic of the environment (i.e. it does not try to model the dynamics). Instead the agent tries through trial and error to build a policy of how to behave optimally to get the most possible rewards.

5.3.2 Model-Based Markov Decision Process

In model-based Reinforcement Learning an agent needs to learn both the model of the transition probabilities and rewards, as well as how to act. In this paradigm one needs to keep track of how many times state s_{t+1} follows state s_t when one takes an action a, and update accordingly the transition probability $P(s_{t+1} \mid s_t, a)$ according to the relative frequencies. One also needs to keep track of all the rewards R(s).

Reinforcement Learning is a learning process by which the agent is observing the environment via some feedback consisting of a reward and the next state, and then acting upon that. This process is a known as the *Markov Decision Process* (MDP). MDP is a mathematical formulation for the problem of learning from interacting with an environment to achieve a goal. The agent and the environment are continually interacting, whereby the agent is selecting actions and the environment is responding to these actions and presenting new situations to the agent.

Formally, an MDP is used to describe an environment for RL, where the environment is fully observable. Almost all RL problems can be formalized as MDPs. The Markov property states that the future is independent of the past given the present. For a *Markov* state **S** and successor state **S′**, the state transition probability function is defined by:

$$P_{SS'} = P[S_{t+1} = s' | S_t = s]$$

It is a probability distribution over the next possible successor states, given the current state. Given that the agent is in a specific state **S**, there is a probability to transition to the first state and another probability to transition to the second state and so on. This transition function could be represented as a matrix, where each row sums to 1:

$$P = from \begin{bmatrix} P_{11} & \cdots & P_{1n} \\ \vdots & \ddots & \vdots \\ P_{n1} & \cdots & P_{nn} \end{bmatrix}$$

The Markov process is a memory-less random process composed of a sequence of random states $S_1, S_2 \ldots, S_n$ exhibiting the Markov property.

The state diagram in Figure 5.2 depicts the example of an Agent attempting to learn three different skills in order to achieve a specific goal. There are several scenarios that could be composed by using different states. One example could be that after acquiring Skill A the agent may acquire Skill B with probability 0.5 or just Wait with probability 0.5. An episode would be for example [Skill A →Skill B → Skill C → Goal], where Goal is the terminal state or absorbing state that terminates this episode.

A Markov Reward Process is a Markov process that measures how much reward was accumulated through a particular sequence that one has sampled. An RL agent tries to maximize the expected sum of rewards from every state it lands in. In order to achieve this objective one must try to get the optimal value function, i.e. the maximum sum of cumulative rewards. This is generally done using the Bellman equation. Richard Bellman was an American applied mathematician who derived the following equations which made it possible to solve MDPs. Using the Bellman equation, the Value function will be decomposed into two components:

- An immediate reward, R_{t+1}, and
- A discounted value for the successor state $\gamma V(S_{t+1})$,

$$V(s) = E[R_{t+1} + \gamma V(S_{t+1}) | S_t = s]$$

The value of the state S is the reward one gets upon leaving that state, plus a discounted average over next possible successor states, where the value of each possible

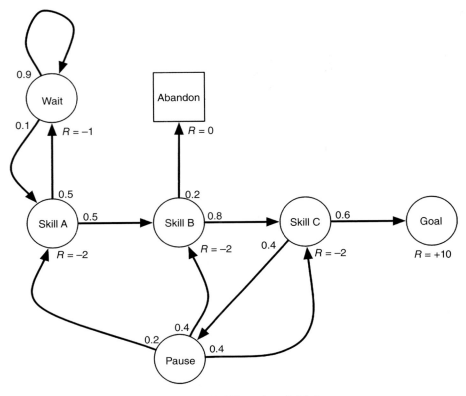

FIGURE 5.2   The graphical illustration of a Markov process.

successor state is multiplied by the probability that we land in it. A *policy* is nothing but a way to choose a certain path (behavior) in a Markov process.

The **state-value** function $v_\pi(s)$ of an MDP is the expected return starting from the state "S" and then following policy "π":

$$v_\pi(s) = E_\pi[G_t| S_t = s] = E_\pi\left[\sum_{k=0}^{\infty} \gamma^k R_{t+k+1}| S_t = s\right] \quad for\ all\ s \in S$$

The **action-value** function $q_\pi(s)$ is the expected return starting from the state "s," taking action "a," and then following policy "π":

$$q_\pi(s, a) = E_\pi[G_t| S_t = s, A_t = a] = E_\pi\left[\sum_{k=0}^{\infty} \gamma^k R_{t+k+1}| S_t = s, A_t = a\right]$$

The **optimal state-value** function **V*(s)** is the maximum value function over all policies.

$$v^*(s) = \max_\pi\ v_\pi(s)$$

The *optimal action-value* function **q***(s, a) is the maximum action value function over all policies.

$$q^*(\text{s}, \text{a}) = \max_{\pi} q_{\pi}(s, a)$$

An optimal Policy could be defined as a stochastic mapping from states to actions, the goal being to know what the best one of these policies is. All optimal policies achieve the optimal action-value function. The Bellman equation models the maximization of the utility of an agent over a time horizon. Very often the problems that one seeks to solve are farming problems where the goal is to maximize the overall utility of a resource over a period of time as opposed to harvesting the resource all at once. Another way of looking at Bellman's equation is as the method used to achieve the proper balance between the local exploitation (in state's space) versus exploring more of the state space so that an optimal harvesting policy can be generated. Some practical examples for the use of MDP:

- Scheduling problems
- Autonomous aircraft navigation
- Manufacturing processes
- Network switching and routing

5.3.3 Model-Free Reinforcement Learning

The other Reinforcement Learning paradigm is the model-free method that has an objective to obtain an optimal policy without a model of the environment. The two most popular model-free RL approaches are the Q-learning and the Temporal Difference (TD) learning.

5.3.3.1 Q-Learning

In Q-learning, the task is to learn the expected discounted reinforcement values, $Q(s, a)$, of taking an action *a* in the state *s* then continuing by always choosing actions optimally. The goal of Q-learning is to learn a policy as a recipe for what action to take under what circumstances. This does not require a model of the environment and can handle problems with stochastic transitions and rewards, without requiring adaptations.

For any finite MDP the method of *Q*-learning finds a policy that is optimal in the sense that it maximizes the expected value of the total reward over all successive steps, starting from the current state. For any given MDP, *Q*-learning can identify an optimal action-selection policy, given an infinite exploration time and a partly random policy. Q stands for quality, and it names the function that returns the maximized reward.

Let's look at the example of a robot that has to cross a maze and reach an end point. Along the way there are traps, and the robot can only move one tile at a time. If the robot steps onto a trap, the robot is considered out. The robot has to reach the end point in the shortest time possible. The reward system works as follows:

1. The robot loses 1 point at each step. This is done so that the robot takes the shortest path and reaches the goal as fast as possible.

2. If the robot steps on a trap, it loses 100 points and the game ends.

3. If the robot advances properly one tile, it gains 1 point.

4. If the robot reaches the end goal, the robot gets 100 points.

A Q-Table is constructed as a simple lookup table where one calculates the maximum expected future rewards for actions taken at each state. This table will guide the algorithm to proceed with the best action at each state. In a Q-table the columns are the actions and the rows are the states. Each Q-table score will be the maximum expected future reward that the robot will get if it takes that action at that state. This is an iterative process, as one needs to improve the Q-Table at each iteration.

The Q-learning algorithm uses the Bellman equation and takes two inputs: the state (**s**) and the action (**a**):

$$Q^\pi(s_t, a_t) = E[R_{t+1} + \gamma R_{t+2} + \gamma^2 R_{t+3} + \cdots] \ [s_t, a_t]$$

$\underbrace{\quad}$ Q-values for state s, given *an action a* $\underbrace{\quad}$ Expected discounted cumulative reward $\underbrace{\quad}$ Given state s and action a

Using the function above, one can get the values of **Q** for the cells in the table. At the beginning all the values in the Q-table are zeros. An iterative process will update the Q-table values. As one starts to explore the environment, the Q-function will give better and better approximations by continuously updating the Q-values in the table.

The Q-learning algorithm consists of (see Figure 5.3):

- *Initialization* of the Q-table: there are n columns → number of actions and m rows → number of states. All be will be initialized to 0.
- Choosing and performing an action: as an example one could use the epsilon greedy strategy. At the beginning, the epsilon rates will be higher. The robot will explore the environment and randomly choose actions. The logic behind this is that the robot does not know anything about the environment. As the robot explores the environment, the epsilon rate decreases and the robot will start to exploit the environment. During the process of exploration, the robot progressively becomes more confident in estimating the Q-values.
- *Evaluation*: after the actions have been taken it is time to measure the rewards and determine the outcome by using the Bellman equation:

$$New \ Q(s, a) = Q(s, a) + \alpha \cdot [R(s, a) + \gamma \cdot max_{a'} Q(s', a') - Q(s, a)]$$

5.3.3.2 *Temporal Difference Learning*

Temporal difference (TD) learning is a technique to learn how to predict a quantity that depends on the future values of a given signal. The label TD derives from its use of changes, or differences, in predictions over successive time steps to drive the learning process. The prediction at any given time step is updated to bring it closer

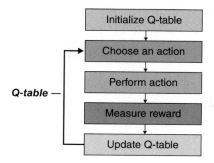

FIGURE 5.3   The Q-learning algorithm.

to the prediction of the same quantity at the next time step. The TD algorithms are often used in RL to predict a measure of the total amount of reward expected in the future. The Bellman equation could be represented as:

$$Q(s,a) = R(s) + \gamma \sum_{s'} P(s'|s,a)max_{a'}Q(s',a')$$

Let's pretend that the currently observed transition (s_t, a, s_{t+1}) is the only possible outcome and let's adjust the Q values toward a local equilibrium:

$$Q^{local}(s,a) = R(s) + \gamma \cdot max_{a'}Q(s',a')$$

$$Q^{new}(s,a) = (1 - \alpha) \cdot Q(s,a) + \alpha \cdot Q^{local}(s,a), \text{ or}$$

$$Q^{new}(s,a) = Q(s,a) + \alpha \cdot [R(s) + \gamma \cdot max_{a'}Q(s',a') - Q(s,a)]$$

At each time step t and from the current state s one should select an action "a" that:

$$a = \quad \arg max_{a'} f(Q(s,a'), N(s,a'))$$

$$\qquad\qquad\qquad | \qquad\qquad\qquad |$$

$$\qquad\qquad Exploration \qquad\quad \#times\ action"a"\ was$$
$$\qquad\qquad function \qquad\qquad taken\ from\ state"s"$$

This will define the state s and perform a TD update:

$$Q(s,a) \leftarrow Q(s,a) + a \cdot [R(s) + \gamma \cdot max_{a'}Q(s\prime,a\prime) - Q(s,a)]$$
$$\qquad\qquad\qquad |$$
$$\qquad\qquad Learning\ rate$$

obs: the learning rate starts at 1 and decays as 1/t. Example: $\alpha(t) = 120/(119+t)$.

At any given time step a prediction is updated to bring it closer to the prediction of the same quantity at the next time step. TD RL is a supervised learning process in which the training signal for a prediction is a future prediction.

Temporal Difference algorithms are used in Reinforcement Learning to predict a measure of the total amount of reward expected in the future.

5.4   CONCLUSIONS

Given the recent progress achieved in developing Computational Intelligence methods that could be applied to a variety of problem domains, the second part of the book will be dedicated to presenting a series of Case Studies that are relevant to the field of Quantitative and Computational Finance.

The goal of achieving Intelligence via computational means has several milestones along the way:

- The first is Automation via Optimization, and it is usually carried out by using Machine Learning algorithms for pattern detection – see Deep Learning in image and sound processing.
- The second is related to the possibility of involving the computational machinery in Prediction, via Learning and Evolution using soft programming techniques.
- The ultimate goal is to achieve a form of *human-like* Intelligence in a setting where the computational algorithms will be able to adapt to the environment without having to be *programmed* as such by the designer – very similar to the concept of Ecorithms.

The second part of the book will examine in more detail the first milestone – how to achieve Automation via Optimization techniques. Since this is a mature field of study, the next chapters will present a series of Case Studies related to the most important components of the Trading workflow: from optimizing trade execution, to valuing derivatives and market making, to more complex topics such as short-time horizon prediction of the limit order book dynamics, real-time risk management and portfolio optimization, or the problem of market surveillance and compliance.

REFERENCES

Atsalakis and Valavanis (2009). Surveying stock market forecasting techniques – Part II: soft computing methods. *Expert Systems with Applications* 36 (3): 5932—5941.

Bacoyannis, Glukhov, Jin et al. (2018). Idiosyncrasies and challenges of data driven learning in electronic trading. NIPS 2018 Workshop on Challenges and Opportunities for AI in Financial Services. https://arxiv.org/abs/1811.09549.

Cavalcante, Brasileiro, Souza et al. (2016). Computational intelligence and financial markets: a survey and future directions. *Expert Systems with Applications* 55: 194–211.

Cheng and Wel (2014). A novel time-series model based on empirical mode decomposition for forecasting TAIEX. *Economic Modelling* 36: 136–141.

Holland (1992). Complex adaptive systems. *Daedalus* 121 (1): 17–30.

Huang and Tsai (2009). A hybrid SOFM-SVR with a filter-based feature selection for stock market forecasting. *Expert Systems with Applications* 36 (2): 1529—1539.

Kerns and Nevmyvaka (2013). Machine learning for market microstructure and high frequency trading. In *High Frequency Trading: New Realities for Traders, Markets and Regulators* (ed. Easley, de Prado, and O'Hara). Risk Books. http://riskbooks.com/book-high-frequency-trading.

Lee, Grosse, Ranganath et al. (2009). Convolutional deep belief networks for scalable unsupervised learning of hierarchical representations. Proceedings of the 26th Annual International Conference on Machine Learning, Montreal, 609–616.

Liang, Zhang, Xiao et al. (2009). Improving option price forecasts with neural networks and support vector regressions. *Neurocomputing* 72 (13): 3055—3065.

Lin, Chiu, and Lin (2009). Empirical mode decomposition – based least squares support vector regression for foreign exchange rate forecasting. *Economic Modelling* 29 (6): 2583—2590.

Ritter (2017). Machine learning for trading. *SSRN Electronic Journal.* https://cims.nyu.edu/~ritter/ritter2017machine.pdf.

Sutton and Barto (1998). *Reinforcement Learning: An Introduction.* MIT Press, 1–220.

Yoo, Kim, and Jan (2005). Machine learning techniques and use of event information for stock market prediction: A survey and evaluation. International Conference on Computational Intelligence for Modelling, Control and Automation and International Conference on Intelligent Agents, Web Technologies and Internet Commerce, Vienna, 835—841.

Zadeh (1997). The roles of fuzzy logic and soft computing in the conception, design and deployment of intelligent systems. *Software Agents and Soft Computing Towards Enhancing Machine Intelligence* (ed. Nwana and Azarmi). Springer, 183–190.

CHAPTER 6

Case Study 1: Optimizing Trade Execution

"The agent is learning about the optimal strategy and the cost without actually building a model. In the training process, the agent tries all sorts of things and gets to observe the reward and basically correct his algorithm."

– Gordon Ritter, GSA Capital Partners

6.1 INTRODUCTION TO THE PROBLEM

The vast majority of problems in Quantitative Finance could be addressed by imposing specific objectives and constraints. One such problem that has attracted a lot of interest from market practitioners since the dawn of the electronic trading era is what is called the market impact or the optimized trade execution problem. If a large transaction cannot be executed promptly due the lack of liquidity at the current market price, it is customary to split it into a sequence of smaller-size transactions. This execution strategy will produce a lesser impact on the price at which the transaction is to be executed. But this optimization process may take a certain amount of time to unfold, and therefore it will expose the market participant to the risk of an adverse market move. This problem has been studied for at least two decades and very interesting results have been reported in the literature (Almgren and Chriss 2000; Bertsimas and Lo 1998; Coggins, Blazejewski, and Aitken 2003; El-Yaniv et al. 2001; Kakade et al. 2004).

Practical solutions range from imposing time limits to the execution process, to enforcing limits on the price at which transactions are to be executed. When these limits are reached, the trading would stop even before reaching the final objective. It is quite easy to understand why these hard limit methods do not result in an optimal execution which should translate into maximizing the wealth while reducing the transaction costs. The execution strategy needs to have an adequate level of robustness that could be insured just when its dynamics is aligned with the dynamics of the market.

This robustness could eventually be achieved by using *Dynamic Programming* (DP) as a general-purpose methodology to achieve optimality. The paradigm of DP is employed to update the execution algorithm such that to reflect changing market conditions and result in an optimal execution. Any Dynamic Programming implementation involves the use of computationally intensive numerical techniques in order to find an optimal trading strategy. Does this problem require a complex mathematical model, or maybe Computational Intelligence could come to the rescue? This problem has been studied also in theoretical Computer Science where it is called the one-way trading problem.

In recent years there was an increased interest in applying Reinforcement Learning to simulate the market impact and find an optimal trading strategy that maximizes the value of the trade adjusted for its risk (Nevmyvaka, Feng, and Kearns 2006; Rantil and Dahlén 2018; Hu 2016). An assortment of Reinforcement Learning–based policies has been developed to specify the optimal action to be taken from any given state according to a discounted future reward criterion. The central idea behind all these RL models is to balance the short-term rewards of actions against the influence that these actions may have on future states. The *Optimized Trade Execution* problem could be defined as the strategy for buying or selling a given volume of a financial asset within a given time horizon such that the transaction's revenue will be maximized while minimizing the costs required to actuate the transaction. This is one of the most common problems for practitioners in financial trading and investing. The parameters of the decision-making algorithm are still underspecified in the current problem definition, since various trade-offs could arise. The speed of execution and the *quality* of the average price at which the execution takes place are anti-correlated variables and they have to be balanced accordingly.

A short execution time requirement for a large order may result in a very unsatisfactory average execution price, and conversely a more relaxed time window could improve the average price for the transaction, but it may expose the execution to adverse market movements, which in turn may result in potentially greater losses. Therefore this problem of *optimized* execution could be framed as a classical optimization problem and it represents one of the most classic problems in Quantitative trading.

Prior to the digitization of the financial industry, the only information available to agents attempting to optimize trade execution was the sequence of prices of already-executed trades and the current bid and ask prices. But the advent of electronic trading has made available to market participants a variety of informational tools that could assist in the process of optimizing the market impact of large volume transactions. Nowadays market participants have access to very granular market microstructure data, or what is called order book data. This type of data has become available in real time and it is represented by two large data structures containing all outstanding buy and sell limit order prices and volumes. Such data is extremely valuable for the problem of optimized execution, since the distribution of outstanding limit orders may help predicting short-term price movements, the likelihood of execution at a given price, as well as what is called buy-side or sell-side imbalances.

The availability in real time of such data coupled with recent advances in the use of Reinforcement Learning, has made possible practical solutions for the *Optimized Trade Execution* problem. A great deal of work has been reported in the field of Market Data microstructure (Smith et al. 2003; O'Hara 1997). This created the conditions for the identification of relevant state variables that could be used in the RL algorithms for the optimization of agent's actions. These state variables could be either *private* variables, such as the amount of time and shares remaining for the algorithm in the execution problem, or *market* variables, which reflect various features of the trading activity in the limit order book. An example of such a microstructure variable is the current cost of a market order submission.

By exploiting the structure of the order book data, customizable RL algorithms are employed to improve the computational efficiency of the optimized execution problem, especially for the case of extremely large data sets. Several studies have shown that combining the availability of market microstructure data with novel RL algorithms could improve significantly the efficiency of the trade execution problem. Nevmyvaka, Feng, and Kearns (2006) have reported improvements in performance for up to 50% compared to baseline cases. By combining Q-learning and Dynamic Programming, the authors implemented efficient RL algorithms to take advantage of the structural features of order book trade execution. The resulting RL policies could be easily interpreted in terms of the state variables and the constraints of the execution problem.

6.1.1 On Limit Orders and Market Microstructure

Modern financial markets are generally limit order markets. A limit order to buy or to sell a certain number N of shares at price P may partially or completely execute at prices at or below the bid or at or above the ask. Let's consider the example of a future contract on the 10-year note ZN (traded on CME's Globex platform) that is currently trading at a price of 121-205 (see Figure 6.1 for the actual snapshot of a ZN order book):

A potential buyer is willing to buy a lot of 116 contracts at the price of 121-180 or lower. If one chooses to submit a limit order with this specification, the order will be placed in the limit order book, which is ordered by price, with the highest price at the top (this price is referred to as the best bid; the lowest sell price is called the best ask). In the example provided above, the order would be placed in the price bracket of 120-180 which has a total of 5,169 bidded contracts. Although the bidder offers to buy at the same price, the other orders (5,053) at this price level have arrived before this one. An execution occurs only when arriving buying limit orders could be matched with selling orders on the opposing side of the book. For example, a limit order to buy 18 contracts at 121-205 will jump in front of the current best bid (121-200) and

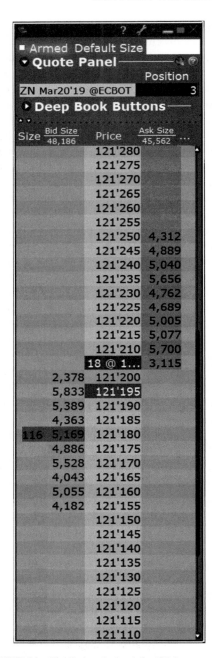

FIGURE 6.1   The limit order book for ZN future contract.

it will generate an instant execution by matching with a lot of limit sell orders for 18 contracts at the same price, 121-205. The 121-200 price level will continue to be the best available bid with 2,378 available contracts, and the 121-205 will represent the best offer level with 3,115 available contracts. As more big orders arrive, they will consume orders deeper on the opposite side of the book, therefore achieving successively worse average execution prices.

The main source of data that is used to train the RL models is composed of limit order book data. This data structure describes the order flow that needs to be modeled and understood in order to find the best possible execution strategy for large orders. This kind of optimization problem requires the development of a generative model (or a simulator) that combines the real-world order flow with artificial orders generated by the execution strategies that one tries to optimize. This simulator needs to maintain order queue priorities and to match the orders in the order book. Therefore historical order book data could be used to run simulations and to capture all costs and uncertainties of trade execution, such as the bid-ask spread, the market impact, or the risk of non-execution. Because of the very granular nature of the order book data and the frequency at which it arrives, these data sets could be extremely large, taking up to several GBs of space per financial instrument and per trading day. A statistically robust study for the *Optimized Trade Execution* problem may require years' worth of data.

6.1.2 Formulation of Base-Line Strategies

How is the dynamics of the order book going to influence the problem of Optimized trade execution? Since the goal is to sell N shares in a specified time horizon T, there are several benchmark strategies that could be used for performance comparison:

1. *Submit at once* is a simple strategy where one market order is submitted at the beginning of the time interval T. This is equivalent to placing a limit order to sell all N shares at price zero, which will have the net effect of obtaining the average execution price at that very moment.

   However, as N grows in size, the average execution price will get progressively worse as one depletes the existing orders of the limit order book. This simplistic strategy could be considered as the primal solution of the *Optimized Trade Execution* problem.

2. *Submit and leave* (S&L) policies are a better class of strategies that would consist of selecting a limit order price P and placing all N shares at that price. After a preset period of time T, the unexecuted orders will be transformed into market orders. Using this approach one would achieve a much better average execution price than using the *submit at once* approach.

   Another advantage of this kind of strategy is the fact that the limit orders do not have to be continuously monitored. Continuous monitoring of limit orders could be expensive and could also expose them to market fluctuations and adverse selection.

3. *Portion out evenly at bid/ask*: This strategy will entail dividing the order into several smaller orders corresponding to the number of time periods allotted for the execution (Hu 2016), If one wants to buy 10,000 units of an instrument in 10 equally spaced time intervals, one order of 1,000 units will be submitted at bid/ask every time period. The leftover portion of the initial order that was not executed within the maximum time period will be executed at the market price.

The application of Reinforcement Learning techniques to the problem of Optimized trade execution involves the consideration of *state-based* strategies. These strategies are aimed at examining relevant features of the order book and coupling them with agent's own trading activity in order to decide the best course of action.

6.1.3 A Reinforcement Learning Formulation for the Optimized Execution Problem

This section will introduce a Reinforcement Learning formulation for the Optimized Execution problem, by defining the terms of state, action, and reward as well as the algorithms used.

6.1.3.1 States

A state is defined as a vector of attributes ($x \in X$) that describes the current configuration of a system. It is important to note that a state is actually an experimentally observed state. The two most important state representations are the elapsed time **t** and the remaining inventory **q**, which represent how much time of the horizon T has passed and how many shares we have left to execute in the target volume N. These variables are typically called private variables because they are known and meaningful just for the execution strategy, and not to the external world. Different resolutions of accuracy are investigated for these variables: Δt and Δq. The time horizon T is divided into distinct intervals (Δt) at which the policy is allowed to observe the state and take an action. As an example, if one wants to execute 10,000 contracts in 10 different episodes, for a time horizon of T = 5 min, one can submit a revised limit order every 30 seconds, and the time remaining variable t can assume values from 0 (start of the episode) down to 10 (last decision point of the episode). One also considers some additional state variables that are called market variables. They encode dynamic properties of the limit order book and its recent activity. Thus, a state could be encoded in the form of $x_n = \langle t|q|o_1, o_2, \ldots o_K \rangle$ where the o_j is a market variable. It is important to note that a state representation is just a model and as such is by no means sufficient to render a perfect picture for a system as complex as modern financial markets.

6.1.3.2 Actions

For the Optimized Execution problem the Action space can be thought of as the collection of limit order prices at which one could reposition the remaining inventory, relative to the current ask or bid. For the problem of selling N shares, an action A corresponds to placing a limit order for all unexecuted orders at price ask A. This means effectively canceling any previous outstanding limit order and replacing with a new limit order. The action A could be positive, negative, or just A = 0 corresponding to an order coming in at the current ask. A positive action A corresponds to *crossing the spread* toward the buyers, and a negative action −A corresponds to placing an order in the sell-side of the book. In the case of buying, A is defined relative to the current bid. For both buying and selling, more positive actions mean movement toward the opposing book, and more negative actions mean placement deeper within our own book.

6.1.3.3   Reward Functions
Any action taken in a given state could result in immediate rewards: cash inflows or outflows, depending on whether selling or buying from any (partial) execution of the limit order placed. But because the execution of the entire lot of N shares is mandatory, any inventory remaining at the end of time T has to be immediately executed at market prices. This translates into consuming all available orders from the opposing side of the book to execute, no matter the quality of the average execution prices.

In order to compare different policies and their performance across instruments, one always measures the execution prices achieved by a policy relative to the mid-spread price at the start of the episode in question. This is representing an idealistic expectation that is assuming an infinite liquidity available at the mid-spread price point. Since this idealized policy cannot be generally realized, one always expects a worse outcome. Therefore one defines the execution cost of a policy as the underperformance compared to the mid-spread baseline. The reward function captures very important features of the execution process, such as the bid-ask spread, the market impact, or the opportunity cost. For practical purposes one generally assumes that commissions and exchange fees are negligible and that the access to exchanges is fast and unhampered by network delays.

6.1.3.4   Algorithms
There is a rich variety of RL algorithms that could be used for the Optimized Execution problem. The best results reported in the literature have been obtained by using RL algorithms that were computationally fast and benefited from an efficient reuse of the market data. One of the most significant assumptions across all RL models is the alleged Markovian nature of trade execution. This feature allows for a significant reduction in the number of state optimizations. If the problem's state space is properly defined, the optimal action at any given point in time is approximately independent of any previous actions. By using the Markov property, the optimal action in a state $\mathbf{s}$ at time $\mathbf{t}$ is independent of the actions in all states with elapsed time $t \le t$. By extending this logic at time $t = T$ (no time left), the optimal actions in the final states are independent from all other actions taken before. When the allocated time runs out, the agent is forced to submit a market order for the reminder of all unexecuted orders in order to bring the inventory to the desired target level N independently of what happened between $t = 0$ and $t = T-1$. The Markovian trade execution model represents an inductive method to solve the Optimized Execution problem. Having assigned optimal actions for the final states (by placing a mandatory market order at $t = T$),

one poses all the information needed to determine the optimal action for all previous states (starting with t = T–1). This will allow for moving one time step back at the time from t = T–2 to t = 0. Attaining the initial time step (t = 0) will guarantee the achievement of a globally optimal policy under the Markovian assumption.

Another significant assumption made is that the agent's own actions do not affect the behavior of other market participants. The consequence of this assumption is that the agent's order submission does not follow any particular strategy in relationship with how orders are submitted by the other market participants, like stepping in front of large orders. From a formal perspective this means that the agent's actions do not affect market state variables $o_1, o_2, \ldots o_K$, but only the private variables t and q. The independence between public and private variables is used in the implementation of the algorithm to use the available data more efficiently and to reduce overfitting. This in turn will ensure that every state encountered could be optimized. As a result for every episode in the order flow data, one could ask the following question: *What is the optimal action to be taken in this state if we were to encounter this particular state with t = 0, 1, 2, or T periods remaining?* The same methodology is to be used for the other private variable, the remaining inventory q. This will ensure that every possible state that can be generated from the dataset $\{t, q\} * \{o_1, o_2, \ldots o_K\}$ will be visited.

6.2   CURRENT STATE-OF-THE-ART IN OPTIMIZED TRADE EXECUTION

This section will review the current state-of-the-art in Optimized Trade execution. The most sophisticated strategies in use for optimizing the execution of large orders require a finite amount of time to trade. Almgren and Chriss (2000) pointed out that the time required for the execution of a large order entails an additional risk, and consequently a risk-return trade-off must be considered. The authors developed families of execution strategies that lie on a risk-return frontier by making specific assumptions about the execution technology employed. Agents who are more risk averse will trade faster, thus incurring higher transaction costs but at lower risk levels. Bertsimas and Lo (1998) derived several dynamic optimal trading strategies that minimize the expected cost of trading of a large block of equities over a fixed time horizon. Given a fixed block of shares to be executed within a fixed time interval, and given a price-impact function (that yields the execution price of an individual trade as a function of the shares traded and market conditions), the authors generated an optimal sequence of trades or the best execution strategy as a function of market conditions.

Coggins, Blazejewski, and Aitken (2003) introduced a new approach for optimizing trade execution in a limit order market. This approach was used for the scenario of trade shortfall where limited liquidity leads to significant transaction costs. The authors described a method for calculating a trade execution plan which balances intraday variations in the supply of liquidity against the risk of adverse future price movements. The trade execution plan corresponded to solutions of discrete time Dynamic Programming problems by specifying transaction costs within a value at risk framework. El-Yaniv and co-authors (2001) addressed the one-way trading problem from the perspective of a time series search problem. In a time series search problem a player is searching for the maximum or minimum price in a sequence that unfolds sequentially, by processing one price at a time. During the game a player could decide just once to accept the current price p in which case the game ends and the player's payoff is p. In the *one-way trading* problem a trader is given the task of trading a certain FX pair. Each day, a new exchange rate is announced, and the trader must decide how many dollars to convert to the foreign currency according to the current rate. The game ends when the trader trades his entire dollar wealth to the foreign currency.

Kakade and collaborators (2004) introduced several online models for Volume Weighted Average Price trading and limit order books. They published an extensive study of competitive algorithms for these problems and related them to earlier online algorithms for stock trading. Algorithmic approaches to the Optimal Execution problem using methods from Stochastic Control have been well studied (Bouchaud, Mezard, and Potters 2002; Cont and Kukanov 2013; Guant, Lehalle, and Tapia 2012; Kharroubi and Pham 2010). This approach starts with the assumption that the underlying real stock price is generated by some known stochastic process. An impact function is defined to specify how arriving liquidity demand pushes market prices away from this true value. Having this information, as well as time and volume constraints, it is then possible to compute the optimal strategy explicitly. This could be done either in closed form or numerically by using Dynamic Programming.

Nevmyvaka, Feng, and Kearns (2006) published one of the first research papers in the area of trade execution optimization using Reinforcement Learning. They presented "the first large-scale empirical application of Reinforcement Learning to the important problem of optimized trade execution in modern financial markets." Their results were based on analyzing 18 months' worth of millisecond time-scale limit order book data from NASDAQ. This paper was one of the first to promote the potential of Reinforcement Learning to address market microstructure problems.

Axel Rantil and Olle Dahlén (2018) published the results of a MS thesis titled "Optimized Trade Execution with Reinforcement Learning" at the University of Linköpings, in Sweden. They reported a series of very interesting findings for the Optimized Trade execution problem following a purely empirical approach. By using historical data to simulate the process of placing artificial orders in a market, the two authors were able to model the problem as a Markov Decision Process (MDP). Within this MDP framework they trained and evaluated a set of RL algorithms having as an objective the minimization of transaction cost on yet unseen test data.

Just a couple of years before, Robert Hu (2016) published a paper on the Optimal Order Execution Using Stochastic Control and Reinforcement Learning. The goal of the thesis was to "find the optimal order execution policy that maximizes the reward from trading financial instruments." Optimal execution policies were devised by using an MDP built using a state space model and the Bellman equation. Simulations on historical order book data have been used to find the state transition probabilities and the rewards associated with each state. An optimal policy was generated using the Bellman equation and tested against a variety of naïve policies on out-of-sample data. This thesis explored whether the MDP is still viable under less constrained assumptions and attempted to estimate the value function using various techniques from Reinforcement Learning.

6.3   IMPLEMENTATION METHODOLOGY

In this section we will address the general methodology used to solve the Optimized Trade execution problem. From a practical perspective the main question is *how to determine the optimal action in a given state*. The availability of large amounts of market microstructure tick-level data has made possible in-depth studies of the Optimized Trade execution problem. The main approach used to interact with the order flow data set and to test several different RL algorithmic implementations is by way of simulating trade executions. The use of simulated orders is needed for emulating the passage through different possible states in order to optimize the RL policy needed to achieve the best execution for a given inventory and specific timeline.

6.3.1   Simulating the Interaction with the Market Microstructure

Historical order flow data could be used to simulate a limit order–based market and its microstructure dynamics. Rantil and Dahlén (2018) described in their study a practical method for simulating the matching of artificial orders with historical order book data.

Their order flow data set was composed of the proximal 10 ask and 10 bid price levels and their associated total order volumes. The order book data was time-stamped with a minute-level granularity and consisted of fields such as the order side (buy or sell), the price level, and the total volume available for that particular price level. Alongside the historical order book depth, aggregated market trades were available for each one-minute interval. This aggregated data consisted of all trades that took place during the succeeding one-minute period of the available depth data.

By placing artificial orders into this simulated market, the authors were able to evaluate the quality of the execution strategies. Depending on the type of the artificial order, the current structure of the order book, and the list of the aggregated trades, orders were matched with:

- Other orders from the depth of the book – immediate matching;
- The aggregated trades – continuous matching; or
- Both types.

For the continuous matching case, the authors assumed that after the occurrence of immediate matching, the unexecuted part of the artificial order was placed in the order book and could be matched with the trades that occurred after the immediate matching took place. This way all the volume traded at a lower (higher) price than the order price when buying (selling) is matched with the artificial order. This is possible because the simulated order was placed in the books before the orders that have been historically traded. All the volume executed during the continuous matching phase is being done at the price of the artificial order and not at the average price of the aggregated trades.

To make the matching process as realistic as possible, the authors encoded into the order-matching simulator several interesting properties:

- If the artificial order is not matched during the immediate matching phase, the trade simulator will take into account the queue for that price by letting the existing volume for that price level be matched during the continuous phase before the artificial order is allowed to match.
- If the artificial order is matched during the immediate matching phase, the trade simulator will adjust so that the same order cannot match with the same historical orders twice.
- For very aggressive orders, like large volume orders that could empty the order book depth for all of the 10 price levels, the assumption made is that the volume for the following price levels will be an average volume of the first 10 price levels.

The outcomes of the matching process are:

- The amount of cash spent if buying, or received if selling, and
- The total volume executed.

After an artificial order has been placed and a matching has occurred, the process could be repeated at the next time step. At specifically chosen time steps, an artificial order is removed and replaced with another one. This could happen several times during an episode until the time limit expires. Therefore a complete episode could be simulated by several matching occurrences. Obviously this simulation method has its own shortcomings since it only considers orders visible in the order book. Orders like hidden orders or iceberg orders are not dealt with. Although hidden orders do not appear in the books, they still could be matched. The iceberg orders will show only part of the volume in the LOB. The ratio of hidden to visible orders can be quite significant for certain markets.

A significant limitation of the market simulator described by Nevmyvaka and co-authors (2006) was represented by the assumption that there is no market impact due to artificial orders on the market as a whole. In a real market setting, the impact of the agent's trading on the order book may persist over time. Another limiting assumption is that the execution strategies and their simulated orders will not affect the behavior of other market participants. Therefore the reaction of the market was not modeled. Market participants could adjust their existing resting orders following a particularly aggressive order.

6.3.2 Using Dynamic Programming to Optimize Trade Execution

Optimizing trade execution is a multistage decision process where the agent decides what orders to place and at what times. It also has a clear objective to minimize the transaction costs. As a consequence the problem of Optimized Trade Execution could be treated as a control problem and it could be potentially solved analytically using the Dynamic Programming paradigm (Almgren and Chriss 2000; Bertsimas and Lo 1998).

Dynamic programming is a well-known method for solving optimal control problems and it can be used for the Markov Decision Process (see Figure 6.2) where the transition matrix and reward function are known. To find the optimal path one could use Bellman's principle of optimality: "An optimal policy has the property that whatever the initial state and initial decision are, the remaining decisions must constitute an optimal policy with regard to the state resulting from the first decision" (Wikipedia 2019).

There are several variants of Dynamic Programming that are currently in use. Rantil and Dahlén (2018) have reported the use of a backward induction method. The author considered the MDP as being represented by an acyclic graph, like in Figure 6.2.

The task is to transact **N** units of an asset during a time interval of **T** steps. The variable i represents the inventory left to transact and the variable t represents the number of time steps elapsed. The action a is encoded by the number of units to transact at time step t and the reward $\mathbf{R_a}$ is the cash flow from the resulting transaction. The goal is to maximize the total reward during the process. Since the process is assumed to be a Markov Decision Process (MDP), an optimal path can be found by using the Bellman expectation equation. This equation allows for the breakdown of the problem into smaller sub-problems.

The algorithm is iterating backwards in time, solving first the state for t = T and then iterating to t = 0 (see Figure 6.3).

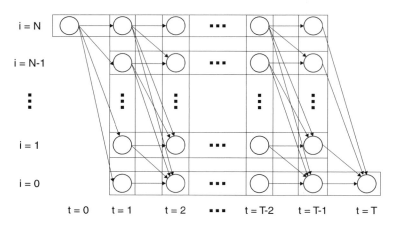

FIGURE 6.2 The Markov decision process represented as an acyclic graph.

f or $t = T - 1$ **to** 0
> **f or** $i = 0$ **to** N
>> $s \leftarrow (t, i)$
>>
>> $v^*(s) \leftarrow max_{a \in A_t} \left[R_s^a + \gamma \sum_{s' \in S} P_{ss'}^a \, v^*(s') \right]$
>>
>> *Record the optimal action f or s*

R_s^a - *reward (cash) in state s from selling due to action a*
$P_{ss'}^a$ - *probability of transition from s to s' given action a*
γ - *discount factor* $\in (0,1)$

FIGURE 6.3   Pseudocode for MDP.

The optimal solution is given by Bellman's principle of optimality and the optimal policy is obtained by chaining together the recorded optimal action for each state one has encountered during the training episode. Solving a control problem in a model-free setting, that is without knowing or modeling the transition probabilities, and the reward function is a more robust approach. Reinforcement Learning is the method of choice to learn a policy through interaction with an environment while maximizing the long-run reward.

6.3.3 Using Reinforcement Learning to Optimize Trade Execution

A more realistic approach would be to use historical market data and define a Markov Decision Process assisted by a trading simulator in order to be able to model the market microstructure dynamics. Reinforcement Learning is an appealing technique (see Figure 6.4) for solving this problem since there is no need for the specification of the transition probability or the reward function. In this new formulation, the problem consists of episodes containing states, actions, and rewards. The environment initiates an episode by returning a starting state. The agent then selects an action $\mathbf{A_t}$ based on the start state $\mathbf{S_t}$ from the set of possible actions $\mathbf{A}$. The environment returns a reward $\mathbf{r_t}$ and the next state $\mathbf{S_{t+1}}$. This is done repeatedly until the episode terminates because some end state was reached.

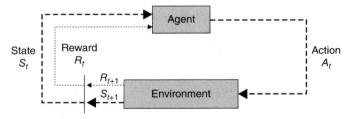

FIGURE 6.4   The reinforcement learning method. **Source:** Adapted from https://i.stack.imgur.com/eoeSq.png.

6.3.3.1 *Learning methods*

There are several classic learning methods for solving the optimal control problem. One category is using the action-value table Q(s, a) to update the value of taking an action **A** in the state **S**. This method is using tables and therefore is limited to handling just discrete states and actions. There are other learning methods that are similar in that they gather information from episodes consisting of a state, action, reward, and the next state where the action is chosen according to some policy. The algorithm runs until the episode terminates. During this time the table Q(s, a) is continuously updated.

Several learning methods are in use:

- Q-learning
- Temporal Differences
- Monte Carlo
- Sarsa(λ)

Nevmyvaka, Feng, and Kearns (2006) reported the use of the *Q-learning* methodology that we introduced in the previous chapter. For every state that one encounters, that is, for every possible combination of time and remaining inventory, the agent checks all possible actions, updates the cost function associated with taking each action, and then it follows the optimal strategy. Any action that is taken will result in an immediate payout when a certain number of shares get bought or sold. This will shift the agent into a new state a time step later. Because the learning moves backwards in time, the new state has been previously optimized and therefore the expected cost of following the optimal strategy from that state is known.

The cost update rule takes the following form:

$$\text{Cost}(s, a) = \frac{n}{n+1}\text{Cost}(s, a) + \frac{1}{n+1}[Cost_{+1}(s, a) + \textbf{arg max } Cost(s_{+1}, a_{+1})]$$

Where:

- **Cost**(s, a) is the cost of taking action **a** in the state **s** and then following the optimal strategy in all subsequent states
- **Cost$_{+1}$**(s, a) is the immediate cost of taking the action **a** in the state **s**
- **s$_{+1}$** is the new state after taking **a** in the state **s**
- **n** is the number of trials for action **a** in the state **s**
- **a$_{+1}$** is the action taken in s$_{+1}$

Nevmyvaka and co-authors reported that in order to learn the optimal strategy, their algorithms had to go through the data set N_T x N_I x N_A times, where N_T represents the number of time steps, N_I is the number of inventory units, and N_A is the number of actions in each state.

According to the authors, the running time of the algorithm was much faster than the worst-case scenario, and it has several interesting properties:

- Running time of the algorithm was independent of the number of market variables.
- Parameters N_T and N_I could be increased arbitrarily without running the risk of overfitting because of the efficient use of the data set.

The optimal strategy for execution reported by Nevmyvaka, Feng, and Kearns could be summarized by the pseudocode shown in Figure 6.5.

The optimal policy is created by selecting the highest-payout action in each and every of the states. One very important aspect to note is that because of the assumption that the private and market variables are considered to be independent, during the training phase one considers that the actions generating a specific policy have no effects on the subsequent evolution of the order book. Therefore after simulating that a certain number of shares have been executed in a given order book state, the agent continues to the next state as if the order book has not been affected by the actions (execution) of the agent in the previous state.

The advantage of using this assumption is that it renders both the computation time and the sample complexity almost independent of the number of market variables, since the agent's actions do not influence market variable evolution. The results reported by Nevmyvaka, Feng, and Kearns validated the assumption made above on the test data set for which this assumption was not made. Consistent empirical results were obtained for the test data set in spite of the independence assumption made for the training data set.

The selected market variables were intended to summarize information from the order books into several of low-resolution features.

Examples of market variables:

- *Bid-Ask Spread* – as a positive value indicating the current difference between the bid and ask prices in the current order books

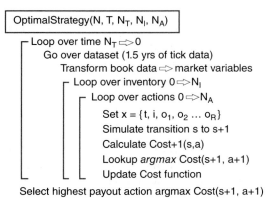

FIGURE 6.5   The optimal strategy pseudocode.

- *Bid-Ask Volume Imbalance* – as a signed quantity indicating the number of shares at the bid minus the number of shares at the ask in the current order book
- *Signed Transaction Volume* – as a signed quantity indicating the number of shares bought in the last 15 seconds minus the number of shares sold in the same time interval
- *Immediate Market Order Cost* – as the cost one would pay for purchasing the remaining shares immediately with a market order

The training data set was partitioned into episodes and the RL algorithm was applied to learn an optimized execution policy over the selected state space. For example, for the two-minute time horizon case, the one-year training data set was split into about 45,000 episodes. One of the advantages of using order microstructure data is that they generate very large training and test sets, which are very beneficial for the learning algorithms. The RL policies represented the outcome of the learning process and these have been compared for the test set with several baseline strategies. The trading costs were measured in basis points over the mid-price at the opening of the episode. The benchmark comparison was made in respect with the optimized Submit-and-Leave strategy. Comparisons between RL policies obtained using different state variables were equally interesting.

6.4   EMPIRICAL RESULTS

In this section we will review the most significant results reported in the literature about the use of Reinforcement Learning algorithms for Optimized Trade Execution.

6.4.1   Application to Equities

Nevmyvaka, Feng, and Kearns (2006) reported an interesting set of empirical results. Their experimental setup consisted of simulating executions for some very liquid stocks, such as NVDA, AMZN, and QCOM. The simulated volumes were 5,000 and 10,000 shares for time horizons of two and eight minutes respectively.

The main conclusions of their study were that:

- The least liquid financial instrument (NVDA) was also the most expensive to trade, and conversely, the most liquid one (QCOM) was the cheapest to transact.
- Trading larger orders is always more costly than trading smaller ones.
- Having less time to execute a trade generally results in higher costs.

In practical terms this means that the agent has to accept the largest price concession when transacting a large number of shares in an illiquid instrument in a relatively short amount of time. The learning process followed by the authors had two variants: using private variables only, or coupling private and market variables together.

6.4.2   Using Private Variables Only

One of the state space configurations consisted of just the two private variables
t – the number of decision points remaining in the episode, and **i** – the remaining
inventory. Even for this very simple setting, the Reinforcement Learning algorithm
used delivered a much-improved performance compared to benchmark policies like
Submit-and-Leave (which was already a major improvement over a simple market
order). The authors reported noticeable improvements over S&L strategies ranging
from 27% to 360% depending on the parameter choices for **T** and **I**. The increase
of either parameter (time and inventory unit resolutions) would lead to much better
results.

These improvements could be explained by RL's ability to find optimal actions
that are conditioned on the state of the environment. The more inventory and less
time remains, the more aggressively the agent should price the orders to avoid sub-
mitting a costly market order at the end. The authors observed that the RL algorithm
was learning the same general shape for a range of different parameter values. On
the other hand, the exact policy specification was found to be instrument dependent.
One of the most interesting results reported in this study was the observation of how
actions were related to the trading costs. The optimal policies were derived from
Q-values. By fixing either the time or the inventory remaining, one could vary the
other private variable and plot the Q-values (or equivalently the trading costs) for
each action.

For each state the action learned was represented by the minimum of the corresponding Q-value function. The shapes of the Q-value functions could explain the
relationship between state variables and the optimal actions to be taken. For large
inventories and little time remaining, the entire Q-value function shifts upwards,
reflecting higher expected costs. At the same time the minimum of the curve shifts in a
way that indicates that optimal action must be more aggressive for these situations. In
the case of small inventories and longer remaining times, the Q-value function shifts
downwards, reflecting lower expected costs, and the minimum of the curve shifts in
the opposite direction, suggesting a more passive behavior for the execution agent.

6.4.3   Using Both Private and Market Variables

By adding market variable to the study, Nevmyvaka, Feng, and Kearns observed further improvements over using just the private variables. The results were averaged
over all instruments, sizes, execution periods, and private variable resolutions T and
I and for each market variable tested.

One of the market variables used in the study was the *immediate market order
cost,* which represents a global measure of liquidity beyond the bid-ask spread. This
market variable measures how much it would cost to submit a market order for the
balance of inventory immediately, as opposed to waiting until the expiration period
T. Another market variable utilized was the *bid-ask volume imbalance,* which is the
signed differences between volumes quoted at the bid and at the ask. *Transaction
volume* represented the signed volume of all trades within the last fifteen seconds

assuming that all buy orders have a positive sign and the sell orders have a negative sign. Each of these market variables could take their values from a relatively small interval.

The authors also explored combinations of two and three market variables. While they succeeded in identifying factors that can improve RL performance significantly, there were many other combinations that did not result in more efficient policies, which is a testimony to market efficiency. Overall, the authors reported an improvement in execution of 50% or more over S&L policies and several times over market orders when using RL together with private and market variables. As such:

- Bid-ask spread resulted in about 8% improvement in the trading cost.
- Immediate market order revenue contributed to about 4.3% cost reduction.
- Signed transaction volume yielded about 2.5% improvement.

By combining all three informative features, a 13% improvement was reported over the original private variables-only state space. These results showed that for each of the features described above, the percentage reduction in trading cost (or the implementation shortfall) was obtained by adding that feature to the original private variables-only state space. The authors reported improvements for three of the four features, with only bid-ask volume imbalance not yielding any discernable usefulness.

This reported improvement in performance is certainly due to the RL algorithm learning different actions for different values of market variables. As an example, larger bid-ask spreads require more aggressive actions from the agent that must go further to chase the opposing book. As was the case for the private variables–only case study, the shape of Q-value function is quite explanatory for the difference of optimal actions across states. For some market variables there is no visible improvement in the performance of the RL algorithm.

6.4.4   Application to Futures

In a recently published study, Rantil and Dahlén (2018) reported a series of very interesting results concerning the problem of Optimized Trade Execution. The authors studied the problem empirically by placing artificial orders in a limit order market simulated with historical order-flow data. The order-flow data was for future contracts in the commodity space (Crude Oil – WTI), stock indexes (FTSE 250, Nasdaq), and fixed income (Gilts). The data sets were selected for a period of 18 months and two thirds of it was used for training and the rest for testing the RL models.

All models and strategies were evaluated in terms of transaction cost. Transaction cost was defined as the difference between the cash flow achieved by the hypothetical scenario of transacting the desired quantity at the mid-price at the beginning of the period and the actual cash flow generated by the model or strategy.

The baseline strategies chosen were:

- *Immediate Execution* (IE), where a market order is submitted for the entire inventory at the beginning of the episode therefore reducing the risk of unfavorable price movement.
- *Submit and Leave* (SL), where a limit order is submitted for the entire inventory at the beginning of the episode and then the remaining volume is executed at market at the expiration of the allotted time horizon.
- This strategy is a trade-off between risk of non-execution and a low cost.
- *Constant Policy* (CP), where one places a limit order for the entire remaining inventory at a constant number of ticks from the bid if buying or ask if selling. This order is replaced with a new order a given number of times (depending on the problem setting).
- Each time the order is replaced, it will be placed with the remaining volume left to execute and with a new price relative to the bid or ask for that particular time point.
- *Constant Policy with Volume* (CPWV) is very similar to the CP policy with the added feature of placing a fixed percentage of the remaining volume instead of all the remaining volume at each order placement.
- *Evenly Distributed* (ED), where the large order is broken into smaller equal sizes and executes at certain time intervals – the most commonly used strategy in practice.

NFK was one of the models developed by Rantil and Dahlén with the goal of validating the results reported by Nevmyvaka, Feng, and Kearns (2006). They also extended their results into the *Dual NFK* model with the goal of regularizing the outputs against external price movement. In addition to these two base models, the authors implemented and evaluated:

- A classical RL algorithm, named *Sarsa(λ)*, which employs a modified reward function, and
- A *Proximal Policy Optimization* (PPO), which is an actor-critic RL algorithm incorporating neural networks in order to find the optimal policy.

The authors evaluated the performance of all these RL-based models, by comparing their results with the ones obtained by using the five simple baseline strategies outlined above.

The results reported by Rantil and Dahlén were very similar with those found by Nevmyvaka, Feng, and Kearns in terms of transaction cost relative to the Submit-and-Leave baseline policies. For some problem settings, like tight bid-ask spreads or small inventory to be executed in very liquid markets, the Submit-and-Leave baseline policies performed better. The Constant Policy strategy has consistently performed better than Submit-and-Leave or NFK in terms of cost by using the same action space and order update frequency as NFK. The NFK performed much better than SL while being relatively simple to train and implement.

The dual NFK model performed on par with NFK, suggesting that one can train the execution model for both sides of the order book instead of training separately for buys and sells. However, there are practical situations when the buy and the sell sides of the order book are not symmetrical and the dual NFK method could not be properly trained. As such the dual model can only be trained when the problem is completely symmetric in respect to buys and sells.

The use of the Sarsa (λ) model with a modified reward function yielded superior results to both NFK models. It outperformed the baseline Constant-Policy strategy for some instruments and problem settings, something that the NFK model did not.

It is worth noting that the baseline policies ED and CPWV performed better than the NFK, dual NFK, and Sarsa (λ) models. However, the comparison is not very relevant since these baseline policies take into account the volume when placing orders. A much better comparison is done with the Proximal Policy Optimization model.

The use of the Proximal Policy Optimization model for one specific problem setting has shown excellent results that outperformed even the best of the baseline strategies and models, showing promise for deep reinforcement learning methods for the problem of Optimized Trade Execution.

As a general conclusion the Proximal Policy Optimization model reduces transaction costs when compared to all baseline strategies by giving robust results on both buying and selling for all instruments with the same hyper-parameters. The training process was reported to be very stable and has produced consistent results on multiple runs.

6.4.5 Another Example

Robert Hu (2016) has published a detailed study for the problem of Optimized Trade Execution. The main conclusions reported by this study are that:

- Naïve baseline strategies were outperforming the RL-based models when the size of the order to be traded was not producing a sizable market impact. The results obtained with a discrete model strongly suggest that naïve baseline strategies perform better when there is no punishment on large volume submissions and aggressive orders.
- The RL-based models implemented via a Markov Decision Process yielded superior results when the market impact was present in order-flow simulations. The superiority of RL-based models in high market impact scenarios could be credited to the fact that MDP takes the average from all the simulations and then incorporates the effect of market impact in the estimated average.
- When considering more realistic market conditions, like slippage on the execution price, the naïve baseline strategies are outperforming the RL-based models.

6.5   CONCLUSIONS AND FUTURE DIRECTIONS

The financial industry has been historically a driving force in promoting the use of novel quantitative and computational technologies. The last decade has seen an increased interest in applying Machine Learning methodologies, specifically Reinforcement Learning, to the problem of Optimized Trade Execution. Designing and implementing strategies that maximize the risk adjusted value of trading has been the object of large research studies (Nevmyvaka, Feng, and Kearns 2006; Rantil and Dahlén 2018; Hu 2016). A wide variety of Reinforcement Learning–based policies have been developed to specify the optimal action to be taken from any given state according to a discounted future reward criterion. These RL models are balancing the short-term rewards of actions against the influence that these actions have on future states.

The previous section has synthetized the latest developments in the area of Optimized Trade Execution. Some important conclusions could be drawn:

- The advent of high-frequency trading and the opportunity to collect vast amounts of tick order-flow data has made possible the empirical study of order book microstructure. The granular analysis of the order book microstructure has facilitated the implementation of the state-based models that in turn could find better optimizations for the market impact problem.
- The appropriate choice of private and market state variables coupled with the utilization of efficient Reinforcement Learning algorithms have resulted in significant improvements over simpler forms of optimization such as submit-and-leave, constant, or evenly distributed policies.
- The availability of novel information regarding order book microstructure has had an important effect on reducing transaction costs. The net effect of using both tabular RL methods (such as Q-learning) and Neural Network function approximations has been the reduction of transaction costs.
- Following a recent surge of interest in Deep Learning and Reinforcement Learning research, new techniques that incorporate DL into RL have been developed (Sutton and Barto 1998; Mnih et al. 2016; Schulman et al. 2015; Schulman et al. 2017). These techniques have been thoroughly evaluated on video games and simulated control tasks.

6.5.1   Further Research

The current body of research could be augmented by expanding the simulations to a wider spectrum of financial instruments. One of the fundamental questions to be answered is whether the Markov Decision Process is a good choice for modeling the Optimized Trade Execution problem and how this assumption depends on the specificity of the financial instrument used.

Making the simulation of artificial orders more realistic is also an important goal for future research. Aspects related to slippage, partial fills, and illiquidity have been topics of interest for some time and they are still under development. The use of larger order-flow data sets could provide very valuable insight into key aspects of the interaction between the executing agent and the market order flow.

New techniques to acquire and process this kind of data need to be developed. These larger data sets could be also instrumental when Neural Networks are used to better estimate the value function rather than just a parametrized function or what is called *Deep Reinforcement Learning*.

REFERENCES

Almgren and Chriss (2000). Optimal execution of portfolio transactions. *Journal of Risk* 3 (2): 5–39.

Bertsimas and Lo (1998). Optimal control of execution costs. *Journal of Financial Markets* 1 (1): 1–50.

Bouchaud, Mezard, and Potters (2002). Statistical properties of stock order books: empirical results and models. *Quantitative Finance* 2: 251–256.

Coggins, Blazejewski, and Aitken (2003). Optimal trade execution of equities in a limit order market. *International Conference on Computational Intelligence for Financial Engineering*, 371–378.

Cont and Kukanov (2013). Optimal order placement in limit order markets. Technical report. https://arxiv.org/abs/1210.1625.

El-Yaniv, Fiat, Karp et al. (2001). Optimal search on one-way trading online algorithms. *Algorithmica* 30 (1): 101–139.

Guant, Lehalle, and Tapia (2012). Optimal portfolio liquidation with limit orders. Technical report. https://arxiv.org/abs/1106.3279.

Hu (2016). Optimal order execution using stochastic control and reinforcement learning. Thesis. KTH Institute of Technology, Sweden. http://www.diva-portal.se/smash/get/diva2:963057/FULLTEXT01.pdf.

Kakade, Kearns, Mansour et al. (2004). Competitive algorithms for VWAP and limit order trading. *Proceedings of the ACM Conference on Electronic Commerce*.

Kharroubi and Pham (2010). Optimal portfolio liquidation with execution cost and risk. *SIAM Journal on Financial Mathematics* 1 (1). https://arxiv.org/abs/0906.2565.

Mnih, Badia, Mirza et al. (2016). Asynchronous methods for deep reinforcement learning. *International Conference on Machine Learning*, 1928–1937.

Nevmyvaka, Feng, and Kearns (2006). Reinforcement learning for optimized trade execution. Machine Learning, Proceedings of the Twenty-Third International Conference Pittsburgh, PA.

O'Hara (1997). *Market Microstructure Theory*. Blackwell, 13–88.

Rantil and Dahlén (2018) Optimized trade execution with reinforcement learning. Master thesis. University of Linköpings, Sweden. https://pdfs.semanticscholar.org/fff0/5d2f0f414eead861a251aeff77f706804f6f.pdf.

Schulman, Levine, Abbeel et al. (2015). Trust region policy optimization. *International Conference on Machine Learning*, 1889–1897.

Schulman, Wolski, Dhariwal et al. (2017). Proximal policy optimization algorithms. https://arxiv.org/pdf/1707.06347.pdf.

Smith, Farmer, Gillemot et al. (2003). Statistical theory of the continuous double auction. *Quantitative Finance* 3 (6): 481–514.

Sutton and Barto (1998). *Reinforcement Learning: An Introduction*. MIT Press, 1–220.

Wikipedia (2019). Bellman equation. https://en.wikipedia.org/wiki/Bellman_equation.

CHAPTER 7

Case Study 2: The Dynamics of the Limit Order Book

"Prediction is very difficult, especially if it's about the future."
— *Niels Bohr, physicist and founding father of atomic structure and quantum theory*

7.1 INTRODUCTION TO THE PROBLEM

This chapter presents several case studies on the use of Machine Learning (ML) techniques to study the dynamics of the limit order book (LOB). This problem could be formulated as follows: *given a large set of order book (microstructure) data, select a suitable set of features to be used by a Machine Learning algorithm with the goal of accurately predicting directional short-time price movements.*

By reviewing a rich collection of recently published literature, this chapter examines the feasibility of applying Machine Learning techniques to the problem of predicting directional price movements for electronically traded financial instruments. The selected case studies are describing models for predicting relatively short-term price movements as measured by the bid-ask midpoint from market microstructure signals.

While the use of ML techniques is becoming more common in today's Quantitative Finance, the vast majority of these efforts are proprietary in nature, and as such most of the published work is originating from academic research. The majority of these studies concluded that developing predictive models for the LOB dynamics could be an achievable goal. One should caution the reader that all analysis is generally performed relative to the midpoint between the bid and ask, which is a fictitious, idealized price. Once we take into account transaction costs and the cost of crossing of the bid-ask spread, profitability is becoming more uncertain.

7.1.1 The New Era of Prediction

After several decades of hope and more than a few false starts, the applicability of Machine Learning to the field of Quantitative Finance is finally coming of age. The advent of inexpensive computing power, data-storage capabilities, and the proliferation of alternative data sets has bolstered the hopes of a successful use of ML in Quantitative Finance. This new phase in the evolution of Quantitative Finance is called the age of prediction. This represents a new paradigm that could bolster efficiency in trading and generate superior returns for firms and individuals that are capable of effectively implementing ML-based strategies.

Although the financial trading industry is still hesitant in hastily adopting the Machine Learning philosophy, there is one aspect in which quantitative trading and investment professionals would agree: that this new paradigm has the chance to change the financial industry in a fundamental way. There is a big wave of expectations for the new age of prediction in which algorithmic trading models will continue to become more and more accurate at predicting the dynamics of market prices. This new paradigm of prediction comes as an innovation to the previous age of estimation in which practitioners relied on classical linear models in order to approximate financial markets outcomes. Practitioners are hopeful that this new age of prediction will empower them to create empirical asset-pricing models that will generate adequate out-of-sample predictions.

Linear state space models, such as Vector Autoregressive (VAR) models, have been heavily used for the modeling of High-Frequency data and in empirical market microstructure research (Hasbrouck 2007; Cont and de Larrard 2013; Guida 2018; Kearns and Nevmyvaka 2013; Lehalle and Laruelle 2013; O'Hara 1997). These linear models provide a natural benchmark for evaluating the performance of forecast algorithms because they are easy to estimate, and they capture in a reliable way trends, linear correlations, and autocorrelations in the state variables. A classic linear Vector Autoregressive model operates on market data, and at each observation it updates a vector of linear features. Then it uses a logistic regression model for estimating the conditional probability of an upward price move.

Modern ML techniques such as Deep Neural Networks have been proven to outperform linear models because of their ability to estimate nonlinear relationships between the price dynamics and the state of the order book (which represents the visible supply and demand for the financial asset under consideration). These observations are consistent with an abundant empirical and econometric literature documenting nonlinear effects in financial time series. The success of these new ML techniques may be attributed to the flexibility of neural networks in representing nonlinearities. More specifically, sensitivity analysis performed on data-driven ML models has uncovered the existence of stable nonlinear relations between state variables and price moves, which are nonlinear features that are useful in forecasting. An example is the relation between the LOB depth and the probability of a price decrease. This kind of relationship has been studied in limit order book queueing models (Cont and de Larrard 2013).

This paradigm shift from estimation to prediction is not necessarily coming from the advent of new tools, since we have been the beneficiaries of statistical machine-learning models for many decades – but from the increased ability to access more data and have access to much faster compute architectures. The recent proliferation of open-source technology, coupled with the surge in computing power and data-storage capacity and the access to more structured and unstructured data, have made possible for financial firms the exploration of novel Machine Learning techniques.

Nowadays financial firms could have easy access to a plethora of advanced satellite and drone technologies that enables them to collect data on consumers' geo-location, spending habits, and advertising preferences, thus providing alternative data inputs to novel ML models.

"We are living in a much more digital world than 20 years ago. All the factors have lined up at the same time, which is benefiting from the trend of using modern approaches for investing," said Tony Guida (2018), portfolio manager in London.

7.1.2 New Challenges

The primary challenge for the financial practitioners is not necessarily technological in nature, but it mostly relates to the implementation process. If a computer scientist strives to get extremely high accuracy for their ML models (usually > 99%), a quantitative financial practitioner considers anything above 50% accuracy a success. The field of Quantitative Finance is not a *Silicon Valley* type culture where open-source code and collaboration is praised or even encouraged. Quantitative Finance has historically thrived on proprietary models and trade secrets. Therefore, according to Guida, "One cannot do a pure copy-paste from computer science into finance."

Again the challenge of the practical implementation is going to supersede the technological aspect. The primary focus of applying ML techniques in Quantitative Finance is to derive computationally and informationally efficient algorithms for inferring good predictive models from large data sets. A natural candidate for application of ML is to problems arising in High-Frequency Trading, for both trade execution and alpha generation.

One major challenge to overcome in training ML models on financial data is coping with the market dynamics, or the market microstructure. Understanding and modeling the dynamics of the price-generating processes is a central aspect for the applicability of ML techniques in Quantitative Finance. It is just unpractical to train an algorithm to categorize and classify all the permutations of every potential market dynamics scenario. From this perspective Market Microstructure is a very low signal-to-noise problem domain, sometimes calling into question the applicability of ML techniques.

While classic quantitative financial models usually prescribe what the relevant features for predictive modeling should be (i.e. excess returns, book-to-market ratios) in many HFT problems one may not have much prior intuition about what the relevant features should be. One typical question is how the distribution of liquidity in the order book is relating to future price movements, if at all. As such the process of selecting the relevant modeling features (feature engineering) is becoming the central theme for the use of ML in HFT.

Artificial Neural Networks are considered to be one of the most emblematic and utilized Machine Learning techniques nowadays. ANNs are considered to be universal function approximators and as such they are extremely flexible and may produce highly nonlinear functions of arbitrary and essentially uncontrollable complexity (e.g. highly non-smooth functions). As a consequence of being universal function approximators, the ANNs exhibit both notable strengths and weaknesses. Let's consider the example of using a generic ANN to build a financial forecasting model. Such a model will most likely be a highly nonlinear function of the input variables, but of an unknown form. It could be as simple as a cubic polynomial or it could take a much more complex mathematical form.

In ML parlance, if the model passes an out-of-sample test, it is considered to be acceptable no matter the functional form it may take. But when one attempts to apply this model to any market data set, one may be surprised by the results. If the market regime has changed since the time when the training data set was collected, the type of nonlinearity fitted by the model from the training data set does not correspond to a current nonlinearity from the actual data one observes.

A large section of Chapter 3 was dedicated to discussing the applicability of Artificial Intelligence to financial data. What makes the problem very difficult to debug is that one cannot detect easily the regime change since this regime is not an observable variable. As a consequence one cannot predict nor control this new type of nonlinearity. It makes it quite impossible to know when or why any ANN model would fail. It is generally accepted that models that are more interpretable would provide a better control of nonlinearities especially in transient situations that are very common in Quantitative Finance.

For problem domains where one deals with human-made, non-smooth, unstructured data such as speech or images, it is hard to find better solutions than ANNs. This is the main reason that Deep Neural Networks have enjoyed such success in applications like image recognition or voice translation.

7.1.3   High-Frequency Data

What really differentiates Quantitative Finance from other problem domains is the specificity of the data generation processes. And this specificity is reflected in the data itself. This section will address the particularity of High-Frequency Trading data as it relates to its use by Machine Learning algorithms. Even as the definition of HFT remains a subjective matter, Quantitative Finance practitioners consider this type of data to be the most granular financial data available. HFT data, also labeled microstructure data, is collected, managed, and distributed by exchanges. Its content details every order placed, every execution and every cancellation, all in real time. The availability of this data is making possible an accurate reconstruction of the full limit order book, both historically and in real time. Market microstructure-level data could be used for a variety of tasks. Besides the forecast of the future price moves other possible applications may include the early prediction of anomalous events, like extreme changes in prices.

The two most important challenges posed by this very granular market microstructure data relate to both its scale and interpretation. The size of recorded microstructure data for a highly liquid stock like GOOG for example could amount to several gigabytes daily. Storing this data for any meaningful periods of time and for a large number of financial assets requires significant storage space and modern compression techniques. In addition, processing this data in an efficient manner requires parsing the data and uncompressing it in small chunks at a time. These requirements may raise some serious technological challenges for the market participants that intend to have access to this data.

The challenge of interpretation is even more significant. What kind of meaningful information, if any, could be extracted from the microstructure data? What features could be inferred from this very granular, low-level data that would be useful in building predictive models for the directional price movement problem? This kind of question is not necessarily specific to HFT data, but it seems especially relevant when used in connection with a Machine Learning training process.

Compared to the more traditional cases like low-frequency market data or generic (not market-related) data, the meaning of microstructure data seems quite opaque. As an example, data like daily opening, low, high, and closing prices which aggregate market activity and integrate information across all market participants or earnings reports could provide actionable signals about the performance of a particular financial instrument. What interpretation could be given to the action of placing a single order in a massive stream of microstructure data? What is the meaning of an intraday snapshot of the order book considering that any existing order could be canceled at any time prior to execution?

Just for comparison let's consider the application of ML to problems in Natural Language Processing (NLP) or Computer Vision. While technically they are both very challenging problems, their degree of interpretability is quite obvious: the basic unit of meaning is the word for NLP and the objects for vision applications. In the case of market microstructure data, the unit of meaning or actionable information is a lot more difficult to identify. In addition to the opacity of meaning this type of data is noisier than in other ML domains.

7.2 CURRENT STATE-OF-THE-ART IN THE PREDICTION OF DIRECTIONAL PRICE MOVEMENT IN THE LOB

This section will review the current state-of-the-art as it relates to the ability to forecast the dynamics of market microstructure LOB data. As in any empirical study it is important to establish some benchmark models against which to compare the results reported in the following case studies. The econometrics literature of the last two decades has published many empirical studies reporting findings like:

- Weekly and monthly stocks returns are weakly negatively correlated, or
- Daily, weekly, and monthly index returns are positively correlated.

The behavior of price returns is very different in Foreign Exchange markets where short-term returns (under a minute) are highly negatively correlated. All these econometric models represent very useful benchmarks for assessing the quality of ML-based models presented in the case studies that will follow.

A great deal of research (Lehalle and Laruelle 2013; O'Hara 1997) has been done recently on the limit order book and its corresponding microstructure, most of the results being reported for individual stocks. The main objective was to characterize features such as liquidity, volatility, and spreads and not necessarily to predict future price action. But the current availability of market microstructure data is making it possible to exploit the more ample dimensionality of the order book when making trading decisions (Zheng, Moulines, and Abergel 2012; Han et al. 2015; Nousi et al. 2018; Ganesh and Rakheja 2018; Tsantekidis et al. 2018; Doering, Fairbank, and Markose 2017). These techniques are far more sophisticated than the standard time series analysis tool set that was used in the past two decades to forecast directional movements in market prices.

Zheng and his co-authors (2012) reported interesting empirical results on the relationship between the bid/ask liquidity balance and the trade sign. They showed that the liquidity balance between the best bid and the best ask prices could be a very informative feature to be used for predicting the direction of future market moves. In addition they defined the price jump concept, as the sell (or buy) market order that could trigger an execution deep into the book at a price which is smaller (or larger) than the best bid (or the best ask) price. Features related to limit order volumes, limit order price gaps, market order information, and limit order event information were built into their model. By using these features a Logistic Regression model was implemented to predict price jumps. Then the authors applied LASSO regularization to select the most informative features for the forecast of price jumps. Their analysis has been performed on the components of the CAC40 French stocks.

Han and his co-authors (2015) developed a multi-class classifier for forecasting price changes using LOB data.

Their predictors were divided into three categories:

- *Basic* set of features – containing 10 levels of bid-ask prices and their corresponding volumes in the limit order book
- *Time-insensitive* set of features – including parameters such as bid-ask spreads, mid-prices, prices differences, mean prices, volumes, and accumulated differences for the 10 levels of the time-sensitive set
- *Time-sensitive* set of features – containing time derivatives for prices and volumes, average intensity of each type of orders (limit, market, and cancellation), relative intensity indicators, and accelerations (market/limit) for the 10 considered price levels

The response variable generated was a label for one of the three possible classes:

- Upward mid-price change (U)
- Downward mid-price change (D)
- Stationary mid-price change (S)

The reported results demonstrated that ML-based techniques could be successfully used to classify mid-price movements using limit order book data as features. The authors proposed and implemented a classifier for predicting mid-price movements in a stationary market microstructure regime. Both Support Vector Machines and Random Forest were used for solving the classification problem, with Random Forest being the most accurate in terms of forecasting mid-price movements. This was largely due to the LOB features being not linearly separable.

Nousi and collaborators demonstrated the use of Machine Learning algorithms for the prediction of future price movements using market microstructure data. The authors employed two different sets of features: one containing handcrafted features based on the raw order book data, and a second one composed of features extracted by ML algorithms, resulting in feature vectors with high dimensionality. Three different classifiers were evaluated using several combinations of these sets of features.

Although a wide variety of ML algorithms have been used to address the price dynamic forecast problem, the most popular ones have revolved around Artificial Neural Networks. The ANN algorithms have the ability to scale up to problems that were previously unsolvable by more classical ML techniques. In recent years a very special type of NN algorithms, Deep Learning (DL), has become increasingly popular. This new family of ANNs has been proved very effective for use in large-scale tasks and for some very specific problem domains, such as voice translation and image processing. The success of DL was mostly due to the advent of modern hardware accelerators such as GPU and FPFA and to the availability of more data for training these ML algorithms. Although there is a lot of hype around the use of DL in Quantitative Finance, there are a lot of questions about its applicability to a problem domain where non-stationarity and noise could be significant challenges to overcome.

Ganesh (2018) published some initial results on the implementation of a DL pipeline which uses information about past trading behavior and current order book microstructure to predict price movement for the very near future.

The training of the deep neural network was divided into:

- An off-line training phase using the data from the previous day, and
- An online training phase done in mini batches, while consuming live data.

Tsantekidis and co-authors (2018) published a report on a new method to construct stationary features that would allow Deep Learning models to be applied more effectively.

Two important classes of DL models were evaluated:

- Recurrent Long Short-Term Memory (LSTM) networks, and
- Convolutional Neural Networks (CNN).

The novelty of their model was reflected in combining the ability of CNNs to extract useful features with the ability of LSTMs to analyze time series. The authors were reporting that the combined LSTM-CNN model was able to outperform the individual LSTM and CNN models in prediction done on short time horizons.

The ability of highly sophisticated ANNs to achieve unprecedented performance across a variety of complex real-world problems was driven by the ability to detect significant patterns autonomously. Research performed by Doering and collaborators (2017) explored a new territory by designing and evaluating a Convolutional Neural Network that could be potentially used for price prediction. Inspired by a visual transformation process, a large set of high-frequency market microstructure data from the London Stock Exchange was mapped into a four-channel market-event based input, which was used to train six deep neural networks. Preliminary results indicated that CNNs behave reasonably well on tackling this task and extracting interesting microstructure patterns, which were in line with previous theoretical findings. This research illustrated a novel approach on using modern Deep-Learning techniques for exploiting and analyzing market microstructure behavior.

In a very recent paper Sirignano and Cont (2018) reported the use of large-scale Deep Learning methods to a HFT database containing billions of electronic market quotes and transactions for US equities. Their goal was to identify a "nonparametric evidence for the existence of a universal and stationary price formation mechanism relating the dynamics of supply and demand for stocks." Their empirical study has necessitated the use of a gigantic High-Performance Compute infrastructure composed of 500 GPU nodes for the training of their DL models on massive amounts of data. The reported results showed that their data-driven approach outperformed linear-model accuracy and it has uncovered a set of universal features that are common across all stocks studied. An even more remarkable result was that the performance of their model in terms of price forecasting accuracy was remarkably stable across time, even a year out of sample. The authors claimed that this empirical result indicates the existence of a stationary relationship between order flow and price changes. This case study will be presented in more detail later in this chapter.

7.2.1 The Contrarians

"We know from physics that rare events might be extremely important for defining the true dynamics of a system."

– Igor Halperin, quant, adj. professor @ NYU

But in all fairness Deep Neural Networks are not popular models across the board in the quantitative financial space. There is a group of academics and practitioners, albeit not very numerous, but quite vocal, that does not fully trust this type of approach. One of the most outspoken contrarians is Igor Halperin, Quant-Researcher and Research Professor of Financial Machine Learning at NYU Tandon School of Engineering. He published a series of papers on the subject of the applicability of DNN in quant finance (Halperin and Feldshteyn 2018). He believes that all of the models currently used by financial practitioners are wrong, and most of them are qualitatively wrong. He explains that by saying that "everyone always complains that financial models fail when you need them the most, namely during periods of market turbulence or crises. I say it's embedded in the way models are constructed, and this applies to both classical financial models and newer machine-learning models, albeit for different reasons."

Halperin describes Paul Samuelson's Geometric Brownian Motion model as an inconsistent model that describes an unstable system characterized by an inverted-parabola potential. According to him, "GBM model cannot be a consistent model of a financial market, nor can it be viewed as a good 'zero-order' approximation to a more general theory with a non-linear potential that would produce stable or metastable dynamics." He adds that "all classical financial models are linear models that are not only not self-consistent because they imply unstable dynamics, but they also miss the whole complexity of financial markets altogether because they correspond to systems without any interactions at all."

But everyone knows that novel ML models can exhibit highly nonlinear behavior and they may have numerous free parameters to fit the market. As an example, Deep Learning could produce highly nonlinear functions with millions, or even billions, of free parameters. And according to Halperin, relying on DL for knowledge extraction from financial data could be even a more ill-conceived idea than relying on linear models in classical finance. Regime changes are fundamentally variations in the underlying type of nonlinearity of the system. Since DNNs are black-box algorithms where one does not have explicit control over the form of the nonlinearity, their use could be very dangerous, according to Halperin. Because financial data could be extremely noisy and nonstationary, it is of a very different nature compared with the data generated from images or speech. By completely ignoring regime changes in the processes that generate financial data, DL could produce highly questionable results. If the underlying nonlinearity driver in the data changes as a result of a regime shift, a model user may not notice that in a timely matter – and this is precisely because Neural Networks in general and DNNs in particular do not explicitly allow the control nonlinearities.

Halperin is advocating for a new type of approach in financial modeling that is to build models with an *explicit control over nonlinearities*. One promising way to do it is to combine ideas from Reinforcement Learning and Physics. One other interesting approach is provided by *Inverse Reinforcement Learning* (IRL) that aims to infer the Reward function from the observed behavior of agents. While IRL is widely used in robotics, Halperin's work (2018) provides a first application of this approach to modeling of financial markets. Instead of using IRL to reverse engineer and learn reward functions of individual traders, Halperin applied IRL to a financial market as a whole, by viewing market dynamics as resulting from actions of an invisible hand. Halperin's idea was that modern methods of IRL can be used to learn the reward function of the invisible hand from observed market prices. This new approach has produced a novel market model with a nonlinear drift given by a quadratic polynomial in price. This is a notable departure from conventional linear models such as the GBM model of Samuelson that behaves well in stable market regimes but is becoming subject to a set of instabilities during market regime changes.

I will conclude this brief literature review by saying that the use of modern ML techniques should be carried out in a way that is fully consistent with the reality of non-stationarity and noisiness in the underlying processes responsible for generating the market microstructure data. One also has to be fully aware of the possibility of rare events and their importance in defining the true dynamics of the system.

The next sections of this chapter will introduce some of the most commonly used methodologies to address the problem of forecasting the dynamics of price movements using the information available in the limit order book. Finding a solution to the problem of forecasting the directional movement of prices in the LOB would entail developing learning models that would generate decisions as to when and under what conditions to trade in a given state space and especially how much (size wise) and in which direction (buy or sell) to transact.

The methodology to address this problem could be divided into two components:

- The engineering of features that will enable a reliable prediction of directional price movements from certain states. The denomination reliable implies a degree of accuracy that is high enough to ensure that profitable trades counterbalance the unprofitable ones.
- The development of learning algorithms for executing trades that could capture this predictability (alpha) at trading costs that will make the strategy profitable.

A viable ML-based methodology must devise profitable predictive signals, and then ensure that they are not going to be obliterated by trading costs. If the former objective is relatively feasible, the latter may be proved to be relatively difficult to achieve. The case studies reviewed in Chapter 6 on Optimized Execution did not consider features that directly captured directional movements in the execution prices. There was no need for forecasting the dynamic of prices since the problem had already specified the direction and the volume to be traded, so predictive signals were less important than those capturing potential trading costs. But for the problem of alpha generation the forecast of directional movement is centrally important.

7.3 USING SUPPORT VECTOR MACHINES AND RANDOM FOREST CLASSIFIERS FOR DIRECTIONAL PRICE FORECAST

Before Deep Neural Networks and Reinforcement Learning techniques were coming of age and started being adopted by the quantitative finance community, more traditional ML methods have been used for directional market price forecast.

Han and collaborators (2015) developed a multiclass classifier for forecasting price changes using market microstructure data. The authors used Support Vector Machine and Random Forest to classify the possible future behavior of the microstructure data into three categories: upward, downward, or stationary mid-price change. SPY index microstructure-level tick data was used for this study. The problem of forecasting the directional move of the price was turned into a classification problem where the mid-price movement has been allocated to one of the three class labels: upward, downward, or stationary.

The authors divided their features into three categories: a basic set, a time-insensitive set, and the time-sensitive set. The selected feature space was represented by a complex feature vector as follows:

Basic *Set*

$v_1 = [0, 39]$ Price and Volume for 10 levels on Bid/Ask

Time-Insensitive *Set*

$v_2 = [40, 59]$ Bid-Ask spreads (10) and Mid-prices (10)
$v_3 = [60, 95]$ Price differences (2 x 18)
$v_4 = [96, 99]$ Mean prices and mean volumes
$v_5 = [100, 101]$ Accumulated differences

Time-Sensitive *Set*

$v_6 = [102, 141]$ Price and Volume derivatives (2 x 2 x 10)
$v_7 = [142, 147]$ Average intensity for limit, market, and cancels @ Bid/Ask
$v_8 = [148, 151]$ Accelerations (limit and market @ Bid/Ask)

Each row in the limit order book data represents a snapshot of the book at a specific time and it records all order events, such as:

- A (Add Order) represents arrivals of limit bid/ask orders.
- D (Order Delete) represents order cancellations.
- CA (Order Execution) can be viewed as arrivals of market orders.

The authors used a 10-fold cross-validation to evaluate the performance of the two classifiers. The training data set was split into 10 buckets, one bucket being the test bucket, and the other 9 being used to train the classifier. This result was repeated 10 times until each bucket had been chosen as the test bucket.

To validate the classification model, performance was measured using three common accuracy measures (averaged for the 10 buckets): Precision, Recall, and F1-Measure:

$$Precision:\ P = \frac{number\ of\ correctly\ predicted\ outcomes\ y}{number\ of\ outcomes\ y\ in\ the\ predictions}$$

$$Recall:\ R = \frac{number\ of\ correctly\ predicted\ outcomes\ y}{number\ of\ outcomes\ y\ in\ the\ sample}$$

$$F_1 - measure:\ F_1 = \frac{2PR}{P + R}$$

7.3.1   Empirical Results

The empirical research study done by Han and co-authors (2015) explored the applicability of ML classification algorithms such as Support Vector Machine (with Linear and Gaussian kernels) and Random Forest to the problem of predicting the directional move for the SPY price. The principal result of this study was that the Random Forest ensemble model performed relatively well in terms of the accuracy of the out-of-sample prediction for the mid-price directional movements in the SPY index while the SVM model was deemed to be inadequate for this task. However the data sample considered for training and testing was small in size and that may impact the generality of the conclusions drawn by the study. The use of linear SVM has exhibited poor results and that fact could be attributed to the linear inseparability of data. By using RBF kernels the performance of classifier has slightly improved, but while Upward and Downward Precision accuracy measure was deemed acceptable, the Recall accuracy measure did not pass the acceptability mark.

The performance of the Random Forest ensemble model was notably superior as compared to the SVM models by producing good accuracy measures. High values for both the Precision and Recall metrics validated the assumption that the three classes were indeed separable. A possible explanation as to why the Random Forest ensemble model has performed better than the SVM counterpart might be due to the nonlinearity of the LOB features. While Support Vector Machines work relatively well for classification problems that could be separated into linear or polynomial kernels, Random Forest ensemble models are a much better choice for problems that exhibit nonlinearity; and from this perspective the LOB feature space is a good testing ground for this type of tool.

For a quantitative trader time is of the essence, and as such the size of the feature space has to be manageable for the sake of faster calculations. For this study the authors selected the 10 most informative features out of the total of 151 features:

1. Volume of the 1st level of bid
2. Volume of the 1st level of ask
3. Mean volume of the first 10 levels of bid
4. Derivative of the 10th level of ask price
5. Accumulated difference of volumes
6. Derivative of the 10th level of bid price
7. Volume of the 3rd level of ask
8. Mean volume of the first ten levels of ask
9. Volume of the 2nd level of ask
10. Volume of the 4th level of ask

The performance of the classifier using just the first 10 most informative features was very similar to the performance of a classifier using all 151 features. The general performance of the classifier for the 10 most informative features has exhibited Precision and Recall values in the interval 0f 80%–90%, which is truly remarkable for a trading problem.

As future developments, the authors of the study have suggested extending the 3-class classifier to a 5-class classifier, together with the use of a more extensive microstructure data set that should cover a larger variety of market regimes.

7.4   STUDYING THE DYNAMICS OF THE LOB WITH REINFORCEMENT LEARNING

Reinforcement Learning has become one of the most utilized ML techniques by quantitative finance professionals. RL methods are applicable to problems that could be framed as "agents acting in environments of quantifiable states that act according to goal-driven reward function."

In one of the most cited research papers on the topic of using Reinforcement Learning methods for directional price movement forecast, Kearns and Nevmyvaka (2013) reported interesting results on a series of empirical studies done on market microstructure data.

The authors used a set of features composed of:

- *Price* – for measuring the recent directional movement of execution price.
- *Bid-Ask Spread* – the price difference between the best offer and the best bid.
- *Smart Price* – a variant of mid-price where the average of the bid and ask prices is weighted according to their inverse volume.
- *Trade Sign* – a feature measuring whether buyers or sellers crossed the spread more frequently in recent N executions.
- *Bid-Ask Volume Imbalance* – a signed quantity indicating the volume of orders placed at the bid minus the volume of orders placed at the ask for the first 10 levels of the order book.
- *Signed Transaction Volume* – a signed quantity indicating the total volume bought in the last 15 seconds minus the total volume sold in the last 15 seconds.

The authors reported the use of these features after normalization and time-averaging over a recent interval. In order to ensure the finiteness of the state space, features were discretized into bins in multiples of standard deviation units. The goal of the study was to examine the feasibility of a directional movement prediction using RL techniques, and not necessarily the development of a practical algorithm that could capture such movements in a cost-efficient way. As such the authors made a set of optimistic execution assumptions by considering just two idealized classes of possible actions for the learning algorithm:

- Buying shares at the bid-ask midpoint, and
- Holding the position for t seconds, after which the position is sold at the midpoint. And conversely, after selling at the midpoint one buys back t seconds later.

The methodology used by Kearns and Nevmyvaka could be summarized as:

- 19 different equity names were in used in the study: AAPL, ADBE, AMGN, AMZN, BIIB, CELG, COST, CSCO, DELL, EBAY, ESRX, GILD, GOOG, INTC, MSFT, ORCL, QCOM, SCHW, and YHOO.

- For each of the 19 names used, several different LOB reconstructions were performed using historical tick data.
- For each trading opportunity a state was computed based on the values of the six microstructure features described above.
- The profit or loss for both actions (buy-sell or sell-buy) was computed via LOB simulation (in order to get the midpoint movement).
- For each state in the state space, the cumulative payoff for both actions was computed across all visits for any given state in the state space for any given training period.
- The Learning process has generated a policy π that was mapping states to action, where (x) was defined to be the action that yielded the greatest training set profitability in the state x.
- Training was performed using a full year (2008) of historical tick data while testing of the learned policy for each name was performed using all 2009 data.

By applying the methodology outlined above, the authors reported that the RL policies that were generated were consistently profitable on the test set and across all the 19 stocks studied.

7.4.1 Empirical Results

The two most important findings reported by Kearns and Nevmyvaka are that:

- Reinforcement Learning has consistently generated profitable policies on the test set, and
- Generated policies were very similar across all the 19 financial instruments used in the study.

By studying the correlation between feature values and the action learned, the authors showed that for virtually every feature used in the study the sign of the correlation is the same across all policies. By convention a $+1$ value was assigned to this correlation for a buying→selling sequence, and a -1 value was attributed to a selling→buying sequence.

A very notable result is that although the use of Reinforcement Learning generates policies that are qualitatively similar, the learning process may generate significantly different quantitative optimizations for each individual instrument. The policies generated by the RL algorithms used in this study have consistently learned momentum-based strategies. For each of the features that embedded directional information (like Price, Smart Price, Trade Sign, Bid-Ask Volume Imbalance, and Signed Transaction Volume) higher values translated into a greater frequency of buying for the learned policies. The meaning of higher values for a specific feature indicates either rising execution prices, rising midpoints, or buying pressure in the form of spread-crossing.

However it should be noted that a simple mapping of the policies onto single features is not an accurate view of the learning process. A lot of complexity could be encoded in the interactions between features. So instead of conditioning on a single directional feature having a high value, the conditioning was done on several features having high values. As such the correlation of a set of features with buying becomes considerably stronger than for any isolated feature.

The authors also examined which of the features were more or less predictive of profitability. Their findings showed that:

- Profitability is maximized by using all six features rather than any single one.
- Smart Price appeared to be the best single feature, sometimes slightly better than using all features together, which may be a sign of mild overfitting in training.
- The bid-ask spread appeared to be the less informative single feature.

While the results of this study exhibited a consistent momentum-like relationship between features and actions across all 19 names, the conclusion might be different when exploring different holding periods. The study has shown that the learning process may discover different models depending on the holding period considered.

For very short holding periods the authors found a consistent momentum-like behavior. For intermediate times ranging from milliseconds to seconds, the price dynamics tends to continue in a momentum-like fashion. At these time scales, buying is more profitable when the recent price movements are strongly moving upwards, and unprofitable when the price are falling. Generally one concludes that features that capture directional moves are positively correlated with future returns.

For longer holding periods (from tens of seconds to minutes) the pattern of the price dynamics may change. For these time horizons the learner discovers new reversion-like strategies. In this new regime buying is becoming more profitable after recent downward price movements, and selling is recommended after upward price movements. All these observations were consistent across all 19 names and their related features. Both the short-term momentum and longer-term reversion strategies exhibit distinctly classifiable outcomes. And this is a desirable property of the learning process. The relationship between the magnitude of the feature values and the extent of future returns is monotonic in nature. This monotonicity breaks when the holding period is extended beyond 30 minutes to several hours. For these holding periods conditioning on any of the features will no longer separate future positive and negative returns.

The behavior of the price formation mechanism for the three different holding periods studied could be summarized as follows:

- When the time interval considered ranges from milliseconds to seconds, the most likely scenario for the price formation process is momentum-like. In this scenario large marketable orders interact with the order book, creating a definite directional pressure.
- When the time interval increases from tens of seconds to several minutes, the observed scenario is mean-reversion. The demand for liquidity pushes prices too far from their equilibrium state, resulting in a price reversion.

- For time scales beyond 30 minutes, the microstructure-based features become less informative, supposedly losing their explanatory power.

It is important to note that the authors did not conclude that microstructure features are immaterial to the price formation process for longer time horizons. As a reminder to the reader, longer holding periods are of a particular interest to asset managers and other quant trading practitioners for which overcoming trading costs (crossing repeatedly the bid-ask spread) is of the outmost importance.

The results of this study conclude in a quite convincing matter that the direction of price dynamics is much easier to forecast over shorter time intervals. But the practicality of these predictions (the ability to cover trading costs) grows with the magnitude of the time holding period. Trading practitioners are looking for an optimal time horizon that is long enough to allow prices to evolve sufficiently in order to overcome the spread, but sufficiently short such that microstructure features are becoming informative of directional movements. The authors suggested a possible path to reducing the influence of long-term directional price drifts by adjusting the learning algorithm. Instead of evaluating the return from a buy action in a given state, one could monitor the relative profitability of buying in that state versus buying in any other possible state. This new methodology could filter out price trends and facilitate the analysis of the price microstructure, thus allowing the learned policies to perform more robustly out-of-sample.

7.4.2 Conclusions

This research study demonstrated that Reinforcement Learning techniques could be successfully applied to a set of handcrafted LOB features in order to forecast price dynamics. It also highlighted two very important aspects worth considering when applying Machine Learning to High-Frequency data:

- What is the nature of the underlying price formation process?
- What is the role and limitations of the learning algorithm itself?

While this study clearly exhibits patterns in the short-term price formation process, devising a profitable trading strategy from this predictability is far from trivial. Because the average magnitude of predictions was measured in fractions of a penny, the reported results cannot be interpreted as a recipe for profitability, since the magnitude of predictability is not sufficient to cover the transaction costs.

What types of remedies are still available to find a practical solution to this problem? According to Kearns and Nevmyvaka (2013), several scenarios should be considered:

1. Hold positions for longer periods so that price changes are larger than the bid-ask spreads, thus producing higher margins. However, the longer the holding period, the less informative market microstructure features seem to become, thus making prediction more difficult.

2. Trade with limit orders, thus avoiding paying the bid-asking spread. Although very promising this direction must be weighed against adverse selection, i.e. the probability of executing only when predictions turn out to be wrong.

3. Design better features that will induce about greater predictability, sufficient to overcome transaction costs.

This case study introduced both the opportunities and the challenges of applying a Machine Learning approach to HFT and market microstructure. The authors constructed a principled framework for how to devise sources of potential profits by defining state spaces, examining LOB handcrafted features and their interplay and using a training-test set methodology.

The main conclusions of this study are:

- Machine Learning does *NOT* provide a wide avenue to profitability, but it does provide a principled approach for data-driven decision-making and optimization.
- Machine Learning techniques should not be used as a black boxes, nor should its users have any expectations about discovering magic strategies via its application.
- The Learning process will succeed with the assistance of informative features that should be expressed and optimized properly.
- Handcrafting and fine-tuning features are necessary to optimize the results.

The authors are firm believers in the fact that there will always be a "human in the loop" for all Machine Learning applications to HFT. They suggest that all these applications should be designed and built "tastefully and with care," in order to become useful and scalable.

7.5 STUDYING THE DYNAMICS OF THE LOB WITH DEEP NEURAL NETWORKS

Sirignano and Cont (2018) recently published a study about the existence of a "universal and stationary price formation mechanism" relating the dynamics of supply and demand in equities, as revealed by the analysis of LOB microstructure-level data. By using a Deep Learning (DL) methodology applied to a very extensive set of High-Frequency microstructure data containing billions of electronic market quotes and transactions for US equities, the authors claimed to have uncovered "nonparametric evidence for the existence of a universal and stationary price formation mechanism" in equities.

The authors assessed their model by testing its out-of-sample predictions for directional price movement using the history of transaction prices and order flow, across a wide range of names and time periods. They demonstrated the existence of a "universal price formation mechanism" that exhibits a remarkably stable out-of-sample prediction accuracy across time, for a wide range of stocks from different US sectors. Their observations hold remarkably well for equity names which are not part of the training sample, showing that the relations captured by the model are universal and not asset-specific. This universal model was trained on a very large data set of equities and it was shown to outperform in terms of out-of-sample prediction accuracy, other asset-specific linear, and nonlinear models trained on time series of individual names.

The current availability of large volumes of order flow and price dynamics data provided quantitative finance professionals with a detailed view of the high-frequency dynamics of supply, demand, and price in the electronic markets (Cont 2011). This data has been recently used to explore the nature of the price formation mechanism which describes how market prices react to fluctuations in supply and demand.

The price formation mechanism could be viewed as the functional mapping between current market prices and the history of prices, order flow, and other information:

$$Price(t + \Delta t) = F(PriceHistory(0 \cdots t), OrderFlow(0 \cdots t), OtherInfo) = F(X_t, \epsilon_t)$$

This functional mapping depends on a set of state variables X_t (like lagged price values, volatility, and order flow), and on a random noise term that represents the arrival of new information and other effects not captured entirely by the state variables. All the models that attempt to explain both empirically and theoretically the dynamic of the market microstructure, albeit stochastic models or ML price prediction models, can all be viewed as ways of representing this functional mapping F, at different time resolutions. One question that has not received a definite answer yet is the degree to which this functional mapping F is universal, in the sense being independent of the specific asset under consideration. Empirical evidence on the universality of certain stylized facts (Cont 2001) has been previously reported, but the current study brings to life new evidence of this universality by using the immense power of data.

Most of the models used in financial econometrics, trading, and risk management are asset-specific and their parameters are estimated using data from a recent time window. This methodology is reflecting the belief that financial data is non-stationary in nature and that it is prone to regime changes which may render older data less relevant for prediction. As a result of this *modus operandi*, financial data sets are fragmented across assets and time and, even in the high-frequency domain, their size is orders of magnitude smaller than those encountered in other fields where Big Data analytics have been successfully applied. By using a nonparametric approach based on Deep Learning, Sirignano and Cont (2018) claimed that the results of their study provide a conclusive evidence for the existence of a universal and stationary relationship between the flow of orders and the market price fluctuations. This alleged universal nature of the price formation mechanism is explained by the fact that a model trained on data from all names outperforms, in terms of out-of-sample prediction accuracy, all name-specific linear and nonlinear models. Remarkably, the universal model is able to extrapolate, or generalize, to stocks not within the training set. The universal model is able to perform well on completely new stocks whose historical data the model was never trained on.

The use of a data-driven approach such Deep Learning enables the model to capture features of the price formation mechanism which are robust across stocks and sectors. Applications in areas such as image, text, or speech recognition have been made possible by the advent of Deep Learning that is using multilayer neural networks and trains them on large data sets to uncover complex nonlinear relations between high-dimensional inputs (or features) and the outputs. From a mathematical perspective a Deep Neural Network (DNN) is a functional mapping $y = f(x)$ between a high-dimensional input vector x and an output y. The mapping is achieved by performing repeated iterations in layers consisting of weighted sums of the inputs, followed by the application of nonlinear activation functions. These Deep Neural Networks can be used as universal approximators for complex nonlinear relationships, by appropriately choosing the weights in each layer. The network weights are estimated by way of optimizing a regularized cost function, so as to minimize the in-sample discrepancy between the network output and desired (labeled) output. In the case of a DNN the optimization problem may have millions of parameters, and the computational requirements for training are extremely high. The most common optimization algorithm employed is Stochastic Gradient Descent, and its practical implementation requires the use of hardware accelerators such as the GPUs.

The authors used this approach to learn the relationship between supply and demand on an electronic equity market as captured by the history of LOB microstructure-level data. The data set used was an HF record of all orders, transactions, and order cancellations for approximately 1,000 stocks traded on the NASDAQ between Jan 1, 2014, and March 31, 2017. The size of this data set amounted to several terabytes. The *time series* aspect of financial market data imposes some very stringent causality requirements, such that the relation between inputs and outputs needs to reflect time ordering. A specially designed network architecture that reflects this constraint is what one calls a Recurrent Neural Network (RNN). One even more special type of RNN is constructed based on Long Short-Term Memory (LSTM) units (see Figure 7.1).

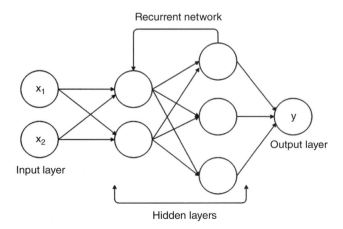

FIGURE 7.1 Typical recurrent neural network architecture.

Each LSTM unit has an internal state which maintains a nonlinear representation of all past data. This internal state is updated as new data arrives. The LSTM units are specially designed to efficiently encode the temporal sequence of data. More details on the functionality of LSTM will follow in the next section. The LSTM network used by Sirignano and Cont involved hundreds of thousands of parameters. The scale of the parameter's space is relatively small compared to the one used in image or speech recognition, but it is enormous compared to the traditional econometric models used in finance. Until very recently the common belief was that financial data is way too noisy to allow for the use of large models while avoiding overfitting. The authors of this study seem to contradict this belief.

Given the extremely large size of the data set and the hyper-dimensionality of the model employed to learn from it, enormous computational resources were required for pre-processing the data as well as for training the network. A very large HPC cluster of about 500 GPU nodes has been employed for this task. The affiliation of one of the authors with the University of Illinois at Urbana-Champaign and the proximity of the National Center for Supercomputing Applications was probably a deciding factor in getting access to these formidable compute resources that are not commonly available to the average quant in trading! Training of DNNs could be highly parallelized on GPUs. Each GPU has thousands of cores, and training is typically 10 to 20 times faster on a GPU than a standard CPU. The authors reported the use of a distributed version of Asynchronous Stochastic Gradient Descent that runs across a mini-cluster of 25 GPU nodes. Batches of data were randomly selected from all equity names and they were sent to the 25 GPU nodes. The gradients were calculated on the GPUs and then the model, which was held on a separate Parameter Server node, was asynchronously updated.

7.5.1 Results

The universe of equities was separated into two groups of about 500 names. The training was done on both transactions and quotes, on two separate groups:

- Name-specific models were trained using data on all transactions and quotes for a specific name, and
- A universal model was trained using data on all transactions and quotes for all the equity names in the training set.

All models were trained to predict the direction of the next price move. The accuracy for the forecast of a given model was measured by the proportion of observations for which it correctly predicts the direction of the next price move:

$$\text{Accuracy}_{\text{model } i} = \frac{\text{\# of price changes } | \text{ correct predictions of direction for i}}{\text{Total number of price changes}} \cdot 100\%$$

A typical out-of-sample data set was composed of transactions and quotes for a three-month time period. A high-frequency data set of such time length is made up of millions of observations and it provides the scope for testing model performance and estimating model accuracy.

The main findings of this very extensive data-driven analysis of the LOB dynamics could be summarized as follows:

- The models trained using Deep Learning substantially outperformed linear models in terms of forecasting accuracy.
- The study uncovered universal features that were common across all equity names considered. The universality held well for names which are not part of the initial training sample.
- The performance of the model in terms of price forecasting accuracy was remarkably stable across time, even a year out of sample. The authors claimed this as an evidence for the existence of a stationary relationship between order flow and price changes which was stable over long periods of time.
- The inclusion of price and order flow historical information into the study was shown to substantially increase the accuracy of the forecast. The authors claimed this as evidence that price dynamics depends not only on the current or recent state of the LOB but on its history, possibly even over long time scales.

These results exhibited evidence for some kind of common structure across different financial instruments. These also illustrated the applicability of deep learning methods for modeling of LOB dynamics by providing some fundamental insights about the nature of price formation in financial markets.

One important question that remains to be answered is the feasibility of such an enterprise outside the realm of a world-renowned Supercomputing center. Can such a complex and resource-intensive process be carried out by any trading firm or investment fund?

7.6 STUDYING THE DYNAMICS OF THE LIMIT ORDER BOOK WITH LONG SHORT-TERM MEMORY NETWORKS

The subsampling of financial time series was until very recently the most common methodology used for the prediction of price dynamics. The best-known example of subsampling is represented by the Open-High-Low-Close (OHLC) candles, which have been used as a technique to reduce the number of features required in the learning phase of the process. Although the use of OHLC candles preserves useful information about market trend and movement ranges within specified time intervals, it discards important microstructure information. Since the arrival of new order events in the LOB happens at random times, the subsampling of features within a predetermined time interval is not possible, and therefore there are no practical ways to preserve all the information it contains.

This problem could be addressed by using more contemporary Machine Learning techniques such as Recurrent Neural Networks (RNN). Novel architectures like

Long Short-Term Memory (LSTM) are capable of natively handling inputs of varying size. This allows one to use the data directly without having to perform any time interval-based subsampling. An example of applying this method was briefly mentioned in the previous case study.

Knowledge and its desired outcome Intelligence, (reflected by thinking and decision-making) have persistence. The thinking process for humans does not start from scratch every time one needs to use it. The usage of a natural language as a communication requires the understanding of each word based on the understanding of previous words. The process of evolution does not discard the acquired information and knowledge in the past and start thinking from scratch again every time. Unfortunately traditional neural networks do not behave this way, and this could be a major shortcoming in learning from time series. Recurrent Neural Networks address this issue by embedding networks with loops in them, and thus allowing information to persist in time (see Figure 7.2).

One of the most appealing characteristics of the Recurrent Neural Networks is the ability to feed the current task with information previously processed and persisted within the network. Long Short-Term Memory networks are a special type of RNNs, capable of learning long-term dependencies. These were introduced by Hochreiter and Schmidhuber (1997), and they find applicability to a variety of problem domains. LSTMs have been explicitly designed to remember information for long periods of time.

Tsantekidis and co-authors (2018) studied the applicability of LSTM in connection with market microstructure data. The market microstructure data used for this study consisted of 10 days' worth of events for five different Finnish company stocks. The data set was composed of consecutive snapshots of the LOB states. The state of the LOB could be altered either by the arrival of a new order, by an execution, or by a cancellation. After an event interacts with the LOB and it changes its state, a new snapshot of the LOB is taken. A total of 4.5 million snapshots were used to train and evaluate the models presented in this work. The goal of this study was to predict price movements based on current and past changes occurring in the LOB.

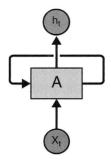

FIGURE 7.2   Diagram of the LSTM concept.

This prediction problem was formally defined as follows:

- Let $x(t) \in \mathcal{R}^q$ denote the feature vector that describes the condition of the LOB at time t for a specific stock, where q is the dimensionality of the corresponding feature vector.
- The direction of the mid-price of that stock was defined as $l_k(t) = \{-1, 0, 1\}$ depending on whether the mid-price increased $(+1)$, remained unchanged (0) or decreased (-1) after k LOB events occurred. The number of events k is also called *prediction horizon*.
- The goal was to learn a model $f_k(x(t))$ where $f_k : \mathcal{R}^n \to \{-1, 0, 1\}$, that could predict the directional move $l_k(t)$ of the mid-price after k orders.

But given the empirical observation that the price of a financial asset could change in a manner that renders its distribution nonstationary, the authors proposed a new method to transform the LOB data into a stationary form. Instead of normalizing the raw values of the LOB depth, suggested to modify the price values to be their percentage difference to the current mid-price of the order book.

The suggested stationary features could be summarized as follows:

Feature	Description
Price level difference	The difference of each price level to the current mid-price: $$p'(i)(t) = \frac{p^{(i)}(t)}{p_m(t)} - 1$$
Mid-price change	The change of the current mid-price compared to the mid-price of the previous time step: $$p'_m(t) = \frac{p_m(t)}{p_m(t-1)} - 1$$
Depth volume cumsum	Total depth volume at each price level: $$v'(k)(t) = \sum_{i=1}^{k} v^i(t)$$

This transformation will remove the non-stationarity from the price time series, and it will make the feature extraction process much easier. The use of these derived features was reported to significantly improve the performance of the models used for the learning phase. The novelty of this study was the introduction of a set of stationary features that could readily be extracted from the limit order book. The feature set described above was used to predict future mid-price movements from large-scale high-frequency limit order data using two different flavors of Deep Learning models:

- Convolutional Neural Networks (CNNs) for feature extraction
- Long Short-Term Memory (LSTM) for the time series analysis

After constructing the three types of stationary features, each of these were separately normalized using a standard z-score concatenated into a single feature vector x_t, where t denotes the time step. Three learning models (CNN, LSTM and CNN-LSTM) were fed with a sequence of vectors $X = \{x_0, x_1, \dots x_w\}$ where w is the total number of events each one represented by a different time step input. These learning models aimed at predicting the future movements of the mid-price. Although mid-price does not represent a tradable price level, the ability to predict mid-price's upwards or downwards movement provides a good estimate for the directional move of the order book in the very near future.

The CNN model had a total of 42 features that were recorded over 300 time steps. This data input matrix was fed into a CNN algorithm that used 16 to 32 convolutional filters of variable sizes. The activation function used for all the convolutional and fully connected layers of the CNN was a Parametric Rectifying Linear Unit. The last layer used a softmax function for the prediction of the probability distribution between the different classes. All the convolutional layers had a Batch Normalization (BN) layer applied right after.

The LSTM network used 32 hidden neurons followed by a feedforward layer with 64 neurons using Dropout and PRELU as activation function. The authors found empirically that the hidden layer of the LSTM should contain 64 or less hidden neurons in order to avoid over-fitting. For a much larger dataset experimenting with a higher number of hidden neurons would be advisable.

Finally the CNN-LSTM model applied the convolutional feature extraction layers on the input and then fed them into the correct temporal order to an LSTM model. The CNN component was composed of the following layers

- 1D Convolution with 16 filters of size (5, 42)
- 1D Convolution with 16 filters of size (5,)
- 1D Convolution with 32 filters of size (5,)
- 1D Convolution with 32 filters of size (5,)

7.6.1 Empirical Results

The study done by Tsantekidis and co-authors (2018) explored the practical applicability of training CNN and LSTM deep learning networks with market microstructure data. The goal of this study was to predict price movements based on current and past changes occurring in the LOB over a number of events k also called the *prediction horizon*.

The LOB microstructure data was split in a 70/30 fashion between the training set and the test set, and all experiments were conducted for four different prediction horizons k. The final results were compared for the models trained on the raw price features with the ones trained using the extracted stationary features. The results confirmed that extracting stationary features from the data significantly will improve the performance of Deep Learning models such as CNNs and LSTMs.

Some of the most interesting results reported by the authors were that the mean values for all the classifier metrics (e.g. Recall, Precision, and the F-1) were noticeably higher for the stationary features as compared to the raw features. (For details see Tsantekidis et al. 2018.)

7.6.2   Conclusions

This research study illustrated a novel method for extracting stationary features from raw LOB data, suitable for use with different DL models. By using CNNs and LSTMs as well as a combination of the two, the authors experimentally demonstrated that the newly suggested features significantly outperform the raw price features.

For the prediction of price time series, a combined CNN-LSTM model was proposed. This novel approach was conducive of a more stable behavior and has led to better results than the individual CNN and LSTM models. As with any Deep Learning applications, using more data would enable the development of bigger networks, but it will not eliminate the risk of overfitting!

As a future direction, the authors suggested the use of a Recurrent Neural Network that could perform an intelligent re-sampling by extracting useful features from a specific and limited time-interval of depth events. This technique would allow for the generation of directional price prediction for a certain time period as opposed to a given number of future events.

Another possible improvement of the model would be the addition of a noise filtering mechanism necessary to improve the quality of the data and allow the deep networks to be trained just on relevant microstructure information.

7.7   STUDYING THE DYNAMICS OF THE LOB
WITH CONVOLUTIONAL NEURAL NETWORKS

Another novel approach to apply CNN learning from market microstructure data was proposed by Doering and collaborators (2017). Their research explored new ways to apply Convolutional Neural Networks in predicting future financial outcomes. The authors suggested a visually inspired transformation process that translates high-frequency market microstructure data into four event-based input channels, which were used to train six different deep networks. The results of this study support the idea that CNN could be successfully applied to extraction of market microstructure patterns. CNN is a special type of Deep Neural Network architecture which has been proven to be especially successful at classifying noisy data sets such as images and speech. CNNs are promoting the use of shared weights within the neural network, which is known to be a contributing factor to improving recognition rates without the downside of overfitting. The principal advantage of using Convolutional Neural Networks is that it automatically identifies basic features that are useful in recognition and that otherwise would have to be hand-crafted. This creates a major advantage when solving problems where meaningful features are hard to extract, as it may be in the case in financial trading. As it is generally the case with any Machine Learning approach, the use of CNN assumes that data encodes some form of repetitive structure that can be eventually transformed into meaningful features. This assumption may very likely be violated when the market undergoes regime shifts.

In this study the authors trained a deep Convolutional Neural Network on a full limit-order book data set obtained from the London Stock Exchange. The data set covered 217 days, with approximately 72,000 events per day in average. The market events from the dataset encoded every bid and ask order, as well as every order deletion and matched trade. Their investigation concentrated on whether deep learning could take advantage of a large amount of available market microstructure data for forecasting purposes. A fair amount of data preparation was necessary to transform the suite of market messages into a format that was acceptable for training the CNN. Snapshots of the limit order book for any point in time were re-created from the list of market messages such that the best bid and ask price were known at any time, together with every trade that ever happened. The resulting time series of limit order book snapshots, events, and prices allowed the authors to calculate training targets and inputs for the CNN.

The targets for the CNN training were the forecasts of market price movement and volatility. The inputs for the CNN were the snapshots of previous order book's state. Because the CNN requires the inputs to be in a matrix form, a mapping was needed to convert the stream of market data into that form. Four different input matrices were generated:

- The LOB's state at time t (A_t)
- The most recent trades (B_t)
- All incoming buy and sell orders (C_t)
- All transmitted order deletions (D_t)

The suggested four-state representation encodes all of the market microstructure information available to all market participants (both humans and algorithms). Each of these matrices has a time axis of recent events and a price information axis. All prices in the LOB were rescaled to the most current mid-price, by including just a limited number of levels β above and below the current price p_t. This formatting transformed the LOB information into a matrix form to be used as an input by the CNN. This way the LOB could be represented as a column vector of volumes corresponding to the total bid and ask size at each price. By concatenating several column vectors of this kind, side-by-side, from a time window of width N, moving forward in chunks of time α, one could build the matrix A_t of dimension 2 β x N/α. The sampling is done from (t–N, t–N+α, ... t).

Similarly any trade matched at time t could be represented as a column vector of zeros everywhere, except at the price level at which the order took place, where the magnitude is set to the log(size) of the trade. As such the matrix B_t is formed by concatenating these order vectors from times t – N to t. Similar procedures were used for the matrices C_t and D_t. Note that α, β, and N are hyper-parameters that have to be chosen in advance. Each of these defines the amount of information that the network is presented with and thus has a significant influence on the outcome. The very important question to be answered is how much information is necessary to build a meaningful and comprehensive representation in order to learn the specific target. Based on their own heuristic approach the authors of the study used some optimized values for the hyper-parameters: N, α, and β.

CNNs are traditionally set up to be able to receive several different input channels. In image analysis, for example, these channels might represent the different red-green-blue content of an image. In the case of microstructure data, the matrices A_t, B_t, C_t, and D_t were each treated as a different input channel. In order to investigate their relative relevance to the forecasting problem, the authors trained three different combinations of these input matrices.

As for the choice of the CNN architecture, the authors chose to adapt the existing CaffeNet (Jia et al. 2014) and GoogleNet (Szegedy et al. 2015) architectures that have been successfully used on very challenging image recognition tasks. The architecture chosen by Doering and collaborators (2017) consisted of:

- 3 convolutional layers (kernel=5 x 5, stride=1)
- 3 ReLU layers
- 2 pooling layers (kernel=2 x 2, stride=2)

The final layers of the network were composed of two fully connected layers and a final softmax-layer for classification. Dropout layers with a ratio of 75% were interconnected to prevent overfitting.

7.7.1 Empirical Results

Three data sets composed of several combinations of the four distinct input matrices A_t, B_t, C_t, and D_t were used:

- Data set I containing just order book inputs.
- Data set II containing order flow inputs $B_t + C_t + D_t$.
- Data set III containing all combined $A_t + B_t + C_t + D_t$.

A Convolutional Neural Network was trained on each of these three data sets, for both the price-trend and the price-volatility prediction tasks. All the six CN networks were implemented and trained using the high-level framework of Caffe (Jia et al. 2014). The choice of the loss function was a cross-entropy function. The network training process was done with optimized base learning rates and RMS decay values. Training took about 200,000 iterations, corresponding to about 100 hours of training time for each network, on a Tesla K80 GPU. The data sets were split into training, validation, and test subsets, in a proportion of 80:15:5. The training process was done in a very homogeneous manner by achieving a gradually decreasing loss for both the training and the validation sets.

The progress achieved in training was validated using the kappa statistic κ which evaluated the prediction accuracy of the class frequency, thus showing the improvement of the current classifier compared to a perfect one. For each of the three data sets, the best performing network snapshot, as measured by its kappa on the validation set, was taken to measure the accuracy on the retained test set.

The results reported in the study showed for both the Accuracy and kappa statistics that all networks started to learn pretty fast with a different degree of success. While some of the networks continued to improve the accuracy of prediction over time, others reached the peak of their performance at the beginning or exhibited rather unstable behavior.

The main results reported in this study indicate that:

- CNNs are capable of dealing reasonably well ($\kappa > 0$) with forecasting price trends and volatility by extracting meaningful features from the microstructure data.
- Predicting the volatility of prices exhibited a better performance than forecasting the direction of the price trend.

Although the prediction time window is short and the accuracy is just slightly higher than random labeling, these results are very relevant to the HFT domain. The highest achieved kappa statistic ($\kappa = 0.223$) for price prediction on combined information source shows that the CN networks are capable of making correct decisions far above random guessing.

The reported results indicate also that the event-flow and the order-book snapshots may encode different exploitable types of information. While the CNNs trained on order flow data for price-move prediction showed a reasonable distinction between class-Up and class-Down, the CNNs trained on order-book data could only learn how to detect if the price will stay in a specific range. Combining patterns from both event-flow and order-book data snapshots had the net result of achieving much higher prediction accuracy than using these individually.

The authors also suggested the use of dropout as a regularization method to reduce overfitting, although overfitting still remains a major obstacle to overcome for most deep networks and great challenge for any financial-data forecasting problem.

7.7.2   Conclusions

This study showed how a set of CNNs could be trained on market microstructure data for financial forecasting purposes. The results indicate that including both limit order book and order-flow information leads to a sufficient prediction accuracy. And these results were achieved without handcrafting any of the input features in advance.

Although extracting actionable knowledge from microstructure data is difficult, this study provided a solid proof of concept for the use of Deep Learning to problems related to market microstructure data. Although good results were reported for short forecasting time frames, future work needs to validate the methodology for longer forecasting time periods.

Future research should concentrate on more experimental setups and different network architectures. The goal will be to achieve a feature extraction ability that is more generalizable to different sets of input data and to gain more actionable insights about market microstructure patterns around specific market events. Given its high computational cost, it will be very useful to compare the accuracy of CNN methods with other Machine Learning techniques.

REFERENCES

Cont (2001). Empirical properties of asset returns: stylized facts and statistical issues. *Quantitative Finance* 1 (2): 223–236.

Cont (2011). Statistical modeling of high frequency financial data: facts, models and challenges. *IEEE Signal Processing* 28 (5): 16–25.

Cont and de Larrard (2013). Price dynamics in a Markovian limit order market. *SIAM Journal of Financial Mathematics* 4 (1): 1–25.

Doering, Fairbank, and Markose (2017). Convolutional neural networks applied to high-frequency market microstructure forecasting. Ninth Computer Science and Electronic Engineering Conference. https://core.ac.uk/download/pdf/146502703.pdf .

Ganesh and Rakheja (2018). Deep neural networks in high frequency trading. https://arxiv.org/abs/1809.01506 .

Guida (2018). Entering the age of prediction in quantitative investment management. https://machinebyte.com/commentary-and-news/entering-the-age-of-prediction-in-quantitative-investment-management, 2018 .

Halperin and Feldshteyn (2018). Market self-learning of signals, impact and optimal trading: invisible hand inference with free energy. https://arxiv.org/abs/1805.06126 .

Han, Hong, Sutardja et al. (2015). Machine learning techniques for price change forecast using the limit order book data. Working paper. http://jcyhong.github.io/assets/machine-learning-price-movements.pdf .

Hasbrouck (2007). *Empirical Market Microstructure: The Institutions, Economics, and Econometrics of Securities Trading*. Oxford University Press, 78–93.

Hochreiter and Schmidhuber (1997). Long short-term memory. *Neural Computation* 9 (8): 1735–1780.

Jia, Shelhamer, Donahue et al. (2014). Caffe: convolutional architecture for fast feature embedding. https://arxiv.org/abs/1408.5093 .

Kearns and Nevmyvaka (2013). Machine learning for market microstructure and high frequency trading. In *High Frequency Trading: New Realities for Traders, Markets and Regulators* (ed. Easley, de Prado, and O'Hara). Risk Books. https://www.cis.upenn.edu/~mkearns/papers/KearnsNevmyvakaHFTRiskBooks.pdf .

Lehalle and Laruelle (2013). *Market Microstructure in Practice*. Hackensack, NJ: World Scientific, chap. 3.

Nousi, Tsantekidis, Passalis et al. (2018). Machine learning for forecasting mid price movement using limit order book data. https://128.84.21.199/abs/1809.07861v1 .

O'Hara (1997). *Market Microstructure Theory*. Blackwell, 13–88.

Sirignano and Cont (2018). Universal features of price formation in financial markets: perspectives from deep learning. https://arxiv.org/pdf/1803.06917.pdf .

Szegedy, Sermanet, Reed et al. (2015). Going deeper with convolutions. IEEE Conference on Computer Vision and Pattern Recognition. https://arxiv.org/abs/1409.4842 .

Tsantekidis, Passalis, Tefas et al. (2018). Using deep learning for price prediction by exploiting stationary limit order book features. https://arxiv.org/abs/1810.09965 .

Zheng, Moulines, and Abergel (2012). Price jump prediction in limit order book. https://arxiv.org/abs/1204.1381 .

CHAPTER 8

Case Study 3: Applying Machine Learning to Portfolio Management

"Science is what we understand well enough to explain to a computer.

Art is everything else."

– Donald Knuth, Turing Award recipient

8.1 INTRODUCTION TO THE PROBLEM

Modern financial markets have evolved into extremely complex systems that are working very efficiently and therefore offering less and less opportunities to the unsophisticated investor. This phenomenon was facilitated by a democratized access to trading tools and information, as well as to an increased technological sophistication of market participants. The use of conventional tools such as basic economic theory or classical market data has become insufficient. Investment professionals are using a wealth of additional data types and they are feeding them into sophisticated quantitative algorithms such as Machine Learning.

In today's financial industry landscape there is a growing appetite for transformation and value creation. There are three main pillars that support the transformation efforts:

- *Alpha generation* – by seeking organic growth in performance through data-driven and ML approaches
- *Boosting operation efficiency* – via cutting-edge automation
- *Managing risk* – through automation of pattern discovery and filtering out of false positives

The financial industry is quickly adapting to a global trend that is fueled by an exponential rise in data generation and storage. IBM estimates that about 90% of the world's data was created just in the past two years. This data deluge is generated primarily by individuals, companies, and sensors. Billions of individuals are producing massive amounts of data via social media, online transactions, and the use of sharing economy outlets like Uber. Companies are generating more transactions than ever before and sensors are becoming ubiquitous, from washing machines to wind turbines.

As a consequence the amount of data generated globally in 2017 was estimated to be around 21 zettabytes (ZB) and is expected to rise to more than 160 ZB by 2025. The *big data* revolution is driven by advancements in computing and storage technology and by a dramatic decline in information technology and communications (IT&C) infrastructure costs. Many industries are now using Data Science paradigms to advance their businesses and the financial industry makes no exception to this trend (see Figure 8.1).

Many have argued for some time that Moore's scaling law should be running up against the limits of physics and as such it will slow down in the near future. Sure enough the clock speed for standard microprocessors has leveled off. But it turns out that the advent of new hardware accelerators such as GPUs and FPGAs has stimulated the latest developments in Machine Learning. Speedups of 20 to 50 times are very common when neural nets are moved from traditional CPUs to GPUs.

8.1.1   The Problem of Portfolio Diversification

Today's financial world is flooded by data: financial data, economic data, alternative data, and news are just the most glaring examples of practically limitless data supplies. Today's successful investors are expecting an almost instantaneous access to these data and the availability of performant Machine Learning algorithms that could help their investment strategies by enhancing returns. There is a widespread optimism

FIGURE 8.1   Data science applicability.

across the financial industry about the use of Machine Learning in the investment process. This is an especially legitimate goal when it comes to the automation of certain tasks that could alleviate the effects of asset mispricing due to behavioral human errors. Combining traditional portfolio management with Machine Learning techniques could generate a substantial financial edge. Building a portfolio management strategy is an essential component of the investment process which includes the selection of important parameters such as:

- Asset and strategies types
- Net worth allocations
- The frequency of rebalancing

The process usually starts by selecting a risk-return profile, as well as the assets and the strategies to be utilized. Active portfolio management involves a consistent and quasi-continuous analysis of market trends with the goal of generating alpha by frequently adjusting the positions and the risk exposure. This is what one calls the beat the market approach. Passive portfolio management, or the buy and hold approach, is associated with making bets on particular markets or financial assets over the long run without constant supervision.

The principal factors that have to be considered when building a portfolio management strategy are:

- *Diversification* – selecting the assets that range in variety across different products with the goal of minimizing the downside risk (Kirchner and Zunckel 2011). Other types of diversification refer to different geographies, economic sectors, or types of assets.
- *Capital allocation* – finding the right balance between the quality and the quantity of assets (Davidow and Peterson 2014).
- *Rebalancing* – as the markets move and assets are repriced, the portfolio needs to be re-optimized. Rebalancing (Jaconetti, Kinniry Jr., and Zilbering 2010) will readjust the weights of the portfolio, and sometimes this may need to go beyond specific asset allocation targets. Strategies may also need to shift, since their profitability can change over time.
- *Marketability* – the availability and liquidity of a certain component (asset) of the portfolio. Assets that have low liquidity will be harder to transact at the desired volume or price.

8.2 CURRENT STATE-OF-THE-ART IN PORTFOLIO MODELING

8.2.1 The Classic Approach

One of the most computationally intensive problems in financial asset management is the topic of portfolio diversification. The problem of portfolio diversification is well known and it was solved mathematically by Markowitz (1952) in his paper, Portfolio Selection. Even though Markowitz's work on Mean-Variance optimization won him a Nobel Prize, the logic of this modern portfolio theory is very intuitive and mathematically tractable. In Markowitz's world, investors are concerned about how to maximize the return while minimizing the risk. Every asset has a unique set of expected returns and standard deviations, and it is defined in respect to all other assets by the covariance matrix. Given these three parameters (i.e. expected return, variance, and covariance matrix), the optimization process revolves around finding the asset weights that will generate the portfolio with the highest risk-adjusted return (the highest Sharpe ratio). This problem is solved in practice by trial and error. An algorithm is testing every possible combination of weights and the associated Sharpe ratios, and it keeps looping until it finds the portfolio with the highest risk-adjusted return.

The computational complexity grows exponentially with the number of assets in the portfolio. A 10-asset portfolio generates a 100-cell covariance matrix while a 10-times-larger portfolio with 100 assets will generate a 10,000-cell covariance matrix, which is 100 times larger. The *Efficient Frontier* optimization is a top-down approach meant to achieve an optimal portfolio. Traditionally, the portfolio optimization problem has been focused on finding the proper balance for allocations to different asset classes based on the mean-variance tradeoff.

8.2.2   The ML Approach

The general problem of Mean-Variance optimization represents an excellent testing ground for the applicability of Machine Learning techniques to portfolio modeling which has such a well-established solution. Among the ML techniques, Deep Learning has been the most popular method used for a variety of financial-related problems. The use of Deep Learning techniques has been reported (Deluard 2018; Heaton, Polson, and Witte 2017) in the training on data sets where the input data was represented by the total returns of an equity portfolio and the output by the optimal weights of the efficient frontier portfolio. Then, an out-of-sample data set was used to test whether the model was able to replicate the optimization process on its own. Interesting findings related to the fact that the vast majority of "the out-of-sample results were generally close to the correct mathematical solution" (Deluard 2018).

Several studies have concluded that Deep Neural Networks are able to quickly learn how to solve this complex optimization problem, and they are doing it without any prior knowledge of the problem and with a relatively small data set (just thousands of data points). One needs to reemphasize that Machine Learning technique in general, and Deep Learning in particular, could be applied just to scenarios where the stationarity of process that generates the data is guaranteed. In other words, the applicability of ML to the Portfolio Diversification problem should be attempted just for situations where "the future resembles the past." As Nassim Taleb said, "a neural network that has only seen white swans will never be able to fathom the existence of a black swan" (Deluard 2018).

The paradigm of scientific discovery is based on the development of new theories and the use of experiments to prove or disprove them. Theories that cannot be disproved are held to be true. *On the contrary, Neural Networks do not rely on theories. They make no assumptions regarding the nature of the relations between variables or the causality between them. They endeavor to infer the relationships between inputs and outputs and learn from repeating this process over more data.*

Neural networks work very much like the biological brain – by example and by experimentation. A toddler has no concept of the laws of gravity and does not understand how the muscular system works. Yet the toddler could learn how to walk after having accumulated enough experience in falling such that she could start using her muscles in a way that will avoid new falls. In a very similar way, in a Deep Neural Network every neuron is trained to look for a specific attribute, and then it synthesizes this raw information into a more complex object.

A similar process could be followed in the case of a portfolio optimization problem. Adding the Deep Learning capabilities to more computing power and data availability could offer significant benefits to risk managers because the more the machines learn from the data sets over time, the better they get at pattern recognition (Heaton, Polson, and Witte 2017; Freitas, De Souza, and De Almeida 2009; Niaki and Hoseinzade 2013; Liang et al. 2018; Fu et al. 2018).

8.3 A DEEP PORTFOLIO APPROACH TO PORTFOLIO OPTIMIZATION

Applying the Machine Learning methodology to portfolio construction problems could produce more effective results than the standard quantitative methods used in finance. In particular, the use of Deep Learning could make possible the detection and the understanding of interactions within the data that are inconspicuous to the current financial economic theory.

In a recent paper, Heaton and collaborators (2017) explored the use of Deep Learning models and introduced the concept of *Deep Portfolios*. These portfolios are constructed based on what the authors defined as *deep features*, which are in effect abstractions of hidden layers that through the process of training could be associated to independent variables. These deep feature abstractions, which are implicit to any Deep Learning algorithm, are becoming the building block of investible *Deep Portfolios*. The goal of this study was to determine how to use available portfolio-data to construct this special type of portfolios. As Deep Neural Networks have the theoretical flexibility to approximate virtually any nonlinear payout function, the consideration of regularization in the process of training and validation was placed at the center of Deep Portfolio theory.

As mentioned in Chapter 7, Deep Learning is a family of Machine Learning algorithms that uses data to train a model with the goal of making predictions on unseen data sets. The use of Deep Learning has dramatically enhanced the ability of computers to classify and label images, translate speech in real-time, or play complex board games at a higher level of performance than humans.

Problems that are specific to the financial markets may sometimes be atypical when compared to more common Deep-Learning applications, like computer imaging. By contrast to image recognition or appropriately answering verbal queries, humans have no inborn ability to select for example a particular financial instrument that is likely to perform well in the future. Yet Deep Learning algorithms may be useful in the portfolio selection process. The reason for having such high expectations is that a deep learner is the best available technique to estimate any functional mapping between data inputs and outputs, or what one calls universal function approximators. A deep learner is expected to find the functional dependency of a return, no matter how complex and nonlinear the features may be. This novel approach is drastically different when compared to more simplistic linear factor models or with very specific quantitative methods like statistical arbitrage techniques.

Because Heaton and collaborators (2017) chose to apply Deep Learning to the problem of portfolio selection by selecting an *autoencoder* implementation, let's introduce the Autoencoder concept.

8.3.1   Autoencoders

An autoencoder is a Deep Learning algorithm that trains a given network architecture to replicate the input itself via a so-called *bottleneck* structure. A key element of an autoencoder is the *information bottleneck*. This bottleneck forces a representation at the intermediate hidden layer that has a smaller number of variables than the input. This representation will require in turn that the autoencoder would keep only the components that are useful for reconstructing the common features of the inputs, and to reject the uncommon ones. As a result, an autoencoder will learn a representation of the hidden layer that rejects most of the noise from the input.

Generally an autoencoder is composed of two symmetrical Deep Belief Networks that could have three to five shallow layers representing the encoding half of the net and a second set of three to five layers that make up the decoding half (see Figure 8.2).

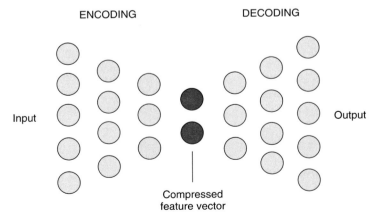

FIGURE 8.2   The autoencoder concept.

Autoencoders are essentially deep neural networks that aim to transform inputs into outputs with the minimum possible error. An autoencoder has three main layers:

- *Encoder* – encodes the input data in a compressed representation of a reduced dimension, also called a *latent space representation.*
- *Code* – represents the compressed input and feeds it to the decoder.
- *Decoder* – decodes the encoded data back to its original dimension. The decoded data is a *lossy reconstruction* of the original data by reconstructing the input from a latent space representation.

Autoencoders are unsupervised ML algorithms (see Figure 8.3) that are used for feature extraction in a manner analogous to nonlinear principal component analysis (PCA). Because an autoencoder could have a high degree of freedom it could become predisposed to overfitting given that it has just too many ways to represent the data. This limitation could be avoided by using the so-called *sparse* autoencoders where a non-sparsity penalty is added to the cost function.

The choice of using an autoencoder algorithm for the problem of deep portfolios relates to the fact that autoencoders eliminate the need to model the variance–covariance matrix explicitly. Heaton and collaborators (2017) pointed out that given an estimated nonlinear combination of deep learners, a variance–covariance matrix is represented implicitly in the network architecture.

The research study published by the authors described a four-step algorithm for building Deep Portfolios. Then they applied this algorithm to showcase a smart indexing example by autoencoding the IBB biotechnology index.

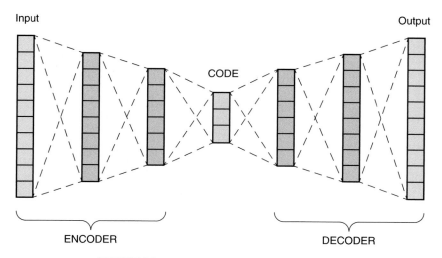

FIGURE 8.3 Another view of the autoencoder concept.

8.3.2   Methodology – The Four-Step Algorithm

Heaton and collaborators (2017) considered in their study the weekly returns for the stock component of the biotechnology IBB index for the period between 2012 and 2016. The goal was to find a selection of investments for which good out-of-sample results could be obtained.

The authors suggested a novel data-driven and model-independent approach in which the Deep Learning algorithm consists of four steps:

- *Auto-encoding* – a pre-processing phase in which an appropriately chosen market-map is used to solve the market-regularization problem and to autoencode the inputs X and therefore create a more efficient representation of them.
- *Calibration* – finding the portfolio-map that solves the portfolio-regularization problem and retrieves the desired target Y; this phase creates a nonlinear portfolio from X to the approximation of the objective Y.
- *Validation* – finding the appropriate trade-off between the two regularization problem errors.
- *Verification* – selecting the proper market-map and portfolio-map according to the validation step.

An important observation to be made is that single-variable activation functions could be often interpreted as mixtures of financial put and call options on linear combinations of the input assets. As such, the Deep Portfolio theory introduced by Heaton and co-authors relies on deep features, or hidden layer abstractions, which through the training procedure could be mapped to the independent variables.

The fundamental question was how to use training data to construct Deep Portfolios. The suggested four-step algorithm made the process of portfolio optimization and inefficiency detection become entirely data-driven and model-free, in sharp contrast to the classic portfolio theory. The authors have defined the deep frontier as the goal to be reached as a function of the amount of regularization.

The autoencoding and calibration steps were done on data from January 2012 to December 2013, and validation and verification on data from January 2014 to April 2016. Both the autoencoder and the deep learning algorithm used one hidden layer with five neurons.

The authors defined a metric called the *degree of communal information* as the two-norm difference between every stock and its autoencoded value and rank all stocks using this measure. By using a bottleneck network structure, the autoencoder reduces the information for the whole universe of stocks to an information subset. Therefore, proximity of a stock to its autoencoded version provides a measure for the similarity of a stock with the stock universe.

In order to eliminate information redundancy (i.e. having multiple stocks contributing the same information), the authors used the 10 most communal stocks plus a certain number of most noncommunal stocks. For the calibration step Rectified Linear Units (ReLU) and fourfold cross-validation were used. The *efficient deep frontier* was represented by the plot of the number of stocks used in the deep portfolio versus the validation accuracy achieved. Model selection was conducted through comparison of efficient deep frontiers.

While the efficient deep frontier still requires that a choice has to be made between two parameters, specifically minimizing either the number of stocks in the portfolio or the validation error, these decisions are purely related to the cut-off sample performance, thus making deep portfolio theory a strictly *data-driven approach*.

8.3.3 Results

In the asset management parlance, the 1% problem deals with finding the best strategy to outperform a given benchmark by 1% per year. Translating this problem into the realm of Deep Portfolios means devising a set of deep features that could improve the performance of a portfolio by 1% annually. According to the Kolmogorov–Arnold theorem (Kolmogorov 1957) hierarchical layers of univariate nonlinear payouts can be used to scan for such features.

The authors reported some interesting results for the construction of a Deep Portfolio composed of stocks from the iShares IBB biotechnology index. They amended the target data during the calibration step by replacing all returns smaller than −5% by exactly 5%, with the goal of creating an anticorrelation index tracker for periods of large drawdowns. As a result *learned* deep portfolio outperformed more classical portfolios during periods of drawdowns. This study has demonstrated that Deep Learning could be an extremely useful framework for processing large financial data sets in order to optimize predictive performance.

8.4 A Q-LEARNING APPROACH TO THE PROBLEM OF PORTFOLIO OPTIMIZATION

The previous case study illustrated the application of Deep Learning to the problem of portfolio construction and the reported results have led to some very encouraging conclusions. But once they are built portfolios need to be optimized. Portfolio Optimization is the process of assigning optimal weights to the individual assets in a portfolio and it represents one of the most fundamental problems in Financial Engineering. The problem of portfolio management falls into the broad category of the Multi-armed bandit problem (MaB). This problem was very well studied in the field of probability theory and could be formulated as follows: "Given set of limited resources, allocate them between competing alternatives in a way that maximizes their expected gain" (Wikipedia 2019). The characteristics of each choice are partially known at the time of allocation, but they may become better understood as time elapses. This is a classic Reinforcement Learning formulation that exemplifies the exploration-exploitation tradeoff dilemma that was discussed at the end of Chapter 5. The goal of the MaB problem is to codify an agent that simultaneously attempts to acquire new knowledge by *exploration* and optimize its decisions based on existing knowledge or *exploitation*. The agent attempts to balance these competing tasks in order to maximize their total value over the period of time considered.

There are many practical applications of the MaB model, such as:

- Clinical trials
- Adaptive routing
- Financial portfolio management

In all these practical examples, the MaB problem attempts to find the proper balance between maximizing the reward based on the knowledge already acquired and attempting new actions to further increase the knowledge already captured. From this perspective portfolio management is an MaB problem where an agent makes decisions on reallocating different financial assets in order to maximize their return.

A variety of approaches have been used traditionally for the problem of portfolio management. Passive investors, for example, could choose a liquidity-based or market capitalization-based weighting approach. But the most common solution is represented by the Markowitz Optimal portfolio, where risk-adverse investors are maximizing their return as a function of their acceptable level of risk.

8.4.1   Problem Statement

Formulating this problem in terms of Reinforcement Learning requires the implementation of an agent that could be trained to determine a set of optimal weights by interacting with the market environment through a series of actions. The RL formulation requires the assumption of a negligible market impact, which means that the agent's actions have a minor impact on the market where the assets are traded. Because the asset prices represent the input data into the RL algorithm, these should not be affected by the agent's actions.

One of the most used RL algorithms is Q-learning. As seen in section 5.3.3 the goal of Q-learning is to learn a policy that an agent could use to take a specific action conditional on a given set of circumstances (states). Q-learning does not require a model of the environment, and it could handle scenarios with transitions and rewards that are stochastic in nature. In the particular case of finite Markov Decision process, Q-learning finds the policy that maximizes the expected value of the total reward over any of the successive steps, starting with the current one. The letter Q stands for the quality of the action taken in a given state, action that was generated by the reward function used to provide the reinforcement.

In a research report published by Jin and El-Saawy (2017), the Q-learning methodology was used to train a neural network with the goal of managing a portfolio of stocks. Given the extreme complexity of the stock market, a model-free algorithm like Q-learning is the preferred technique to achieve the balance between *exploration* and *exploitation* in order to determine the optimal outcome. The portfolio under study was composed of a high-volatility stock and a low-volatility stock, but that could be generalized to a more complex scenario. The portfolio was fed into a neural network in order to generate a recommended action for the agent, like either buying more low-volatility stocks while selling more high-volatility stocks, or just the opposite.

8.4.2 Methodology

Jin and El-Saawy trained a neural network using end-of-the-day historical market data prices from Google Finance for 20 different stocks and for a period of time period ranging from July 2001 to July 2016. A Python implementation using the Keras library was used to build and train the NN models. Keras is an easy-to-use interface that is built on top of efficient multidimensional numerical libraries such as Theano or TensorFlow. The goal of the study was to build a Reinforcement Learning (RL) agent that could manage a two-stock portfolio where one of the assets was significantly more volatile than the other. The inputs used by the NN in each of the states were the historical prices for a fixed time window (2, 7, or 30 days), the position in each of the stocks, the total value of the portfolio, and the amount of cash available.

The action space was discretized into seven different regions: $a_t \in$ (−0.25, −0.10, −0.05, 0, 0.05, 0.10, 0.25) where each region represented one of the seven possible compositions of the portfolio. A value of $a_t = 0.25$ signifies for example that the stock A makes up 25% of the portfolio's total value. For each action a_t the portfolio sells a certain amount of the low-volatility stock and buys the corresponding amount of the high-volatility stock (and vice versa for $a_t < 0$). This discrete action space, alongside the simplified state space, helped in making the problem tractable. The NN architecture chosen by the authors was composed of four hidden layers with 100 neurons per layer. The main idea was that the architecture is simple enough to allow for a quick yet robust training to adequately approximate the Q-function.

8.4.3 The Deep Q-Learning Algorithm

Jin and El-Saawy (2017), used an ε-greedy exploration strategy, where the agent chooses a random action with probability $1 - \varepsilon$. Because the dimensionality of the state space was relatively small, being represented by the tuple (8, 18, 64), where (2, 7, 3) were the numbers of days taken into account ($8 = 2 \times 2 + 4$, $18 = 7 \times 2 + 4$, or $64 = 30 \times 2 + 4$), the authors chose to use a fully connected feedforward architecture instead of the more common convolution and pooling layers (which have typically high dimensionality, like in image processing).

The performance of the model was compared against two very simplistic benchmarks:

- *Do-nothing* benchmark – allocated in a 50–50 manner at the beginning and then it does nothing. This benchmark acts as a very crude approximation of the market since it represents the raw performance of the two stocks.
- *Rebalance* benchmark - reevaluated its holdings every 30 days and then it bought or sold stock to ensure the total portfolio value is split 50–50 between the two stocks.

8.4.4   Results

All models were trained using a penalized reward of $\lambda = 0.5$. In terms of returns, the two benchmarks outperformed all but two of the models tested. However, these results came at the cost of a higher volatility in the portfolio's value. But overall, the NN models had a much higher Sharpe ratio and significantly less volatility than the benchmarks. These results were a good illustration of the potential for neural networks to manage financial portfolios using the Q-learning methodology.

It is likely that the choice of very simple network architecture (with just four hidden layers) could have impacted its flexibility and that the convolution layers tasked with looking at the differences between successive stock prices could have performed significantly better. This effect could have been compounded by the sparsity of the action space and the simplicity of the state space. By encoding the states with more meaningful features, the authors could have potentially increased the performance of the outcomes.

8.5   A DEEP REINFORCEMENT LEARNING APPROACH TO PORTFOLIO MANAGEMENT

In a recently published study, Jiang and collaborators (2017) suggested the use of a Deep Reinforcement Learning framework as a solution tool kit for the portfolio management problem.

Their Deep Reinforcement Learning framework consisted of several components:

- Ensemble of Identical Independent Evaluators
- Portfolio-Vector Memory component
- Online Stochastic Batch Learning scheme
- Explicit Reward function

This framework was implemented using three different network architectures:

- Convolutional Neural Network
- Recurrent Neural Network
- Long Short-Term Memory

All these Deep Learning models could be applied to any type of financial assets, but the authors chose to train and test these on cryptocurrency market data.

8.5.1   Methodology

The portfolio consisted of 11 different cryptocurrencies and it was rebalanced every 30 minutes. The Ensemble of Identical Independent Evaluators (EIIE) was the central component of this Deep RL framework. An Identical Independent Evaluator is a

Neural Network tasked to inspect both the price history of a basket of assets and the associated portfolio weights for the previous trading period. Based on this analysis the EIIE is then forecasting the potential growth of the portfolio over the next time period. The evaluation score obtained for each of the assets is then fed into a softmax of the deep neural network layer, whose output will represent the new set of portfolio weights for the next trading period. This set of portfolio weights defined the market actions to be taken by the RL agent. As a result of this evaluation process, the position of an asset that has earned a higher weight within the portfolio will be increased accordingly, and the position of an asset that has acquired a smaller weight within the portfolio will be decreased proportionally.

The portfolio weights for each trading period are recorded in a data structure labeled Portfolio Vector Memory (PVM). The EIIE is trained using the Online Stochastic Batch Learning scheme (OSBL) proposed by the authors, which is compatible with both pre-trade and online training.

8.5.2   Data

The market data used for training and testing of the EIIE was acquired from the cryptocurrency exchange Poloniex, where about 65 cryptocurrencies were traded at the time the analysis was performed. However, the study has used only a subset of the most traded 11 cryptocurrencies plus the Bitcoin Cash.

Historical prices for these 12 cryptocurrencies were fed into the IIEs to generate the output portfolio vector.

The input to the neural network IIE at the end of the time period t is a tensor of rank 3 called $\mathbf{X_t}$. This tensor has three dimensions (see Figure 8.4):

- $m = 11$ – the number of selected non-cash assets,
- $n = 50$ – the number of trading periods before t, and
- $f = 3$ – the number of features.

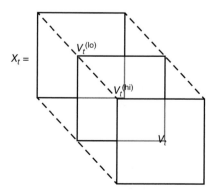

FIGURE 8.4   The market data tensor. **Source:** Adapted from Jiang, Xu, and Liang (2017).

8.5.3   The RL Setting: Agent, Environment, and Policy

In a portfolio management setting, the Reinforcement Learning agent is represented by the portfolio manager. This agent is looking to gain awareness of the state of a very complex environment. The main features that the agent could access are transaction prices and order flow information, specifically the history of all orders placed into the market since the beginning of the time period under consideration. Because a potentially large amount of order flow data could hinder the performance of the RL agent, shorter time periods were taken into consideration (n = 50 periods of 30 minutes, which amounts to 25 hours).

The actions taken by the agent were redefining the composition and the weights of the portfolio at each time step (trading period). The Reward function employed by this Deep RL framework was represented explicitly by the average of the logarithmic returns over the trading periods under consideration. By using an explicit Reward function, during training the EIIE evolves along the gradient ascending direction of the function. The Deep RL method implies that the learned deep network is used as the RL policy. Given the large variety of states for both the assets and the portfolio, the deep network is used to extract features and suggest the necessary actions. The deep neural networks were trained to maximize the reward at each time step.

Three different network architectures were used to implement the IIEs: Convolutional Neural Networks, Recurrent Neural Networks, and Long Short-Term Memory networks. In all cases, the input to the networks is the price tensor X_t and the output is the portfolio vector w_t.

8.5.4   The CNN Implementation

As described in Chapter 7, Convolutional Neural Networks are considered to be a good choice when the dependency on the history of the asset price is short-dated. The inputs that define the states could be shared sequentially. If L is defined as the total number of assets in the portfolio and N as the number of different states, each input is an $N \times L$ log return matrix plus a vector of length L representing the portfolio at the previous time step.

For each asset the CNN will output a prediction score based only on its historical return and its previous portfolio percentage. The individual scores are then combined using a softmax layer to generate an action recommendation for the portfolio. The input to the network is a $3 \times 11 \times 50$ price tensor, composed of the high, low, and closing prices of m non-cash assets over the past n periods. The outputs are the new portfolio weights.

8.5.5   The RNN and LSTM Implementations

By using a recurrent version of the deep network architecture, the authors intended to utilize input sequences of arbitrary length. For a basic RNN architecture, the hidden state h_t of a cell at time t could be expressed by using a nonlinear activation function f that could be either a sigmoid or a tanh function:

$$h_t = f(W_h \cdot h_{t-1} + W_x \cdot x_t)$$

In order to take a specific action based on the states of the N previous time periods, the log return at each time step is fed into the RNN and an action is taken based on the output generated. The prices of individual assets are fed into small recurrent subnets. These subnets are identical for both basic RNNs and LSTMs. The structure of the ensemble network past the recurrent subnets is the same as the second half of the CNN. In order for the neural network to account for transaction costs, the portfolio vector from the last period, w_{t-1}, is inserted just before the softmax voting layer.

8.5.6   Results

Different metrics have been traditionally used to measure the performance of a particular portfolio selection strategy:

- Cumulative Portfolio Value
- Sharpe Ratio – or risk-adjusted mean return, defined as the average of the risk-free return by its deviation
- Maximum Drawdown – the biggest loss from a peak to a trough

The performance of the three different implementations of the EIIE ensemble has been compared with a series of benchmark portfolio selection strategies (Li and Hoi 2014; Li, Sahoo, and Hoi 2016).
The three benchmarks used for comparison were:

- The Best Stock – the asset with the best final cumulative portfolio value
- The Uniform Buy and Hold – an equally weighted portfolio of the preselected assets that were held until the end of the period without rebalancing
- Uniform Constant Rebalanced Portfolios (Cover 1991, 1996).

The authors of this study (Jiang, Xu, and Liang 2017) claimed that their implementation of the Deep RL approach yielded superior results compared to other work (Li and Hoi 2014; Li, Sahoo, and Hoi 2016; Cover 1991, 1996). In terms of Cumulative Portfolio Value and Sharpe Ratio, the best performing algorithm was the CNN EIIE. These results were showing the effectiveness of the RL policy and the potential that useful information could be extracted from historical prices in order predict the future dynamics of the portfolio. Note that at the beginning of the training process, the CNN exhibits a lower performance compared to the baseline, but its performance improves substantially in time due to the online learning when the policy gets better through the process of exploration and exploitation.

Interestingly enough the RNN does not outperform either the CNN or the Uniform Buy and Hold. An explanation could be due to the fact that the RNNs are depending on an infinitely long price history, while CNN only depends on a finite time horizon. Also the lower complexity of the RNN architecture coupled with the poor quality of the market price data (noise) could have negatively impacted the RNN learning process.

We conclude the chapter on the applicability of Machine Learning techniques to the portfolio selection and management problem with this brief introduction of the Deep Reinforcement Learning framework by Jiang and collaborators. Their results exhibited a superior performance when compared to more traditional methods, like Uniform Buy and Hold or Uniform Constant Rebalanced Portfolios (Cover 1991, 1996).

REFERENCES

Cover (1991). Universal portfolios. *Mathematical Finance* 1 (1): 1–29.

Cover (1996). Universal data compression and portfolio selection. *Proceedings of 37th Annual Symposium on Foundations of Computer Science*, 534–538.

Davidow and Peterson (2014). A modern approach to asset allocation and portfolio construction. Schwab Center for Financial Research. https://content.schwab.com/web/retail/public/asset_allocation/assets/MKT81752HL-02.pdf .

Deluard (2018). An artificial intelligence solution to portfolio diversification. *International Banker*. (21 May). https://internationalbanker.com/brokerage/an-artificial-intelligence-solution-to-portfolio-diversification/ .

Freitas, De Souza, and De Almeida (2009). Prediction-based portfolio optimization model using neural networks. *Neurocomputing* 72 (10): 2155–2170.

Fu, Du, Guo et al. (2018). A machine learning framework for stock selection. https://arxiv.org/abs/1806.01743 .

Heaton, Polson, and Witte (2017). Deep learning for finance: deep portfolios. *Applied Stochastic Models in Business and Industry* 33 (1): 3–12.

Jaconetti, Kinniry Jr., and Zilbering (2010). Best practices for portfolio rebalancing. Vanguard Research. https://www.vanguard.com/pdf/ISGPORE.pdf .

Jiang, Xu, and Liang (2017). A deep reinforcement learning framework for the financial portfolio management problem. https://arxiv.org/abs/1706.10059 .

Jin and El-Saawy (2017). Portfolio management using reinforcement learning. Report. Stanford University. http://cs229.stanford.edu/proj2016/report/JinElSaawy-PortfolioManagementusing ReinforcementLearning-report.pdf .

Kirchner and Zunckel (2011). Measuring portfolio diversification. https://arxiv.org/abs/1102.4722 .

Kolmogorov (1957). The representation of continuous functions of many variables by superposition of continuous functions of one variable and addition. *Dokl. Akademia Nauk SSSR* 114: 953–956.

Li and Hoi (2014). Online portfolio selection: a survey. *ACM Computing Surveys* 46 (3): 35. https://ink.library.smu.edu.sg/cgi/viewcontent.cgi?article=3263&context=sis_research .

Li, Sahoo, and Hoi (2016). OLPS: A toolbox for online portfolio selection. *Journal of Machine Learning Research* 17: 1–5. http://www.jmlr.org/papers/volume17/15-317/15-317.pdf.

Liang, Chen, Zhuet et al. Adversarial deep reinforcement learning in portfolio management. https://arxiv.org/abs/1808.09940 .

Markowitz (1952). Portfolio selection. *Journal of Finance* 7 (1): 77–91.

Niaki and Hoseinzade (2013). Forecasting S&P 500 index using artificial neural networks and design of experiments. *Journal of Industrial Engineering International* 9 (1): 1–9.

Wikipedia (2019). Multi-armed bandit. https://en.wikipedia.org/wiki/Multi-armed_bandit.

CHAPTER 9

Case Study 4: Applying Machine Learning to Market Making

"We are drowning in information but are starved for knowledge."

– John Naisbitt, futurist

9.1 INTRODUCTION TO THE PROBLEM

Market Making represents one of the most fundamental aspects of trading. This chapter will address the topic of Market Making, which is the process of providing liquidity by continually posting offers to buy and sell a financial asset. From a practical perspective this problem is very challenging, and its complexity is due to factors like adverse selection and inventory risk, which is the risk of accumulating an unfavorable position and ultimately losing money. A Market Maker (MM) is defined as the agent who facilitates trading in a double-sided auction market by simultaneously quoting bids and offers and thus supplying the necessary liquidity that enables markets to be functional and efficient.

In this framework, *liquidity* is defined as the availability of immediate trading opportunities at prices that reasonably reflect current market conditions. As a result of providing liquidity to market participants, an MM will profit from the spread or the difference between the bids and offers they are executing transactions at. In addition to providing liquidity, Market Making has also a major contribution in stabilizing prices and facilitating an accurate price discovery process (Schwartz and Peng 2013).

Market Making is a straightforward trading strategy:

- Buy at the bid,
- Sell at the offer (ask), and
- Repeat this as frequently as possible in order to make a profit.

In actuality, the execution of this apparently simple strategy is rather complex. The size of the spread (that is the difference between the best offer and the best bid) is the most influential factor in the success of MM – the larger the spread, the greater are the MM's profits. But there are two factors that are adversely impacting the efficiency of MM:

- A possible *accumulated inventory*, as this could limit the MM's ability to maintain two-side quotes, and
- The necessary available *information*, as every market participant is relying on having an informational edge.

Since the amount and the quality of the *information* sought through price discovery is hard to gauge in real-time, a typical MM strategy is to quote a pair of bids and offers that will maximize the profit while minimizing the accumulated inventory. Therefore an optimal market making strategy is the ability to quote a bid-ask spread with the least amount of risk (inventory build-up).

This process requires:

- A comprehensive analysis of the order flow for the financial assets traded via the examination of the limit order book microstructure.
- A near *real-time* resolution of the side on which more trades are happening, which in fact equates to a very short-term forecast of the price movement.
- The ability to accurately model the current volatility of the market and adopt the quoting of the spreads to current market conditions (a proper volatility model of the traded instrument is absolutely crucial to MM problem).
- Hedging in correlated instruments.
- Filtering out noise from the market data feeds.
- Incorporating in the quoting algorithm the feedback from the existing accumulated inventory and the daily risk parameters.

All this information will be factored into a model and then will be fed in *real-time* to the MM algorithm. In order for the strategy to be successful, the process of sending the quotes to the market has to be executed faster than any other competing MM while having the quickest possible access to the market data.

As a result, the market maker must be proficient at consistently updating the prices of the asset based on the relative supply and demand provided by market participants via the limit order book. The connection between the *Market Making* problem and the *Price Dynamics Forecast* problem addressed previously becomes quite evident. Obviously the ability to properly analyze and use market microstructure information is central.

The two most important aspects for the success of a market-making strategy are:

- The ability to properly manage the accumulated inventory, or what one calls *Inventory-Driven* Market Making, and
- The aptitude to forecast successfully the very short-term dynamics of the price movement, also called *Information-Driven* Market Making.

The proliferation of High Frequency and Algorithmic trading has triggered a profound change in the microstructure of markets during the last two decades. The abundance of highly granular HFT data, the fragmentation of the markets, and the existence of ever more sophisticated trading algorithms has rendered the microstructure of markets harder to understand and to exploit. As a result most of the theoretical and empirical models used to explain market microstructure are outdated and they may no longer be considered reliable for practical use. According to Maureen O'Hara (2015), traditional models used in market microstructure might have become obsolete and are in need of a profound rework.

From this perspective, Machine Learning methods are of great interest especially given the availability of massive amounts of data and inexpensive computing power. But traditional supervised ML approaches are not generally useful given the complexity and the nonlinear dynamics of financial markets. The MM agents must be able to adapt and dynamically learn their optimal behavior. As such, Reinforcement Learning has become the tool of choice when it comes to studying the problem of *Market Making* (Spooner et al. 2018; Elwin 2018; Sutton 1998).

This chapter will focus on the study of market microstructure trading dynamics, such as the clustering of bid-ask spread, optimal trade execution, and optimal inventory management. Most of the use cases presented will be applications of Reinforcement Learning agents.

9.2   CURRENT STATE-OF-THE-ART IN MARKET MAKING

The main goal of Market Making is to provide liquidity by facilitating transactions with other market participants. Like many other major aspects of trading, Market Making has become increasingly automated with the advent of the electronic limit order book. The necessity for automation came with the need to handle ever more data and to react to ever-changing market conditions on much shorter time scales.

Market Making has been studied across a number of disciplines, from Finance and Economics, to Machine Learning and Operational Research. The most common approach used in the finance literature is to treat market making as a problem of *Stochastic Optimal Control*. Models for order arrivals and executions have been developed, and control algorithms for driving the Market-Making process have been suggested (Avellaneda and Stoikov 2008; Chakraborty and Kearns 2011; Guilbaud and Pham 2011).

More recent publications have reported studies on price impact, the role of adverse selection and predictability (Abergel et al. 2016), as well as the importance of risk measures and inventory constraints (Guéant, Lehalle, and Fernandez-Tapia 2013).

A popular topic in Market Making research has been the study of *zero-intelligence* (ZI) agents. The ZI agents are tasked to be fully aware of inventory constraints (Gode and Sunder 1992) while being oblivious to observing, remembering, or learning from the microstructure. More intelligent variants have been recently suggested and they are incorporating modern learning mechanisms (Vytelingum, Cliff, and Jennings 2008). The agents are typically evaluated in simulated markets without the use of real market data. A significant amount of research has been reported on the relationship between Market Making and the short-term predictability of price dynamics (Othman 2012; Othman et al. 2013). In this context, the MM agent's main task is to extract information from informed market participants.

The specific role of an MM could vary substantially across market segments. In what is called a pure dealer market, multiple MMs will competitively quote prices and therefore incoming market orders from market participants will trade at the best available MM price (Huang and Stoll 1996). In a pure limit-order market, both investors and MMs submit orders with limits in price. Whenever an incoming market order matches an existing limit order, a trade occurs at the resting order's limit price. This market mechanism is called the *Continuous Double Auction* (CDA). For the so-called specialist markets there is usually a unique designated MM that acts as a dealer with a mandate (obligation) to maintain fair and orderly markets. In modern electronic markets, pure limit-order markets are the predominating MM type (Frey and Grammig 2006).

The activity of providing liquidity to the market participants could generate profits, while running the risk of adverse selection. This happens when traders with more current or otherwise better information may be able to take advantage of the MM's standing offers. The vast majority of the Market Making literature has historically focused on the tradeoff between profit potential and adverse selection risk and its implications for MM strategies (Glosten and Milgrom 1985; Kyle 1985). The impact of the MM activity may depend on the number of market makers acting in a specific market and at a specific time. Several authors considered the effect of MMs competing for the orders of other traders. Their studies examined the MM competition in models where orders are split across separate markets or in the same market through a common Limit Order Book (Glosten and Milgrom 1985; Biais, Martimort, and Rochet 2000).

Most of the literature on Market Making is centered predominantly within the field of *market microstructure*, which examines the process by which prices, information, and transactions are constructed by the stochastic-like interactions between traders in a market setting (Biais, Glosten, and Spatt 2005; O'Hara 1997).

Early work focused on dealer markets, in which a monopolistic MM (the dealer) controls trading by acting as the middleman. The seminal model of Glosten and Milgrom (1985) framed spreads as arising from adverse selection. The standard Glosten and Milgrom model assumes conditions of perfect competition and constrains the MMs to set prices to achieve zero expected profit. A separate line of research investigated models where MMs could achieve positive outcomes (profits). This research derived the prices that would be set by rational market makers, either as monopolists (Das 2008) or in competition with each other. The model of Biais, Martimort, and Rochet (2000) suggested that multiple market makers in an imperfect competition setting could potentially earn positive expected profits. Nevertheless these profits will vanish as the number of MMs goes to infinity. Much of the relevant theoretical literature relies on simplifying assumptions about MM behavior and trader interactions (Biais, Glosten, and Spatt 2005). Empirical studies provide insight into the effects of market makers in real-world markets (Conrad, Wahal, and Xiang 2015; Shelton 2001). One of the conclusions of the study was that historical data alone cannot elucidate the strategic choices faced by market participants.

As we have seen in the previous two chapters, Reinforcement Learning was applied successfully for many other financial trading problems, including but not limited to optimal execution and the short-term prediction of price movement. The first published study on applying RL to market making (Chan and Shelton 2001) focused on the impact that the uninformed traders (noise) may have on the MM agent's quoting behavior.

The results demonstrated that the Reinforcement Learning agent successfully converges on the expected strategies in controlled environments. However, the RL methodology does not capture the complexity of handling order placement and cancellation. These results could be attributed to partial observability of state variables and to the excessive noise in the problem domain. In contrast Spooner and co-authors (2018) found that temporal-difference RL could be an effective technique for tackling the market making problem, provided that one uses eligibility traces and carefully designed function approximators and reward functions.

Abernethy and Kale (2013) report the use of an online learning approach to develop a market making agent. The authors produced very interesting theoretical results for a stylized model and was able to empirically evaluate their agents under strong assumptions on executions (like a market that has sufficient liquidity in order to execute market orders entirely at the posted price with no slippage).

Market Making has been one of the early adopters of Machine Learning techniques (Nevmyvaka, Sycara, and Seppi 2005). The study by Nevmyvaka and collaborators demonstrated the effectiveness of learning algorithms for this kind of control problem. The authors' approach was to create an electronic MM whose primary goal was to optimally change the spread over the very next iteration instead of finding the best model for the past transactions. The authors attempted to create a more normative (as opposed to explanatory) model, and therefore they tried to determine which factors are more important for generating a good spread update in response to the actions of other market makers.

In one of the most recently published studies, Elwin (2018) used Reinforcement Learning to understand the market microstructure of assets transacted on NASDAQ Nordics and trained MM agents on a simulated electronic market with similar characteristics. The author was using Deep-Q-Network (DQN) and Proximal Policy Optimization (PPO) algorithms on these simulated environments. The MM agents were reported to successfully reproduce stylized facts in historical trading data, such as mean reverting prices and the absence of linear autocorrelations in price changes. The interactions between the simulated MM agents exhibited realistic aspects of the trading dynamics such as bid-ask spread clustering and optimal inventory management, indicating that the use of RL with PPO and DQN could yield to relevant choices when modeling market microstructure. The next section will illustrate some interesting Machine Learning approaches that could be used to address the problem of market making.

9.3   APPLICATIONS OF TEMPORAL-DIFFERENCE RL IN MARKET MAKING

In one of the most recently published papers on the topic of Market Making modeling, Spooner and co-authors (2018) described a methodology to design a MM agent using Temporal-Difference Reinforcement Learning (TD-RL). By using a "high-fidelity simulation of the limit order book" the authors suggested a linear combination of tile codings as value function approximators, and of a custom reward function that controls the inventory risk. The goal of this study was to demonstrate the effectiveness of this TD-RL method (Sutton 1988) by showing that the MM agent could outperform both simple benchmark strategies, as well as more recently published online learning approaches.

9.3.1   Methodology

This research study revisited some of the most important aspects of Market Making modeling previously reported in the literature (Shelton 2001; Chan and Shelton 2001). By using a novel approach the authors developed a "high-fidelity simulation" using high-frequency historical data. This study found innovative solutions to previously unresolved issues associated with reward attribution, noise, and partial observability. The authors proposed new formulations for both the Reward function and the State representation, and they successfully demonstrated that these choices are key factors in the success of the MM agent. The methodology employed by the authors to construct the Market Making TD-RL agent could be summarized as follows:

- *Developing a data-driven simulation of the Limit Order Book.*
  This was done by using a basket of 10 equities across 5 different venues. The LOB data included 5 levels of depth and millisecond-level transaction updates.
- *Investigating the performance of a wide range of TD-based learning algorithms.*
  The authors addressed previously raised concerns about the efficacy of one-step temporal-difference learning, by demonstrating that eligibility traces are a simple and effective solution. Eligibility traces are one of the basic mechanisms used in Reinforcement Learning. In general any temporal-difference method, such as Q-learning or Sarsa, could be combined with eligibility traces to obtain a more general method that may learn more efficiently.
  A more theoretical view sees eligibility traces as a bridge between TD to Monte Carlo methods. When TD methods are augmented with eligibility traces, they produce a family of methods spanning a spectrum that has Monte Carlo methods at one end and one-step TD methods at the other.

Another way to view eligibility traces is more mechanistic in nature. An eligibility trace is viewed as a temporary record of the occurrence of an event, such as the visiting of a state or the taking of an action. The trace marks the memory parameters associated with the event as eligible for undergoing learning changes.

- *Showing that the use of incremental PnL (profit and loss) as the natural choice for the Reward function does not lead to the best performance.*

  The authors showed that the use of PnL as a Reward function actually induces instability during the learning process. They proposed a novel solution in the form of an asymmetrically dampened Reward function which they claim improves learning stability and produces "higher and more consistent returns."

- *Suggesting a series of three different State space designs and proposing a linear combination of tile codings as the final representation.*

  The authors showed that the proper choice of the Reward function and the Space state representation will generate a much better performance of the MM strategy due to a more stable learning process.

- *Introducing a consolidated design for the MM agent.*

  The authors showed that a consolidated MM agent will generate the best risk-adjusted out-of-sample performance compared to a set of simple benchmarks, basic RL agents, or compared with more recently published online learning approaches (Spooner et al. 2018). Moreover, the authors claimed that the performance of the consolidated MM agent could be competitive enough to represent a potentially viable approach for practical use.

9.3.2 The Simulator

Spooner and collaborators (2018) developed a market simulator by reconstructing the LOB from historical data. Their data set contained 8 months' worth of data for 10 securities chosen from 4 different sectors. Their simulator has tracked the top 5 price levels in the LOB and allowed the MM agent to place quotes within these price levels. Since the market simulator was fed with historical data, the orders placed by the MM agent could not have impacted the market. For all intents and purposes, the size of the orders used by the MM agent were small compared to the total amount traded in the market, so the impact of the agent's orders would have been negligible.

One limitation of this LOB simulator was related to the fact that the data has been previously aggregated per price level. Variations of the amount of volume at a particular price level may indicate that some of the orders at that level either have been executed or have been canceled. Because there is no discrimination between the sizes of different orders for each level one does not know precisely which orders have been canceled versus executed. This shortcoming may cause problems when the MM agent's order was simulated for that price level, because one does not know whether the canceled order was ahead or behind the simulated order in the queue.

The solution chosen by the authors was to assume that cancellations were distributed uniformly throughout the queue, which means that the probability that the canceled order is ahead of the agent's order is proportional to the amount of volume ahead of the agent's order compared to the amount of volume behind it.

9.3.3   Market Making Agent Specification

9.3.3.1   Trading Strategy

Spooner and collaborators (2018) considered a state-based MM agent that acted on events as they occurred in the LOB and was subject to inventory constraints. An event was defined as a possible change in price, in volume, or the redistribution of the orders in the LOB, that is, any observable change in the state of the environment. This translates into the fact that the agent's actions were not spaced regularly in time. The MM agent was designed to quote prices at which it was willing to buy and sell at all times unless the inventory constraints were violated. In that case the MM agent was restricted just to orders that would bring the agent closer to a neutral position.

The action space suggested by the authors was based on a typical MM strategy in which the agent is restricted to a single buy and sell order and cannot exit the market (Chakraborty and Kearns 2011). There were 10 possible actions that the MM agent could perform:

- The first 9 actions correspond to a pair of orders with a particular spread and bias in their prices. Limit orders will be placed at fixed distances relative to a reference price, $Ref(t_i)$ – the mid-price. At each time step the agent revises 2 control parameters, θ_a and θ_b.

    Smaller values of the parameter $\theta_{a,b}$ lead to quotes that are closer to the top of the book while larger $\theta_{a,b}$ values cause the quotes to be deeper in the book. The MM agent may choose to quote wide or tight – or even to skew its orders in favor of the buy/sell side.

- The last category of possible actions allowed for the MM agent to clear its inventory using a market order. This market order was sized proportionately to the agent's current inventory. Note that volume is defined to be negative for buy orders and positive for sell orders.

The full specification of the agent's pricing strategy is:

$$p_{a,b}(t_i) = Ref(t_i) + Dist_{a,b}(t_i)$$

$$Dist_{a,b}(t_i) = \theta_{a,b}(t_i) \cdot Spread(t_i)$$

The parameter Spread (t_i) was a time-dependent scale factor which was calculated by taking a moving average of the market half-spread, or $s(t_i)/2$.

9.3.3.2 Reward Functions

The more traditional reward function for trading agents was considered to be the PnL (profit and loss). Under this reward function, the MM agent is encouraged to maintain quotes and hold an inventory which will appreciate in value over time.

For a given time t_i, one could define the parameters $Matched_a(t_i)$ and $Matched_b(t_i)$ as the amount of volume matched (executed) against the agent's orders since the last time t_{i-1} for asks and bids respectively. Let $m(t_i)$ denote the mid-price at time t_i.

Given the executions of the agent's orders relative to the mid-price, let's define two functions to calculate the PnL:

$$\varphi_a(t_i) \triangleq Matched_a(t_i) \cdot [p_a(t_i) - m(t_i)] \tag{9.1}$$

$$\varphi_b(t_i) \triangleq Matched_b(t_i) \cdot [m(t_i) - p_b(t_i)] \tag{9.2}$$

If both orders are executed within the same time interval $[t_{i-1}, t_i]$, then $\varphi_a(t_i) + \varphi_b(t_i)$ will simply become just the agent's quoted spread.

If the agent's inventory at time t_i is denoted as $Inv(t_i)$, one could define the incremental (non-dampened) PnL function $\Psi(t_i)$ by setting $\Psi(t_0) \triangleq 0$ and:

$$\Psi(t_i) \triangleq \varphi_a(t_i) + \varphi_b(t_i) + Inv(t_i)\Delta m(t_i) \tag{9.3}$$

The inventory term corresponds to the change in the agent's cash holdings due to changes in price in the market. Note that this term is only necessary because we accounted for the PnL from the agent's trades relative to the mid-price. While the above definition for the reward function was traditionally considered as a natural choice for this problem domain, the authors showed that such a basic formulation of the reward function ignores the specific objectives of a market maker, often leading to instability during learning and unsatisfactory out-of-sample performance.

The authors suggested (Spooner et al. 2018) two alternative definitions of the reward function which were engineered to discourage trend-following and reinforce the capture of the spread. The three reward functions that we study are as follows:

PnL:

$$r_i = \Psi(t_i) \tag{9.4}$$

Symmetrically dampened PnL:

$$r_i = \Psi(t_i) - \eta \cdot Inv(t_i)\Delta m(t_i) \tag{9.5}$$

Asymmetrically dampened PnL:

$$r_i = \Psi(t_i) - \max[0, \eta \cdot Inv(t_i)\Delta m(t_i)] \tag{9.6}$$

For the last two versions of the reward functions, the dampening is applied to the inventory term using a scale factor η. This damping factor η reduces the incentive for the MM agent to seek gains from trend-following speculation. The symmetric version dampens both profits and losses from speculation while asymmetric dampening reduces the profit from speculative positions but keeps losses intact. The remarkable finding was that in both cases, the amount of reward that could be gained from capturing the spread is larger compared to the amount of reward that can be gained through speculation, thus encouraging market-making behavior.

9.3.3.3   State Representation

The state of the environment is constructed from attributes that describe both the condition of the agent and market, that is, agent state and market state, respectively. The agent-state is described by:

- The *inventory*, $Inv(t_i)$ – the quantitative measure of the asset owned or owed by the agent – is a measure of risk exposure (a large absolute position could open the agent to sizable losses).
- The active quoting distances, normalized by the current spread scale factor, $Spread(t_i)$; these are the effective values of the control parameters, $\theta_{a,b}$, after stepping forward in the simulation.

But the most challenging aspect comes from the market. Unlike the agent's internal features, the market state is subject to partial observability and may not have a Markovian representation. In order to select the most representative market state variables, one must balance expressivity with informational value while avoiding Bellman's curse of dimensionality. The authors of this study included the following market state attributes:

- Market (bid-ask) spread(s)
- Mid-price move (Δm)
- Book/queue imbalance
- Signed volume
- Volatility
- Relative Strength Index

Based on these attributes three different representations of market state were considered. The *agent state* and the *full state* were represented using a conventional tile coding approximation scheme. The third state takes into account approximations of the agent state, the market state, and the full state simultaneously using a linear combination of these three tile codings (LCTC). This approach is equivalent to learning three independent value functions, each of which is updated using the same TD-error for gradient descent.

The authors argued that a coarse state representation may improve learning efficiency by directing the MM agent toward more optimal regions of the policy space. This approach is exploiting the alleged independence between the agent-state and market-state variables. This novel technique could be particularly relevant for problems where a lot of domain-specific knowledge is available a priori. Learning the value for the agent state, market state, and full state representations independently enables the MM agent to learn this much faster as it does not rely on observing every permutation of the full state to evaluate the value of its inventory. It is plausible that this will also help the MM agent converge much more efficiently by guiding it away from local optima in the policy space.

9.3.3.4   Learning Algorithms

The authors considered general-purpose TD-RL algorithms (Sutton 1988) such as Q-learning (QL), Sarsa, and R-learning. Each algorithm was implemented using eligibility traces (ETs). They used 1,000 days of training episodes with a typical training sample of 120 days and a testing sample of 40 days.

During the training process a learning rate $\alpha = 0.001$ was used and an R-learning step-size of $\beta = 0.005$. The value of the discount factor chosen was $\gamma = 0.97$ and the trace parameter $\lambda = 0.96$. From a market-making perspective an order size of 1,000 shares was employed and the limits for the inventory were 10,000 for both long and short sides.

For each set of experiments, the data set was split into disjoint training and testing sets, where all of the training data was older that the testing data. In addition to that, separate validation data sets were used for hyper-parameter optimization and for drawing comparisons between the various types of agents considered.

9.3.3.5   Performance Criteria

Customarily the primary metric used to assess the performance of a trading strategy is the amount of returns. While this approach makes sense in terms of capital returns, it certainly does not make much sense from a market maker optimization perspective, especially because a multitude of strategies were tested across a variety of stocks, each with varying prices and liquidity.

Instead of dollar returns the authors used a normalized daily PnL that rated how well the strategies performed in terms of capturing the spread. This metric was defined on a daily basis as the total profit divided by the average market spread which normalizes the profit across different markets. This metric expresses to the number of market spreads that would need to be captured in order to obtain that profit.

Another important goal for market makers is to avoid keeping large inventories. To assess how well the TD-RL MM agents accomplish this task, a mean absolute position (MAP) metric was introduced. High values of this metric indicate that the agent has taken a sizeable amount of risk and therefore took a speculative approach to trading. On the other hand, smaller values would suggest that the agent is relying less on market trends and more on pure market making techniques.

9.3.4   Empirical Results

The most notable finding by Spooner and co-authors was that the Temporal-Difference Reinforcement Learning implementation of the MM agent was shown to outperform both simple benchmark strategies as well as more recently published online learning approaches.

9.3.4.1 Benchmarks

In order to relate the performance of the TD-RL agent to published literature let's quickly review the set of benchmarks used by this study. The benchmarks used for comparison were represented by:

- A group of spread-based strategies based on the online learning approach introduced by the work of Abernethy and Kale (2013), and
- A pair of basic agents, using an agent state representation, coupled with a non-dampened PnL reward function and QL or Sarsa methods. These basic agents represented the best prior reported results using standard techniques and they were closely related to those introduced by Chan and Shelton (2001).

9.3.4.2 Spread-Based Strategies

The spread-based benchmark strategy uses an online learning meta-algorithm inspired by the original work of Abernethy and Kale. The results this study tried to reproduce were less conclusive compared to the ones reported by the original Abernethy and Kale paper, where the online learning strategy was found to be profitable over all time frames and all the stocks considered. This inconsistency could be attributed to the use of less realistic market simulation capabilities in the original work (the tracking of the LOB microstructure by Abernethy and Kale did not exhibit the same level of accuracy as the one in Spooner and co-authors (2018)).

Another set of benchmarks were considered by using random policies over the MM action space. These strategies were quoting at fixed, symmetric distances from the chosen reference price ($\theta_a = \theta_b$) at all times. This different approach accounts for market liquidity in a much better way by adapting the quoting prices to changes in the bid-ask spread. Fixed strategies with $\theta_{a,b} > 1$ were found to be profitable on average, with decreasing MAP as $\theta_{a,b}$ increases.

But in all cases this strategy was found to suffer from high volatility that was most likely caused by a lack of proper inventory management, as indicated by the consistently high mean average positions.

9.3.4.3 Basic Agent

The basic agent used a state representation comprising:

- The agent-state, that is the inventory,
- The normalized bid/ask quoting distances, and
- The non-dampened PnL reward function (Equation 9.4).

This agent was trained using a one-step Q-learning and Sarsa algorithms. The addition of eligibility traces (i.e. $Q(\lambda)$ and Sarsa(λ)) was reported to improve the agents' performance, yielding strategies that occasionally generated profits out-of-sample.

9.3.4.4 Extensions

Three different extensions to the basic agent were proposed. They were related to variations of the following:

- Learning algorithm
- Reward function
- State representation

9.3.4.5 Learning Algorithms

The first variation on the basic agents addressed the impact of using different learning algorithms, like Q-learning and Sarsa. The study reported that variants based on off-policy learning tended to perform worse than their on-policy counterparts.

The reason that Q-learning is an off-policy algorithm is that it updates its Q-values using the Q-value of the *next* state and a *greedy action*. In other words, it estimates the *return* (total discounted future reward) for state action pairs assuming a greedy policy were followed despite the fact that it's not following a greedy policy. On the other hand, Sarsa is an on-policy algorithm because it updates its Q-values using the Q-value of the *next* state and the *current policy's* action. It estimates the return for state-action pairs assuming the current policy continues to be followed.

Although some variants were found to outperform the basic agent for some equities, none of them were as consistent as the Sarsa version. This suggests that while each stock could be optimized individually for maximal performance, Sarsa may be used reliably as a baseline.

9.3.4.6 Reward Functions

The results of the study showed that the classical choice of reward function (the non-dampened PnL) does not represent the best out-of-sample performance across the basket of securities. Although the symmetric dampening was found to exacerbate the flaws in the basic agent, the asymmetric dampening of the trend-following term in Equation 9.3, with sufficiently high damping factor (η), was found to produce superior risk-adjusted performance in most cases.

The results showed that there is a critical value of $\eta \sim 0.1$ beyond which the agent begins to converge on fundamentally different policies than those promoted by the non-dampened PnL function. This shift in the final policy corresponds to a reduction in the risk exposure. This was manifested by a change from holding large, unbalanced inventories toward smaller and more neutral positions. This reduction in exposure comes along with a change in PnL that exhibits a much lower variance. The impact of asymmetric dampening was very noticeable by providing strong evidence that the inventory term in Equation 9.3 was the main driver for the MM agent's behavior, and it should represent the main parameter to be manipulated to match a given risk profile. The study has also observed that asymmetric dampening of the reward function would lead to improved stability during learning and better asymptotic performance compared to the basic agent. Another important conclusion was that the inventory component in Equation 9.3 is not only driving behavior, but it is also the main source of instability – increasing the value of η seems to yield better and more consistent performance.

9.3.4.7 State Representation
Three state representations were considered:

- An *agent state* (as used by the basic agent)
- A *full state* (agent and market variables)
- A Linear Combination of Tile Codings

The idea behind considering these different states was to identify and address challenges associated with increased state complexity when including market parameters. The consideration of market parameters was found to have a strongly negative impact on returns. The study did not detect any measurable improvement in performance with increased training, but instead the TD-RL agent was regularly seen to degrade and even diverge.

One of the findings was that the basic agent was a lot more efficient at learning than the full-state variant and tended to be more stable – most likely because the state-space was much smaller in size.

In order to capitalize on stability and efficiency while incorporating market information, the authors considered what they called a *Linear Combination of Tile Codings* (LCTC). This variant has considerably outperformed the full-state agent and did not exhibit any issues of divergence as seen for the full-state variant. The conclusion was that the LCTC combines expressivity and efficiency and helps to prevent divergence even when the market variables have little informational content.

9.3.4.8 The Consolidated Agent
The study considered a consolidated version of the best variants on the basic agent by using the asymmetrically dampened reward function with an LCTC state space and training it using Sarsa. The study found that the consolidated agent generated slightly lower returns than the best individual variants, but it had a much improved out-of-sample stability.

In addition, the consolidated agent showed the tendency to hold smaller inventories, which may have been a contributing factor toward the reduced uncertainty on PnL and thus a better risk exposure. In conclusion, the consolidated agent was found to produce superior risk-adjusted performance over the basic agent and extended variants overall.

By comparing the basic and the consolidated agents' out-of-sample tests the study showed that the former is highly volatile while the latter is stable. In general, the basic agent holds non-zero inventory, therefore creating risk exposure to changes in the security's value for extended periods of time, thus contributing to some noise observed in the equity curve.

The consolidated agent learned a policy that usually targets a near-zero inventory, relying less on speculative trading and thus yielding the consistency one expects from a good market-making strategy.

9.3.4.9 Conclusions

By developing a realistic simulation methodology and by using eligibility traces Spooner and co-authors (2018) developed a TD-RL-based MM agent that has produced competitive out-of-sample performance across a basket of securities.

The study investigated different learning algorithms, reward functions, and state representations and consolidated the best techniques into a single agent which was shown to produce superior risk-adjusted performance.

The authors also outlined the directions of future research:

- Apply more advanced learning algorithms such as Greedy GQ, Q(σ), and true online variants which could provide convergence with linear function approximation.
- Explore Deep Reinforcement Learning, specifically the use of Recurrent Neural Networks that should be well-suited to the sequential nature of the problem.
- Introduce a parametrized action space as an alternative to discrete action sets.
- Extend the analysis to multiple orders and variable order size action spaces.
- Investigate the impact of market frictions such as rebates, fees, and latency on the agent's strategy.
- The use of sequential Bayesian methods for more efficient and accurate LOB reconstruction and estimation of order queues.

9.4   MARKET MAKING IN HIGH-FREQUENCY TRADING USING RL

A recently published research study authored by *Ye-Sheen Lim* and Denise Gorse (2018) described the application of Reinforcement Learning to optimal Market Making in High-Frequency Trading. The authors suggested a novel formulation for states, actions, and reward functions that are specific to market making in High-Frequency Trading, including a novel use for *CARA utility* as a terminal reward measure for improving the learning process. CARA is a risk aversion measure and stands for *Consumption with Constant Absolute Risk Aversion* (Babcock, Choi, and Feinerma 1993). The results reported by this study showed that an optimal policy trained using Q-learning "outperforms state-of-the-art market making algorithms." The work has also analyzed the optimal RL policies and the influence of the CARA utility from a trading perspective.

Given the challenging aspects of modeling the dynamics of financial markets, even the most complex mathematical models could not entirely capture the reality of the financial landscape. This challenge is even more notable in High-Frequency Trading, a battlefield of great interest for both financial institutions and market regulators. Given the complexity of this field, that is using ultra-high-speed communication technology to enable microseconds-level market data to drive all trading decisions, generally HFT traders are considered to function as *de facto* market makers.

There was relatively little work published in the area of HF Market Making (Fernandez-Tapia 2015). The vast majority of previously published work on HF Market Making has proposed strategies derived from mathematical models that made strong assumptions about market behavior. As such these models relied heavily on parameters that had to be fitted from recent market data. Since these parameters are subjected to regime changes, the fitting process could be extremely unreliable. In addition to these limitations, the inherently nonlinear action space of the models has been proven to be very unstable. As such very small perturbations in the action space could lead to extreme control values.

A much more effective strategy will aim at building a framework that learns effective MM strategies from historical data and eliminates the need for such unstable and unreliable market models. Lim and Gorse (2018) introduced a novel formulation of a discrete Q-learning algorithm for market making, tested it against the model used by Fernandez-Tapia (2015), and analyzed the resulting optimal policy. Market-making control policies refer to the offsets from the best bid and best ask in the LOB at which to post the bid and ask quotes. The authors also used the CARA utility (Babcock, Choi, and Feinerma 1993) in a very creative fashion to improve learning based on the measure of an agent's risk aversion.

9.4.1   Methodology

9.4.1.1   States
Lim and Gorse (2018) have assumed that state transitions are Markovian in nature, and they considered that the partially observable variables were fully observable. The ultimate test of these assumptions will be considered in the final empirical evaluation of the algorithm.

The two main states considered were the inventory i, and the remaining time τ. In order to reduce the computational complexity, the inventory states were binned into six categories (states) representing small, medium, and large inventory imbalance for both bids and offers, with an additional category representing the flat (zero) inventory.

The trading period T was partitioned into k time steps; therefore the remaining time could be encoded as:

$$\tau \in \left\{ \frac{1}{k}T, \frac{2}{k}T, \cdots, T \right\} \tag{9.7}$$

9.4.1.2   Actions
The authors defined the action of simultaneously quoting bid/ask limit orders at a given time step as a tuple $a = (d_b, d_a)$. The MM strategy employed dictates that at every time step, any unexecuted orders previously placed will be canceled and new limit orders will be submitted according to the action selected from the optimal policy at any given state.

9.4.1.3 *Rewards*

A traditional approach to the Market Making problem looks to maximize the expected utility of the PnL measure for the MM agent. This type of utility is meant to evaluate the performance of the agent at the end of a trading period and does not accurately represent immediate rewards at each time step t.

The authors proposed a more suitable utility through the reward function R_t as described below:

$$R_t = a(V_t - V_{t-1}) + e^{b\tau_t} sign(|i_t| - |i_{t-1}|) \tag{9.8}$$

where a and b are constants, V_t is the equity value at time t, i_t is the inventory of the agent at time t, and τ_t is the remaining trading time at t.

At the end of a trading period, the authors formulated a terminal reward based on the Constant Absolute Risk Aversion (CARA) utility (Babcock, Choi, and Feinerma 1993) to represent the attitude of the agent to the gains or losses caused by having inventory i_T at the end of the trading period. The CARA utility takes the form:

$$R_t = \alpha - \exp(-r(C_T - i_T S_T)) \tag{9.9}$$

where α is a constant, r is the risk aversion parameter, C_T is the profit or loss (PnL) made during the trading period, and S_T is the average price (including costs) at which we can immediately liquidate i_T shares.

9.4.2 Experimental Setting

A discrete Q-learning algorithm (Sutton and Barto 1998) was used to find the optimal action-selection policy. Since the selected states and actions are naturally discrete there was no need for a reward function approximation. Given the lack of a good starting policy for an environment as complex as the HF market, the authors suggested the use of an off-policy algorithm instead of an on-policy algorithm (for better exploration).

During the learning process, the optimal actions are chosen in an ε-greedy manner. Both the ε and the learning rate were set to diminish as more episodes were run. As for the experimental setup, each trading period was set to 120 seconds, with $k = 12$ time steps. As for the inventory state i, a small inventory was defined to be in the range $0 < i \le 200$, a medium inventory in the range $200 < i \le 400$, and a large inventory as $i > 400$. In total there are 66 combinations of possible time and inventory states.

A Poisson model was used to simulate the LOB dynamic. The RL agent was trained for 10,000 episodes. For every episode, the simulation was first run for 5 minutes just to initialize the order book. By selecting the optimal offsets from Q, the RL agent could submit simultaneous quotes every 10 seconds until the end of the trading period. As already mentioned, any previously submitted orders that have not been executed are canceled.

As a result Q is updated using the reward function R_t as described in Equation 9.8. At the end of the trading period, a terminal reward R_T is used to update the value of the last encountered state, regardless of the action taken so far (see Equation 9.9). This action signifies that the CARA utility is propagated through all previous states and enables the agent to take into account its risk aversion in accumulating inventory throughout the trading period.

The RL-based market maker could choose to quote an offset from the set {0, 1, 2} ticks for each bid and ask side respectively, giving a total of 9 different tuples as actions. The Zero Tick Offset method represents the simplest form of market making where the bid and ask prices of the limit orders are set to the best bid and best ask. Another experiment consisted of randomly choosing from the action set available to the RL agent.

9.4.3   Results and Conclusions

The study performed by Lim and Gorse (2018) simulated trading scenarios for 2,000 trading periods. At the end of each period, the total inventory accumulated was liquidated with a market order and the final total profit obtained by the agent was computed.

This research study claimed that their RL agents outperformed in terms of profit all the other methods, including the mathematical model of Avellaneda-Stoikov (2008), which is still considered state-of-the-art in the literature. In addition, the study showed that the RL agent was the most inventory neutral compared to all other methods.

The use of the CARA utility has demonstrated that there is a lot of potential in the integration of more classic mathematical models and Machine Learning methods. The risk aversion parameter in the CARA utility represented the willingness of the agent to risk these natural price movements.

For future work, the authors will consider the use of Reinforcement Learning to tune the actions of the Avellaneda-Stoikov algorithm, depending on the limit order book states.

9.5   OTHER RESEARCH STUDIES

A variety of other research studies on the topic of Market Making have been published. One of them, authored by Wah and collaborators (2017), investigated "the effects of market making on market performance, focusing on allocative efficiency as well as gains from trade accrued by background traders." The authors used empirical simulation methods to evaluate heuristic strategies for market makers in a variety of trading environments. A novel market model was introduced to incorporate both private and common valuation attributes, with dynamic fundamental value and asymmetric information.

The authors reported the presence of a surplus achieved by background traders in strategic equilibrium, for use cases with and without a market maker.

One of their main findings indicated that the presence of a market maker tends to increase total welfare across various environments. The authors reported that Market Making strategies tend to benefit investors in relatively illiquid markets and in situations where background traders are impatient due to limited trading opportunities. The presence of additional market makers tends to enhance these benefits, as competition drives the market makers to provide liquidity at lower price spreads.

In a separate research study by Li and collaborators (2014) a two-tier MM framework was presented. This framework included a trading signal generator based on a supervised learning approach and an event-driven MM strategy. The trading signal generator component was fed with market microstructure information from the LOB and generated directional price movement predictions. The Market Making strategy was implemented in a second tier and it was producing quotes based on the signals generated by the first tier.

This interesting combination of directional movement prediction and Market Making was reported to add an extra layer of risk control by preventing losses due to market trending. The empirical results showed that when MM strategies were coupled with directional forecasting signals, they would perform better than strategies without any signal in terms of average daily profit and loss (PnL) and Sharpe ratio (SR). Correct directional predictions may help the MM strategies to readjust their quoting along with market trending, which avoids the strategies triggering stop losses.

Dixon (2017) authored a study on the use of High-Frequency trade execution models and used them to evaluate the economic impact of supervised machine learners. The author extended the concept of a confusion matrix to introduce that of a trade information matrix by attributing the expected profit and loss of the high-frequency strategy under execution constraints, such as fill probabilities and position dependent trade rules, to correct and incorrect predictions. Dixon applied this novel trade execution model market microstructure data to the E-mini S&P 500 futures contract. His approach used *Recurrent Neural Networks* to directly evaluate the performance sensitivity of a market-making strategy to prediction errors.

Other studies (Kanagal, Wu, and Chen 2017; Gil and Zahavi 2012; Jumadinova and Dasgupta 2010) addressed the problem of agent-based Market Making. The general conclusion is that the fundamental challenge in constructing Market-Making strategies comes from the need for the MM to balance conflicting objectives of maximizing trading utility and market quality, or in other words to find the right balance between reaching the profit goals (PnL) and fulfilling the role of an MM (i.e. to ensure fair and stable markets).

REFERENCES

Abergel, Chakraborti, Jedidi et al. (2016). *Limit Order Books*. Cambridge Press, 9–44.

Abernethy and Kale (2013). Adaptive market making via online learning. *Proceedings of 27th Annual Conference on Neural Information Processing Systems*, 2058–2066. https://papers.nips.cc/paper/4910-adaptive-market-making-via-online-learning.pdf.

Avellaneda and Stoikov (2008). High-frequency trading in a limit order book. *Quantitative Finance* 8 (3): 217–224.

Babcock, Choi, and Feinerma (1993). Risk and probability premiums for CARA utility functions. *Journal of Agricultural and Resource Economics* 18 (1): 17–24.

Biais, Glosten, and Spatt (2005). Market microstructure: A survey of microfoundations, empirical results, and policy implications. *Journal of Financial Markets* 8 (2): 217–264.

Biais, Martimort, and Rochet (2000). Competing mechanisms in a common value environment. *Econometrica* 68 (4): 799–837.

Chakraborty and Kearns (2011). Market making and mean reversion. *Proceedings 12th ACM Conference on Electronic Commerce*, 307–314.

Chan and Shelton (2001). An electronic market-maker. AI Memo 2001-005. MIT AI Lab. https://pdfs.semanticscholar.org/bef0/3da46b778d2cc305907452da1598b6b15be5.pdf.

Conrad, Wahal, and Xiang (2015). High-frequency quoting, trading and the efficiency of prices. *Journal of Financial Economics* 116 (2): 271–291.

Das (2008). The effects of market-making on price dynamics. *Proceedings of 7th International Joint Conference on Autonomous Agents and Multi-agent Systems*, 887–894.

Dixon (2017). A high frequency trade execution model for supervised learning. https://arxiv.org/abs/1710.03870.

Elwin (2018). Simulating market maker behavior using deep reinforcement learning to understand market microstructure. Thesis. KTH Institute of Technology, Sweden. http://www.nada.kth.se/~ann/exjobb/marcus_elwin.pdf.

Fernandez-Tapia (2015). High-frequency trading meets reinforcement learning: exploiting the iterative nature of trading algorithms. https://papers.ssrn.com/sol3/papers.cfm?abstract_id=2594477.

Frey and Grammig (2006). Liquidity supply and adverse selection in a pure limit order book market. *Empirical Economics* 30 (4): 1007–1033.

Gil and Zahavi (2012). Supervised learning of market making strategy. https://pdfs.semanticscholar.org/56a8/5b0b6d8e6096687939583131b675ad3edfea.pdf.

Glosten and Milgrom (1985). Bid, ask and transaction prices in a specialist market with heterogeneously informed traders. *Journal of Financial Economics* 14 (1): 71–100.

Gode and Sunder (1992). Allocative efficiency of markets with zero-intelligence traders: market as a partial substitute for individual rationality. *Journal of Political Economy* 101 (1): 119–137.

Guéant, Lehalle, and Fernandez-Tapia (2013). Dealing with the inventory risk: a solution to the market making problem. *Mathematics and Financial Economics* 7 (4): 477–507.

Guilbaud and Pham (2011). Optimal high frequency trading with limit and market orders. https://arxiv.org/abs/1106.5040.

Huang and Stoll (1996). Dealer versus auction markets: a paired comparison of execution costs on NASDAQ and the NYSE. *Journal of Financial Economics* 41 (3): 313–357.

Jumadinova and Dasgupta (2010). *A comparison of different automated market-making strategies. 12th Workshop on Agent-Mediated Electronic Commerce*, 141–154.

Kanagal, Wu, and Chen (2017). *Market making with machine learning methods*. Report. https://web.stanford.edu/class/msande448/2017/Final/Reports/gr4.pdf.

Kyle (1985). *Continuous auctions and insider trading. Econometrica* 53 (6): 1315–1335.

Li, Deng, Zhu et al. (2014). An intelligent market making strategy in algorithmic trading. *Frontier of Computer Science* 8 (4): 596–608. https://www.researchgate.net/publication/273823137_An_intelligent_market_making_strategy_in_algorithmic_trading.

Lim and Gorse (2018). Reinforcement learning for high-frequency market making. *ESANN 2018 Proceedings, European Symposium on Artificial Neural Networks, Computational Intelligence and Machine Learning*. Bruges, Belgium (25–27 April). https://www.elen.ucl.ac.be/Proceedings/esann/esannpdf/es2018-50.pdf.

Nevmyvaka, Sycara, and Seppi (2005). Electronic market making: initial investigation. *Artificial Intelligence in Economics and Finance*. World Scientific. http://www.cs.cmu.edu/~softagents/papers/CR_nevmyvaka_sycara_seppi.pdf.

O'Hara (1997). *Market Microstructure Theory*. Blackwell, 13–88.

O'Hara (2015). High frequency market microstructure. *Journal of Financial Economics* 116 (2): 257–270.

Othman (2012). Automated market making: theory and practice. Ph.D. dissertation. Carnegie Mellon University. http://reports-archive.adm.cs.cmu.edu/anon/2012/CMU-CS-12-123.pdf.

Othman, Pennock, Reeves et al. (2013). A practical liquidity-sensitive automated market maker. *ACM Transactions on Economics and Computation* 1 (3): 1–25.

Schwartz and Peng (2013). Market makers. *Encyclopedia of Finance*. Springer, 487–489.

Shelton (2001). Importance sampling for reinforcement learning with multiple objectives. Ph.D. dissertation. Massachusetts Institute of Technology. https://www.researchgate.net/publication/37596455_Importance_Sampling_for_Reinforcement_Learning_with_Multiple_Objectives.

Spooner, Savani, Fearnley et al. (2018). Market making via reinforcement learning. https://arxiv.org/abs/1804.04216.

Stadie, Yang, Houthooft et al. (2018). Some considerations on learning to explore via meta-reinforcement learning. *32nd Conference on Neural IPS*, Montreal. https://papers.nips.cc/paper/8140-the-importance-of-sampling-inmeta-reinforcement-learning.pdf.

Sutton (1988). Learning to predict by the methods of temporal differences. *Machine Learning* 3 (1): 9–44.

Sutton and Barto (1998). Reinforcement learning: an introduction. *IEEE Transactions on Neural Networks* 9 (5): 1054–1054.

Vytelingum, Cliff, and Jennings (2008). Strategic bidding in continuous double auctions. *Artificial Intelligence* 172 (14): 1700–1729.

Wah, Wright, and Wellman (2017). Welfare effects of market-making in continuous double auctions. *Journal of Artificial Intelligence Research* 5 (59): 613–650.

CHAPTER 10

Case Study 5: Applications of Machine Learning to Derivatives Valuation

"Everything should be made as simple as possible, but not simpler!"

– Albert Einstein

10.1 INTRODUCTION TO THE PROBLEM

One of the most momentous developments in the history of Quantitative Finance was the publication of the Black-Scholes-Merton (BSM) options pricing theory in 1973 (Black and Scholes 1972, 1973). The significance of this event and its influence on later developments in Quantitative Finance cannot be overstated. This event represented the beginning of a new field in Quantitative Finance: Derivatives Valuation. The BSM formula quantifies the value of an option through its dependency on the future volatility of the underlying asset, rather than on its expected return. The BSM theory formulates the price of an option based on several input parameters, such as the price of the underlying asset, the market's risk-free interest rate, the time interval until an option's expiration date, the strike price of the contract, and the volatility of the underlying asset. The revolutionary idea behind BSM was that it is not necessary to use the risk premium when valuing an option, as the asset price already contains this information.

This option pricing formula represents a *theory-driven* model based on the assumption that asset prices follow a geometric Brownian motion. At the time of the BSM publication, most of the computational tools that we are accustomed to today were a decade away from becoming mainstream. Using a more *data-driven* approach to value options would not have been a viable prospect at that time. Although the BSM theory was, and continues to be a remarkable development in the evolution of Quantitative Finance, its inability to reproduce very important empirical facts represents a serious drawback. Its biggest flaw is represented by the mismatch between the model volatility of the underlying option and the observed volatility from the market, or what is called implied volatility. For several decades a new research field developed in order to cope with this serious limitation. The development of modern computational tools enabled more complex models to be calibrated on real market data and to alleviate some of the BSM limitations. For a very long time, quantitative researchers and academics in finance have been busy trying to model the derivatives markets and come up with new and more realistic models.

Market practitioners are using nowadays more sophisticated models such as:

- *Levy* models – formulating a price dynamics of a higher mathematical complexity than the Brownian motion.
- *Variance-Gamma* models.
- *Stochastic volatility* models.
- *Heston* volatility models.

The advent of modern computational technology enabled the valuation of exotic options in a timely manner and has sped-up a plethora of computationally hungry numerical methods such as Monte Carlo, Fast Fourier Transforms, and Partial Differential Equations.

Quantitative professionals are passionate not just about the mathematical aspects of problem solving, but they are also very interested in the latest technological breakthroughs and in the development of new computational methods that could be successfully applied to existing problems. The field of Quantitative and Computational Finance is an ever-demanding taskmaster. The progress achieved by Moore's Law seems to never be sufficient to the impetus of the financial industry. An ever-growing body of quantitative professionals is employed to develop new techniques that deliver more accurate valuation models with as little computational effort as possible. At the same time, computationally demanding tasks are becoming commonplace in the landscape of derivative valuation and pricing of financial derivatives (Green 2015). New financial regulations are adding even more pressure to an already very competitive landscape.

As recent advances in algorithmic development and hardware accelerators have been widely adopted by the financial industry, Machine Learning has become an integral part of the basic Quantitative and Computational modeling tool kit. The addition of Machine Leaning to this toolbox is a direct consequence of the growing availability of low-cost computational power and easy-to-access data (financial or alternative). The most conspicuous outcome of this new trend is the advent of a new paradigm – a data-driven approach to derivatives pricing. One of the most important advantages of using ML methods compared with model-driven approaches is that they are able to reproduce most of the empirical characteristics of financial derivatives.

The general appeal of ML algorithms, especially the subfield of Artificial Neural Networks, is that they are able to approximate a function based on the function's inputs and outputs if the number of data points is sufficiently large. If one considers an option as a functional mapping between the contracted terms (inputs) and the premium of the option (output), ANNs could be used to infer this relationship based on empirical data. If the data sample is large enough and the ANN algorithm is complex enough, then the function that the network will learn from the data set will be close enough to the real one for any practical purpose (Hornik, Stinchcombe, and White 1989). Although the training process could be quite time-consuming, once the process is completed, the use of the ML model for prediction could be extremely fast. Artificial Neural Networks are perhaps best known in finance in the context of predictive algorithms used in trading strategies. But there are also many other financial problems (e.g. credit scoring or bankruptcy prediction) that have pioneered the use of ANN models.

An example could be the problem of Credit Value Adjustment where a classifier approach has been used to map credit default swaps (CDS) to illiquid counterparties (Brummelhuis and Luo 2017). Alongside Artificial Neural Networks, a variety of other ML techniques have been applied to the problem of derivatives valuation, the two most used ones being Deep Neural Networks and Reinforcement Learning. The field of Quantitative and Computational Finance has changed fundamentally since Black, Scholes, and Merton published their seminal papers on options pricing in 1973. The exponential growth over the past decade in computational power and data has allowed researchers to apply ML techniques to price derivatives with precision unforeseen decades ago when options pricing was done by theoretical models based on the foundation of stochastic calculus.

This chapter is dedicated to the study of modern Machine Learning techniques that could be applied to the problem of derivatives valuation. The goal is to first introduce the problem of derivatives valuation using ML, to quickly review the relevant published literature, and then to present a series of case studies related to common valuation tasks.

10.1.1 Problem Statement and Research Questions

- How feasible is it to use Machine Learning as a tool set for the development of valuation models in financial derivatives?
- What are the criteria to select the most efficient architectures for training these models?
- What is the proper metric to be used to assess the computational performance?
- How could hyper-parameter tuning affect the final valuation results?

The problem at hand is to efficiently price financial derivatives in a way that is both fast and accurate. From this perspective a derivatives valuation model is a functional mapping of inputs, like market data and contract specific terms, to an output representing the fair value of the financial derivative. This functional representation may have a tractable analytic form, or it may be numerically approximated using methods like Monte Carlo simulation, binomial trees, or finite difference. Simple derivatives like European stock options could be valued with a relatively small number of inputs, while more complex products like Bermudan swaptions, for example, may require many more inputs, involving all the properties of the underlying swap and option exercise schedule.

Ultimately the parametrization of the mapping function may require a pretty large number of parameters (could be in the hundreds or thousands for more complex derivate products). The need for a large number of inputs is not a stringent requirement for Neural Networks. As an example, Deep Neural Network architectures used for image recognition tasks could be trained quit efficiently on millions of parameters.

When it comes to training an ANN model to approximate a derivatives valuation function, one has to make some up-front decisions that are specific to the application domain. One could choose to train the network on all the parameters (specified by a classical valuation model) or only on a subset of them. Additionally one could choose to train over a larger or a smaller domain for a given parameter. The trade-off is usually dictated by model-complexity versus the training time. In the case of path-dependent derivatives (e.g. Bermudan options) one may choose to take as inputs the properties of a specific trade and then train the model against a variety of input market data scenarios.

This specific choice will generate a considerable reduction in the size of the parameter space, thus relaxing the training requirements such as the size of training data set and the amount of time spent training. A very important aspect to keep in mind is that the learned model could only be trusted to approximate the function well just over the parameter ranges that were used in training. Outside these ranges it is very unlikely that the functional approximation will perform effectively.

10.2 CURRENT STATE-OF-THE-ART IN DERIVATIVES VALUATION BY APPLYING ML

The theory of options pricing is solidly based on the seminal work by Black, Scholes, and Merton (Black and Scholes 1972, 1973). They devised a set of closed-form solutions for option prices by using a dynamic hedging strategy and a no-arbitrage requirement. The Black-Scholes formulas are classical examples of traditional parametric, no-arbitrage pricing formulas, the derivations of which depend heavily on the assumptions and knowledge of the stochastic process that determines the price dynamics of the underlying asset of the option. If for any reason the specification of the stochastic process is incomplete or incorrect, the resulting model will generate pricing errors.

Among market practitioners it is common knowledge that the Geometric Brownian Motion (GBM) assumption is violated in practice; therefore a variety of other *corrective* models have been used to extend the GBM assumption. In addition, *fair* prices generated by these *corrective* models are further adjusted using traders' *judgment*. This makes impossible the knowledge of the exact mathematical function that is generating the market prices.

One attractive solution to this challenge is to use a data-driven, nonparametric approach. Because nowadays market data is plentiful and readily available, there is the possibility to train an algorithm to learn the function that is collectively generating option prices in the market.

10.2.1   The Beginnings: 1992–2004

The first attempt to use this new methodology was done by Hutchinson and his co-authors in 1994 (Hutchinson, Lo, and Poggio 1994). Their publication is considered to be a seminal study on this topic. The authors demonstrated that a neural network is an excellent vehicle to approximate the market's option pricing function. Hutchison proposed a nonparametric method for estimating the pricing formula of a derivative asset using neural networks. Hutchison indicated that when the underlying asset's price dynamic is unknown, or when the pricing equation associated with the no-arbitrage condition cannot be solved analytically, neural network-pricing methods could be more accurate and computationally more efficient alternatives to the more traditional arbitrage-based pricing formulas.

Hutchinson studied the use of three different NN models using American-style S&P 500 index futures calls, and they found that all of the neural network models yielded superior results to the older parametric valuation models. They also showed that the NN models could learn the Black-Scholes pricing formula with very-high-degree accuracy from simulated data. The progress engendered by the work of Hutchinson and co-authors was truly remarkable, especially because the use of NN makes possible the capture of subtle nonlinearities in the data that was not possible previously using linear statistical approaches.

In 1992 Trippi and Turban published one of the first books on this subject. They titled it *Neural Networks in Finance and Investing: Using Artificial Intelligence to Improve Real World Performance* (Trippi and Turban 1992). Back then the authors speculated that Neural Networks will revolutionize "virtually every aspect of financial and investment decision making." Their vision has come to life nowadays when financial firms worldwide are employing NN to tackle difficult tasks involving data patterns detection. More than 25 years ago the two authors claimed that "neural networks will eventually outperform even the best traders and investors."

Earlier work done by Malliaris and Salchenberger (1993) studied the pricing performance of NN models with American-style S&P 100 call options. The authors found that the NN model yielded superior results in the case of out-of-the-money options, but that Black-Scholes was superior for the in-the-money options.

Anders, Korn, and Schmitt (1996) published a study comparing the pricing accuracy of a neural network with European-style calls written on DAX 30 and has also found that the results were superior to classical methods. Amilon (2003) compared both the pricing and hedging performance of a neural network with European-style calls on the OMX index with both implicit and historical volatilities and found that the use of NN was yielding superior results in both cases.

Bennell and Sutcliffe (2004) compared the pricing accuracy with FTSE 100 call options to a dividend-adjusted Black-Scholes formula and found that the neural network was producing superior results in terms of accuracy. The work published by Hanke (1999) reported that the performance of the Black-Scholes model became superior to the use of NN after the parameters for volatility and risk-free rate were optimized. Yao, Li, and Tan (2000) conducted a study to forecast the option prices of Nikkei 225 index futures by using back-propagation neural networks. Their results suggested that for volatile markets an NN integrated option pricing model outperforms the traditional Black-Scholes model, but that the performance of Black-Scholes is generally better for at-the-money options.

Morelli and co-authors (2004) applied NN algorithms to the problem of option pricing and used it to simulate the nonlinear behavior of such financial derivatives. The authors used two different types of neural networks: multilayer perceptron and radial basis functions. Their analysis was carried out for both standard European and American options, including evaluation of the Greeks, necessary for hedging purposes. They published a detailed numerical investigation showing that after a careful phase of training, NNs are able to predict the option values and the Greeks with a high degree of accuracy and very fast.

In general, the results of the earlier studies indicated that neural networks are indeed capable of learning pricing formulas up to high degree of accuracy from real market data. However, there are some serious limitations of these early studies. First off the data used for training was relatively sparse given the limited availability of market data at the beginning of the electronic trading era (1990s). Then the level of computational resources available at that time was quite modest compared to today's availability. Given the significant increase in both available data and computational power, the last decade made possible the development of deeper, more computationally intensive data-driven models such as the Deep Neural Networks. Therefore, it is of great interest to study the performance of such a deep neural network models in pricing derivatives in general, and options in particular.

10.2.2   The Last Decade

Gradojevic and co-authors (2009) proposed a *nonparametric modular* NN model to price S&P 500 European call options. The modules were constructed based on time to maturity and moneyness of the options. The option price function of interest was chosen to be homogeneous of degree one with respect to the underlying index price and the strike price. When compared to several parametric and nonparametric models, the method introduced by the authors consistently exhibited superior out-of-sample pricing performance. This study found that modularity improves the generalization properties of standard feedforward neural network option pricing models.

The paper published by Wang and Lin (2009) promoted a new approach: the integration of an *asymmetric volatility* model into an ANN option pricing model to improve forecasting ability of derivative securities price. The introduction of a new hybrid asymmetric volatility method had as an effect the reduction of the stochastic and nonlinearity of the error term sequence and has captured the asymmetric volatility simultaneously. The published results demonstrated that the *Grey-GJR-GARCH* volatility provides a much higher predictability than other volatility approaches.

The complexity of the NN models used for valuation has increased substantially during the last decade, and the paper published by Hong-yan, Hui, and Jiang (2010) was one of the first to tackle this new trend. The authors suggested a hybrid Wavelet-Neural Network model based on the Black-Scholes model. Within this new approach, options are classified according to their moneyness and the weighted implied volatility rates are regarded as the inputs of the NN. A genetic algorithm was used to determine the optimal weights of the implied volatility rates of different kinds of options. The authors used this model for a case study on the Hong Kong derivative market showing that these hybrid models are performing better than the conventional Black-Scholes model or the other neural network models.

Another attempt to combine neural networks and evolutionary algorithms to optimize pricing policies was done by Shakya and co-authors (2012). The authors introduced the design of an NN-based demand model and the use evolutionary algorithms to optimize policy over this model. Two key benefits of this approach were reported. First, the use of MM provided the necessary flexibility to model a range of different demand scenarios occurring within different products and services. Secondly, the use of a genetic algorithm made it versatile enough to solve very complex models. The results showed that their model was more consistent, adapted well to a range of different scenarios, and found more accurate pricing policies than other models.

Mitra (2012) published a study showing that the Black and Scholes formula for theoretical pricing of options exhibits certain systematic biases. Past studies attempted to reduce these biases by incorporating correction mechanisms for the data used as inputs. Among all nonparametric approaches used to improve accuracy of the BS model, Artificial Neural Networks were found to be the most promising alternative. Mitra's study made an attempt to improve the accuracy of option price estimation using ANNs with adjusted input parameters (using suitable multipliers). The adjustment factors were determined by a process that minimized the valuation errors.

Chen and Sutcliffe (2012) compared the performance of ANNs with that of the modified Black model in both pricing and hedging short sterling options. By using high-frequency data, both standard and hybrid ANNs were trained to generate option prices. The study showed that hybrid ANNs are "significantly superior to both the modified Black model and the standard ANN in pricing call and put options." The performance of hedge ratios from ANNs directly trained on actual hedge ratios was significantly superior to those based on a pricing model and to the modified Black model. Finally the article by Park, Kim, and Lee (2014) provides an excellent overview of the literature on parametric models and nonparametric machine learning models for option pricing.

In conclusion it should be noted that most of the well-established nonparametric models have one thing in common: they are calibrated using supervised learning techniques. As many of the studies mentioned previously have shown, this approach could work very well in a variety of scenarios. But one has to be aware of the fact that there are some disadvantages to this approach as well. First off, in order to come up with a good model, in general a large amount of data is required for training. This makes the process applicable just for financial assets or markets where there is enough historical data provided by an active and liquid derivatives market. Secondly, if the historical market data contains biases, the valuation model is likely to learn them as well.

10.3   USING DEEP LEARNING FOR VALUATION OF DERIVATIVES

Analytically tractable solutions to the derivatives pricing problem are known for just a small subset of derivative products and they are generally based on rather stringent assumptions. Practitioners are frequently resorting to the use of numerical approximation techniques. The most common approaches rely on using Monte Carlo simulations (Broadie and Glasserman 1997; Longstaff and Schwartz 2001) or Dynamic Programming (Ben-Ameur et al. 2007), which is an ingenious technique to relate the fair price of a derivative to the optimal value function of a Markov Decision Process (MDP).

But even purely numerical techniques could be quite restrictive in their usage. As an example, Monte Carlo methods would require the knowledge of the probability distribution of the state space in order to generate random samples from which they can extract their fair price estimates. In order to determine the optimal value, Dynamic Programming methods would require the explicit knowledge of the transition probabilities for the associated Markov Decision Process.

Fortunately there is a more efficient method to address this problem that is a model-free, data-driven approach that is using Machine Learning. The general appeal of ML algorithms, especially Neural Networks, comes from their ability to be universal function approximators. If one considers an option as a functional mapping between the contracted terms (inputs) and the premium of the option (output), one could use NN to infer this relationship based on empirical data. Feeding a large enough data sample into a powerful NN algorithm will generate a functional mapping between the inputs and the outputs therefore inferring a model for the problem at hand.

The objective of this section is to illustrate the application of Deep Learning to the problem of valuation of derivatives by tapping into the most recently published literature. The main study to be referenced in this section (Ferguson and Green 2018) was written by two market practitioners and it responds to the need to address the derivatives valuation from a model-free data-driven perspective. The authors proposed the use of the Deep Learning methodology to value an option call on a basket of stocks. Their results suggest that this new methodology could yield very accurate and fast results, according to the authors, "capable of producing valuations a million times faster than traditional models."

The use of computationally complex models is a common practice in modern finance. This is especially true in the field of derivative products, where complex and computationally expensive valuation adjustments are becoming increasingly important. The classical approach used to cope with these computational challenges is to develop approximations for these hard-to-compute valuation functions. Approximation Theory methods such as the Chebyshev interpolation have been applied to XVA models where trades are valued in the context of a Monte Carlo simulation. The advent of Deep Neural Networks and its successful applications in computer vision and image recognition has been a catalyst for new ideas in the field of Quantitative Finance. For almost two decades financial quantitative researchers and academics have suggested that neural networks may be successfully used to learn option pricing models directly from the markets. The recent wave of interest in the deep version of NN has attracted a lot of interest from the financial industry, specifically when it comes to the use of universal nonlinear function approximators.

What really makes the Deep Neural Networks more attractive than the standard econometric models? The most plausible answer is that DNNs deal reasonably well with nonlinearities. The majority of econometric models are either linear functions or just simple transformations of linear functions. In practice, however, the relationship between inputs and outputs are profoundly nonlinear. This is where DNNs could be very proficient at modeling nonlinearities. As the input data is transformed from one layer of the network to the next, nonlinearity gets filtered away. Using this approach one could learn almost any function to a high degree of accuracy. This ability to detect and isolate nonlinearities makes DNN a very interesting candidate for a wide range of applications in Finance, derivatives valuation being just one of them.

According to Ferguson and Green (2018), Deep Neural Networks present a series of major advantages to more classical methods when it comes to approximating nonlinear functions. The most important advantage of using DNNs is the universality aspect of the approximation, in the sense that feedforward networks could encode almost any variety of functional dependency under very relaxed assumptions about the activation function to be used by the network. Another advantage is that DNNs could address independently the demand for accuracy from the computation speed requirements (valuation time). DNNs are also ideal candidates for functional approximators because they are not impacted by the curse of dimensionality. Therefore their use does not impose any limitations on the size input parameter space.

10.3.1 Implementation Methodology

Ferguson and Green illustrated in their study a practical example for the use of DNNs to the problem of derivatives valuation. The authors introduced a Deep Neural Network that could learn to price a European call option on a worst-of basket with six underlying stocks. This option valuation is done traditionally by using a Monte Carlo simulation under the assumption that each of the stocks follows a geometric Brownian motion.

This simple example was introduced for two very practical reasons:

- The dimensionality of the valuation function is at a reasonable level. For a basket of n = 6 stocks, the number of input parameters is 28 leading to a 28-dimensional input space: 6 stock prices, 6 volatilities, 1 time-to-expiration and 15 correlations.
- To test the viability of using DNNs versus the more computationally intensive Monte Carlo simulation.

The authors used Monte Carlo simulation to generate random sets of training data [$x(i)$, $y(i)$]. All parameters were generated independently with the distribution selected individually for each parameter. The choice of the sampling distribution was considered to be a very important aspect of the data generation process and it was made on a case-by-case basis. The parameters were sampled independently and randomly, with the exception of correlation matrices, which were handled separately. As such a lognormal distribution was used for the six stock prices, whereas for volatility and expiry uniform distributions were employed. The correlation matrices were sampled from a β-distribution using a C-vine method (Lewandowski, Kurowicka, and Joe 2009).

The process started by randomly generating a set of parameters. Then the function to be approximated was called to generate a value. By using this approach a large number of training samples could be created. In spite of the fact that this process could be computationally intensive (the derivative valuation function is called many times) this process needs to run just once for the initial training of the model. Because the training examples are independent, the procedure could be readily parallelized.

The selection of a representative data set is central to the success to learning process, because the primary goal of the Deep Learning model is to minimize the error between its estimates and that of the training data that it's presented with. Another important consideration relates to the nature of the function being learned. As a result, more training data needs to be fed to regions where the function values are more volatile (change more rapidly). As such the authors generated more data for short dated maturities since the convexity of the basket option valuation function is greatest for at the money short dated options. Three different training data sets were generated, ranging from several millions to several hundreds of millions of examples and Monte Carlo paths. It took approximately a week of computer time to generate each of these three data sets.

The weights of the models were initialized using a pseudo-random number generator. They were sampled either from a uniform or standard normal distribution. The models were then trained in mini-batch sizes of 50,000 samples. The test set, which consisted of 5,000 samples, was drawn randomly from a separate set of highly accurate MC-generated data (~100mm paths) used only for testing. The authors reported that by using a 24-core AMD server they computed the values for the test set in a little more than a week by fully using all of the cores. The use of 100 million Monte Carlo paths yielded an accuracy of about 1%. However, the valuation time for a single option was about 300 seconds, making it impractical for a production environment. For a reduced accuracy of 5% (using just 1 million MC paths) or 20% (100k paths) the valuation time was a lot more acceptable (i.e. one hour and 45 minutes, or 10 minutes, respectively). All models were trained using an Adam optimizer.

Different network architectures with six hidden layers were used. The models were differentiated by the training set used and by the number of nodes used in each hidden layer. Each hidden layer used a ReLU activation function with the exception of the final output layer, where a simple linear function was employed to generate a real valued output. The first experiment used models trained with the first training set (A). The largest network employed (with about 600 nodes per layer) yielded negative results due to overfitting. For this example the out-of-sample performance was "materially worse than that of the smaller models." The second data set (B) was used to train the second set of models. These models used 400, 600, 1,200, 1,400, and 1,600 nodes per layer. The final set of experiments were conducted with training models with the same number of neurons per layer as case B, but using the third training set C, with only 10,000 Monte Carlo paths.

10.3.2 Empirical Results

One of the most significant results reported by this study was that the use of larger training data sets while employing Monte Carlo noise in each training example has yielded significantly better results. The explanation offered by the authors was that employing a much broader (noisier) distribution of the Monte Carlo scenarios through the model domain is in effect much more beneficial to reducing overfitting as opposed to just concentrating on generating highly accurate training data via Monte Carlo. Feeding more data into larger models could lead to successful training before overfitting sets in.

Another key observation was that the test results were of better quality compared to the training results. This is an indication of the fact that "the DNN models have learned to average out the numerical noise associated with the lower-quality training data." The authors conclude that "the best approach may be obtained by using single Monte Carlo paths directly."

10.3.2.1 *Benchmarks*

The authors benchmarked their DNN approach against a classical Monte Carlo valuation method using QuantLib. The Monte Carlo valuation method required about 10 minutes to complete its calculations using all 24 cores of an AMD server. On the other hand, the Deep Learning inference results needed less than 6 milliseconds to compute on an NVIDIA GTX 1080ti GPU.

The whole process could be broken down into the three key phases:

- Generation of the training set
- Training the DNN
- Final inference step

The authors generated three training data sets, balancing off the size of the data set against the number of Monte Carlo scenarios per sample (quality of data). Each dataset took approximately 1 week to generate using all 24 cores of an AMD server. The complexity of the training phase is a function of the number of layers, the nodes per layer, the size of the training set, the size of mini-batch, and the learning rate. The time needed to train the models introduced in this study was anywhere between three hours and one week. The time necessary to generate the training data set and to train the model could be considered as one-off costs. One could compare these phases to the time spent developing traditional models.

From a practical perspective the inference time, or the time necessary for a trained model to return a valuation, is the only time one needs to be concerned about. This time varies with the size of the model:

- For less complex architectures (e.g. 6 layers with 300 nodes per layer) the authors reported that more than 20,000 valuations could be returned in parallel in less than 50 microseconds.
- For more complex architectures (e.g. 6 layers with 1400 nodes per layer) 50,000 valuations could be returned in less than 6 milliseconds.

10.3.3   Conclusions and Future Directions

Ferguson and Green (2018) demonstrated that DNNs can be successfully used to generate highly accurate derivatives valuations for a basket of options. Their models were able to compute valuations approximately one million times faster than traditional Monte Carlo models. The authors developed a unique methodology to generate a training data set. Their main finding was that using small numbers of Monte Carlo paths in the training set could be very effective because the neural network learns to "average out the random error component of the Monte Carlo model found in the training set."

The authors also suggested the exploration of other important aspects of the valuation problem, such as:

- Scaling the dimensionality of the derivatives pricing model.
- Developing scoring techniques to determine the suitability of the trained model to input data being applied.
- Using DNNs to approximate both valuation model and model calibration steps.
- Using DNNs to accelerate derivative valuations for XVA.
- Exploring the impact of the mini-batch size. Smaller mini-batches allow GPU memory to be used for other purposes, such as building larger models.

10.3.4   Other Research Studies

Stark (2017) has recently defended a thesis on the subject of "Machine Learning and Options Pricing: A Comparison of Black-Scholes and a Deep Neural Network in Pricing and Hedging DAX 30 Index Options." This work provides a comparison of the pricing and hedging performance of a Deep Neural Network model with the classical Black-Scholes model. In this study the author applied the DNN methodology to a data set of daily closing prices of DAX 30 call options for the time period between 2013 and 2017, for a total of 1,231 days.

The data set used contains a total of 668 different call options with 25 different strike prices. The total number of observed options prices was very large (>130,000). The proposed model was a *Multilayer Perceptron* with four hidden layers, and it was implemented using the Theano library (widely used in Deep Learning applications). The sizes of the hidden layers were 100, 80, 60, and 40, respectively, and all neurons in the hidden layers were using the logistic sigmoid as the activation function. The output layer consisted of one neuron which used the SoftPlus as the activation function. The optimization algorithm used was stochastic gradient descent with a mini-batch size of 128. The number of training epochs (i.e. iterations) was 1,000.

The principal conclusion of this study was that a properly trained DNN would exhibit superior performance in pricing and delta hedging European-style call options than the classical Black-Scholes model. The pricing performance was measured as both mean error and root mean squared error, and the delta hedging performance was measured as the total value of the dynamic delta hedging portfolio at the expiration of the option contract. The author presented a detailed analysis of the pricing performance at different moneyness levels and maturity times. The results revealed that Black-Scholes outperforms the neural network model in pricing short-maturity options at all moneyness levels. But for medium- and long-dated options, the pricing performance of the neural network is far superior to BS especially for out-of-the money options, and this result is consistent with previous reports from the literature.

In another recently published study by Culkin and Das (2007), a fully connected feedforward DNN was used to reproduce the Black and Scholes option pricing formula to a high degree of accuracy. The authors investigated the applicability of DNN to option valuation problems and tried to revisit the original problem that Hutchinson and collaborators examined in their seminal 1994 paper (Hutchinson, Lo, and Poggio 1994). They suggested the use of a much larger neural network than the one used by Hutchinson more than two decades ago.

The advantage of using neural networks with many layers is the ability to capture subtle nonlinearities in the data that were not possible with more or less linear statistical approaches. Although this fact was known in 1994, the adequate compute technology was not available at that time. Nowadays progress in hardware acceleration has rendered this problem computable, so that training a DNN on high-performance CPUs, GPUs, and other specialized hardware is absolutely feasible. These DNNs currently provide remarkable performance on tasks such as language translation, image recognition, self-driving cars, etc.

The authors have reported on the details of the DNN architecture they have used:

- The input space had 6 parameters.
- Four hidden layers of 100 neurons each were used. The neurons at each layer were chosen based on different activation functions that are LeakyReLU, ELU, ReLU, and ELU respectively.

- The final output layer consisted of a single output neuron which we set to be the standard exponential function (the output to be non-negative).

In order to counter overfitting, a dropout rate of 25% was used for each hidden layer. The loss function used for optimization was the Mean-Squared error (MSE) and a batch size of 64 was used with 10 epochs. The entire exercise resulted in fitting a total of more than 31,000 weights for the DNN model. The model was trained using Google's TensorFlow package. An RMS error of 0.0112 for the in-sample results has been reported (all the strike prices were normalized to $1). The average percentage pricing error (error divided by option price) was 0.0420, or about 4%. For the out-of-sample results both the RMS error and the average percentage pricing error were very similar to the results obtained from training. Therefore no overfitting was evidenced. Another observation was that moneyness was not correlated with the pricing error. Their results showed that simple DNN architectures could learn to price options very accurately and efficiently.

10.4   USING RL FOR VALUATION OF DERIVATIVES

This section will illustrate the use of Reinforcement Learning in solving the derivatives valuation problem in a data-driven, model-free fashion. Two research papers will be discussed.

10.4.1   Using a Simple Markov Decision Process

Grassl (2010) published a paper where he has formulated a novel solution for finding the fair price of a derivative. By using a simple Markov Decision Process (MDP) the author suggested the equivalence between its optimal value function and the derivative's fair price function. This formulation is equivalent to translating the derivatives pricing problem in terms of a Reinforcement Learning MDP problem by using the *Kernel-Based Reinforcement Learning* algorithm. Analytically tractable fair price models are available for just a small subset of derivatives and are generally based on rather strict assumptions. The world of practitioners usually turns to numerical approximation techniques in order to estimate the fair price of a derivative contract. In a Reinforcement Learning (RL) setting both the state space and the transition probabilities are used in an implicit manner as the learning is based on trajectory samples from the MDP. The biggest promise of RL is that one could learn a pricing model directly from market data without making any assumptions that the underlying's price follows a specific price process. Hopefully one of the biggest drawbacks of classic derivatives pricing methods could be therefore overcome.

10.4.1.1   *Implementation Methodology*
The author showed that the fair price of a specific derivative could be determined by learning the optimal value function of a simple Markov Decision process. In order

to generalize this methodology to any derivative, and avoid models that are product specific, the author defined an enhanced state as the tuple (state, parametrization) that defines a bijective (one-to-one) relationship between a given derivative and its parametrization. Trading processes could be represented as finite MDPs. As market participants need to act only at discrete times (when new information becomes available), prices and quantities could only change in discrete increments and the action space in the MDP consists of only two choices, sell and buy. But as the dimensions of the MDP could grow very rapidly, the problem may quickly become computationally impractical.

To avoid this possibility the authors made the assumption that trading happens in a continuous MDP state space. It is generally very difficult to generalize finite state RL algorithms to the continuous state case. Instead, the use of RL in continuous state space often attempts to approximate the optimal value function directly from a given sample of trajectories from the MDP. One such approach is called Kernel-Based Reinforcement Learning (Ormoneit and Sen 2002). The study by Grassl showed that finding the approximate value function of an exact, continuous MDP is the equivalent of finding the exact value function of an approximate, finite MDP while still maintaining the same convergence guarantees. Applying this approach essentially translates to interpreting the samples of a high-dimensional discrete MDP as samples from a continuous MDP that could be solved by approximating it with a simpler discrete MDP.

10.4.1.2 Empirical Results

Grassl (2010) implemented a version of the Kernel-Based Reinforcement Learning algorithm by using a Euclidian distance metric d and a Gaussian kernel φ. Initial numerical experiments showed that the function approximation was consistently overestimating the fair price for out-of-the money options. This observation translates into the fact that high prices from far away regions of the state space could be propagated through to regions where the option is nearly worthless. This problem was due to the choice of the Euclidian distance metric. These initial results were improved by modifying the distance function d such that its contours were egg-shaped curves tilted toward smaller values of $\sigma\sqrt{(T\text{-}t)}$. This change greatly improved the quality of the model. Learning was based on data from 1,000 randomly generated European calls and about 11,000 randomly generated transitions. The returns of the underlying prices were sampled from a log-normal distribution and the spot prices of the derivatives were assumed to be equal to the exact Black-Scholes price. The resulting RMS error of this approximation corresponded to less than 2 cents in absolute $ value, which could be considered a promising result. The model's behavior was consistent across successive runs that used different initializations of the random number generator. The work by Grassl showed how the derivatives pricing problem could be represented by a Markov Decision process for which RL techniques can readily be applied. The algorithm proposed by Grassl's version of Kernel-Based Reinforcement Learning yielded encouraging results on a simple test problem – pricing a vanilla European call option.

10.4.2   The Q-Learning Black-Scholes Model (QLBS)

In several recently published papers, Halperin (2017, 2018) reported the use of a risk-adjusted Markov Decision process that was applied to a discrete-time version of the classical Black-Scholes-Merton model. In this model the option price was the optimal Q-function while the optimal hedge was the second argument of this optimal Q-function. The pricing of the option was done by "learning to dynamically optimize risk-adjusted returns for an option replicating portfolio" in a similar fashion to the Markowitz portfolio theory. The remarkable conclusion of this paper is that once the Q-Learning model is created in a parametric setting, it will able to perform model-free and learn to price and hedge the option "directly from data generated from a dynamic replicating portfolio which is rebalanced at discrete time intervals."

In a risk-averse BSM-like setting, given enough training data the suggested Q-Learner will always converge to the true BS price and to the hedge ratio of the option in the continuous time limit $\Delta t \to 0$. According to Halperin, in spite of randomly generated hedges at the stage of data generation, the Q-Learner will always converge because it is an off-policy algorithm. The reason that Q-learning is an off-policy algorithm is that it estimates the total discounted future reward (return) for state-action pairs assuming a greedy policy was followed despite the fact that it's not following a greedy policy. In other words, it updates its Q-values using the Q-value of the next state and the next *action*. By contrast, Sarsa which is an on-policy algorithm, updates its Q-values using the Q-value of the next state and the *current policy's* action. It estimates the return for state-action pairs assuming the current policy continues to be followed.

If the conditions were different from a BSM-like world, the Q-Learner would perform as well as before, because the Q-Learning is a model-free algorithm. For finite time steps Δt the Q-Learner is able to efficiently calculate in a model-free fashion both the optimal hedge and optimal price of the option directly from trading data. This is a convincing example of the fact that Reinforcement Learning could provide efficient data-driven and model-free methods for optimal pricing and hedging of options in a discrete time setting. The suggested Q-Learning model is both simple and tractable by using just basic Linear Algebra and Monte Carlo simulation for generating synthetic data.

10.4.2.1   *Implementation Methodology*

Extending the BSM model to a discrete-time setting was extensively studied and reported in the literature. Halperin re-formulated some of this research and encoded it as a risk-adjusted Markov Decision Process (MDP) problem. Within this new formulation, an option seller is modeled as an agent that hedges its risk in the option by trading in the underlying stock at discrete times. The author calls this model the QLBS model. This model is based on the Q-Learning method introduced by Watkins. This algorithm computes both the optimal price and the optimal hedge in a time-discretized BS model directly from data.

The author derived the Bellman optimality equation for the action-value function of the QLBS model and then presented its solution using a backward-recursion

Value Iteration Dynamic Programming (DP) method, which could be used when the model parameters are known. This procedure generated both the optimal hedge and optimal option price of the QLBS model that converge to their respective BSM values in the strict continuous-time limit $\Delta t \rightarrow 0$. An interesting observation made by Halperin was that the normally labor-intensive policy optimization step for the DP backward recursion method could be done analytically in the QLBS model, due to a particularly simple (quadratic) form of a proper objective function arising in this optimization problem. For situations where the QLBS dynamics is unknown, Reinforcement Learning could be used to learn the optimal hedge and price directly from trading data for a dynamic hedge portfolio. Solving the Bellman optimality equation could be done without any knowledge of model's dynamics but relying solely on sample data. An important note is that the suggested QLBS model could be formulated either as a continuous-state or a discrete-state model, the latter being a finite-state approximation for the former. While continuous-state financial models are more relevant to practitioners, the discrete-state models are easier to interpret.

For benchmarking purposes the author generated data by means of MC simulation of stock price history, actions (re-hedges) that implement the risk-minimization strategies, and all risk-adjusted returns associated with these strategies. The simulated data was then fed into a Q-Learner that was tasked to finding the best hedging (risk minimization) strategy directly from the data, without requiring any knowledge about the dynamics or the hedge strategy that generated the data. The simulation process also included randomization of actions. As an example the author generated sometimes actions that corresponded to suboptimal hedges. The goal was to task the Q-Learner with finding the best hedging strategy, specifically using data generated associated with suboptimal strategies. In a real trading environment a straightforward application of this process would be to feed both historical market data and a specific trading strategy to a Q-Learner agent that will be tasked to improve the outcomes of the strategy. Off-policy algorithms like Q-Learning are very efficient at learning an optimal policy even when the data used for training was generated in accordance with a suboptimal policy. The suggested framework is truly general and can be extended to more complex multi-asset portfolios. The QLBS model represents one of the most recent contributions to the literature on hedging and pricing in incomplete markets. Unlike most of the previous models on hedging and pricing, the QLBS provides consistent hedging and pricing (in the same model) at each time step, by using an efficient, model-free data-driven Q-Learning algorithm.

10.4.2.2 Conclusions

The QLBS model introduced by Halperin (2017, 2018) represents one of the most recent attempts to model derivatives pricing using Reinforcement Learning. The author's goal was to develop a model for derivatives pricing "that would implement the principle of hedging first and pricing second in a consistent way for a discrete-time version of the classical Black-Scholes-Merton model." An optimal Action-Value Q-function was devised to perform the tasks of hedging and pricing by learning. Based on this Q-function both hedging option pricing are determined simultaneously.

By stepping aside from the academic setting of $\Delta t \to 0$, the QLBS model achieves model independence through the use of Q-Learning. The author's original goal was to develop a BSM-like simulated environment in a simple discrete-time and -space setting that could eventually be used for pedagogical purposes to explain RL algorithms such as Q-Learning. From this perspective the QLBS model could potentially be used for benchmarking other RL algorithms (e.g. Policy Gradient methods, Actor-Critic algorithms, or Deep Reinforcement Learning) in simulated environments.

The QLBS model is in many respects a much simpler mathematical representation than the continuous-time BSM model, which involves non-elementary functions such as cumulative normal distributions of composite arguments. The QLBS model involves only Linear Algebra concepts and finite sums, and both hedge and price are contained in the same formula as opposed to two different ones in the BSM model. The famous Black-Scholes formula could be re-created using the QLBS model by feeding data generated by random strategies into a Deep Neural Network to approximate the value function for very small-time steps. This approach does not require the use of any Partial Differential Equations.

Besides its mathematical simplicity QLBS could be used to price and hedge options directly from data without the need to know anything about the process dynamics or the nature of the hedge strategy employed. A complex problem such as the volatility smile that is an important matter in the BSM world is solved implicitly by QLBS, due to Q-Learning and reliance on data instead of a model. The term *volatility smile* is just a label given by market practitioners to a specific pattern in the option data. Unlike the classical BSM model that is rooted in Ito's calculus, the QLBS model is grounded in Dynamic Programming and Reinforcement Learning and exploits the convergence properties of Q-Learning to establish its own convergence to the classical BSM model in the academic limit $\Delta t \to 0$.

REFERENCES

Amilon (2003). A neural network versus Black-Scholes: A comparison of pricing and hedging performances. *Journal of Forecasting* 22 (4): 317–335.

Anders, Korn, and Schmitt (1996), Improving the pricing of options: A neural network approach. *ZEW Discussion Papers* no. 96-104. https://www.econstor.eu/bitstream/10419/29448/1/257772065.pdf.

Ben-Ameur, Breton, Karoui et al. (2007). A dynamic programming approach for pricing options embedded in bonds. *Journal of Economic Dynamics and Control* 31 (7): 2212–2233.

Bennell and Sutcliffe (2004). Black-Scholes versus artificial neural networks in pricing FTSE100 options. *Intelligent Systems in Accounting, Finance and Management* 12 (4): 243–260.

Black and Scholes (1972). The valuation of option contracts and a test of market efficiency. *Journal of Finance* 27 (2): 399–417.

Black and Scholes (1973). The pricing of options and corporate liabilities. *Journal of Political Economy* 81 (3): 637–654.

Broadie and Glasserman (1997). Pricing American-style securities using simulation. *Journal of Economic Dynamics and Control* 21 (8–9): 1323–1352.

Brummelhuis and Luo (2017). CDS rate construction methods by machine learning techniques. https://ssrn.com/abstract=2967184.

Chen and Sutcliffe (2012). Pricing and hedging short sterling options using neural networks. *Intelligent Systems in Accounting, Finance and Management* 19: 128–149.

Culkin and Das (2017). Machine learning in finance: The case of deep learning for option pricing. https://srdas.github.io/Papers/BlackScholesNN.pdf.

Ferguson and Green (2018). Deeply learning derivatives. https://arxiv.org/abs/1809.02233.

Gradojevic, Gencay, and Kukolj (2009). Option pricing with modular neural networks. *IEEE Transactions on Neural Networks* 20 (4): 626–637.

Grassl (2010). A reinforcement learning approach for pricing derivatives. http://cs229.stanford.edu/proj2010/Grassl-AReinforcementLearningApproachForPricingDerivatives.pdf.

Green (2015). *XVA: Credit, Funding and Capital Valuation Adjustments*. Wiley, 25–194.

Halperin (2017). QLBS: Q-learner in the Black-Scholes-Merton worlds. https://arxiv.org/abs/1712.04609.

Halperin (2018). QLBS: Q-learner goes NuQLear: Fitted Q iteration, Inverse RL and options portfolios. https://arxiv.org/pdf/1801.06077.pdf.

Hanke (1999). Neural networks vs. Black/Scholes: An empirical comparison of two fundamentally different option pricing methods. *Journal of Computational Intelligence in Finance* 7 (1): 26–34.

Hornik, Stinchcombe, and White (1989). Multilayer feedforward networks are universal approximators. *Neural Networks* 2 (5): 359–366.

Hutchinson, Lo, and Poggio (1994). A nonparametric approach to pricing and hedging derivative securities via learning networks. *Journal of Finance* 49 (3): 851–889.

Lewandowski, Kurowicka, and Joe (2009). Generating random correlation matrices based on vines and extended onion method. *Journal of Multivariate Analysis* 100 (9): 1989–2001.

Longstaff and Schwartz (2001). Valuing American options by simulation: A simple least-squares approach. *Review of Financial Studies* 14 (1): 113–147.

Malliaris and Salchenberger (1993). A neural network model for estimating option prices. *Applied Intelligence* 3 (3): 193–206.

Mitra (2012). An option pricing model that combines neural network approach and Black Scholes formula. *Global Journal of Computer Science and Technology* 12 (4): 6–16.

Morelli, Montagna, Nicrosini et al. (2004). Pricing financial derivatives with neural networks. *Physica A: Statistical Mechanics and its Applications* 338 (1–2): 160–165.

Ormoneit and Sen (2002). Kernel-based reinforcement learning. *Machine Learning* 49 (2–3): 161–178.

Park, Kim, and Lee (2014). Parametric models and non-parametric machine learning models for predicting option prices: Empirical comparison study over KOSPI 200 Index options. *Expert Systems with Applications* 41 (11): 5227–5237.

Shakya, Kern, Owusu et al. (2012). Neural network demand models and evolutionary optimizers for dynamic pricing. *Knowledge-Based Systems* 29: 44–53.

Stark (2017). Machine learning and options pricing: A comparison of Black-Scholes and a deep neural network in pricing and hedging DAX 30 index options. http://urn.fi/URN:NBN:fi:aalto-201803281865.

Trippi and Turban (1992). *Neural Networks in Finance and Investing: Using Artificial Intelligence to Improve Real World Performance*. McGraw-Hill.

Wang and Lin (2009). The political uncertainty and stock market behavior in emerging democracy: The case of Taiwan. *Quality and Quantity* 43 (2): 237–248.

Watkins (1989). Learning from delayed rewards. PhD thesis. Kings College, Cambridge, England. https://www.cs.rhul.ac.uk/home/chrisw/new_thesis.pdf.

Watkins and Dayan (1992). Q-learning. *Machine Learning* 8 (3–4): 179–192.

Yao, Li, and Tan (2000). Option price forecasting using neural networks. *OMEGA: International Journal of Management Science* 28 (4): 455–466.

Zhang, Hui, and Jiang (2010). Study on option pricing by applying hybrid wavelet networks and genetic algorithm. *Journal of Systems Engineering* 25 (1): 43–49.

CHAPTER 11

Case Study 6: Using Machine Learning for Risk Management and Compliance

"With the advent of big data and the ability to link much more data than we could have years ago, it should now be possible to know in advance when risks are emerging."

– Oliver Maspfuhl, Commerzbank

11.1 INTRODUCTION TO THE PROBLEM

Although the declared objective of this book is to illustrate the applicability of Computational Intelligence to Data-Driven decision-making in trading, I have used consistently the label Machine Learning throughout as a proxy term for CI. Machine Learning represents today the most advanced and the most applicable component of Computational Intelligence in solving practical problems in Quantitative and Computational Finance. The great promise of applying Computational Intelligence techniques to this problem domain is about increasing profits and operational efficiencies, through automation, innovation, and pattern discovery. At the same time one should acknowledge the emergence of a series of practical limitations that could constitute significant barriers to a widespread adoption of CI by the financial industry. These limitations are related to the availability and quality of data, to an insufficient understanding of technology risks, as well as to regulatory constraints and the need to transform the corporate culture.

11.1.1 Challenges

According to a recent Deloitte study, the biggest challenge for financial firms "is less about dealing with completely new types of risks and more about existing risks either being harder to identify in an effective and timely manner or manifesting themselves in unfamiliar ways" (Bigham et. al. 2018). One of the biggest challenges in adopting ML technologies is the understanding and the interpretation of relationships between the data driving the models and the value and the quality of the outcome. ML algorithms continuously learn from new data, and make decisions which are driven by complex statistical methods, rather than by predefined or clearly interpretable rules. The use of modern ML techniques could render auditability and traceability very challenging. At the same time the speed at which the outcomes of models could evolve may result in large scale, sometimes catastrophic errors. Nevertheless the potential to deploy Machine Learning technology as a tool to support Risk Management, Compliance, and Supervision could become a real game changer for the financial industry. The last financial crisis was a manifestation of the failure to forecast, detect, and deal with important sources of systemic risk. But nowadays the ability of modern ML technology to detect patterns and anomalies in large data sets has become the tool of choice to better protect the integrity of the financial system. The rising complexity of the financial markets coupled with an increased technological sophistication of trading and processing activities has driven the interest of market practitioners to apply the most current ML-based technologies to fundamental business problems. The most important drivers are boosting profits, coping with new regulations, cutting costs, and improving operational efficiencies.

Nevertheless, applying the paradigm of Machine Learning in Risk Management remains a work in progress and a considerable business challenge. "Risk management will profit greatly from the opportunity to use more data sources than in the past, because the complex dependencies between events have always been notoriously difficult to quantify. But with the advent of big data and the ability to link much more data than we could have years ago, it should now be possible to know in advance when risks are emerging from high dependencies in the system and then mitigate such risks," said Oliver Maspfuhl, from the Credit risk and Capital management group at Commerzbank (O'Hara and Clark 2017). Some of the most promising applications of Machine Learning are related to cybersecurity and market surveillance, which are two topics of particular interest to market practitioners and regulators. The need to protect from cyber-intrusion and to monitor internal staff activity has increased dramatically during the last decade. Both domains require a real-time monitoring of extremely large volumes of data, and this process could benefit from the use of ML technology. The application of ML to financial data offers a multitude of possible use cases: from alpha-seeking through order-book data mining, to cybersecurity and market surveillance. Nevertheless the technical infrastructure required by ML remains a major barrier of entry for a large segment of the financial industry, specifically because this new technology requires a sophisticated data infrastructure and considerable computing power that is still not widely available today to the majority of financial firms.

The technology infrastructure required for the usage of Machine Learning techniques could be classified into two main categories:

- *Data storage* and *retrieval* – it generally demands very large volumes of disk space for data storage.
- *Compute power* – that is required to train ML systems on large amounts of data and in reasonable amounts of time.

One of the most critical aspects that financial firms are considering when applying Machine Learning methods to their Risk Management and Compliance needs, is whether they could afford to hold all of the necessary data within their own infrastructure or alternatively to use commercial-grade cloud-based infrastructure. Despite the proliferation of cloud-based services, most financial firms are still reluctant about storing sensitive client and transactional information outside their premises. This reluctance could become a major impediment in the effective adoption of ML, as in some cases it would be practically impossible to store all of the data needed internally without outsourcing it to a third-party cloud provider. Reservations about cloud-based data storage are not strictly related to just data security but also to data accessibility when needed. Financial firms cannot afford to give up control over their data if they choose to store it in the cloud. As the data requirements for more advanced ML algorithms, such as Deep Learning, are becoming more demanding, financial firms may soon be forced to commit all their data storage and computer infrastructure to external vendors, incurring significant capital investments, and generating potential accessibility and security implications.

11.1.2   The Problem

How to understand and control financial risk through the use of ML-driven solutions? This formulation covers a wide spectrum of problems, from deciding how much a bank should lend to a customer (credit risk), to providing warning signals to traders about market risk, and from detecting customer and insider fraud (operational risk), to improving compliance and reducing model risk (regulatory compliance risk). This chapter will present a series of case studies related to the applicability of ML to financial risk management by category of risk: credit risk, market risk, operational risk, and regulatory risk.

11.2   CURRENT STATE-OF-THE-ART FOR APPLICATIONS OF ML TO RISK MANAGEMENT AND COMPLIANCE

11.2.1   Credit Risk

Credit risk is defined as the exposure to a potential loss that could arise from the failure of a counterparty to fulfill its contractual obligations or from an increased risk of default during the term of the transaction. Financial firms have traditionally employed classical linear or logistic regression techniques to model credit risk (Altman and

Edward 1968). The practice of credit risk demonstrated that traditional statistical methods do not provide a rigorous approach to model this type of risk. The advent of modern ML methods raised the hope that credit risk management capabilities could be significantly improved through leveraging the ability of the algorithms to gain a semantic understanding of unstructured data. The use of ML to model credit risk dates back to 1994 when Altman and collaborators performed the first comparative analysis between traditional statistical methods of distress and bankruptcy prediction and a Neural Network algorithm. Their conclusion was that a combined approach of the two methods could significantly improve the accuracy of credit risk models (Altman, Marco, and Varetto 1994).

The globalization and technological sophistication of modern financial markets increased the complexity of assessing credit risk, and these conditions opened the door for the applicability of Machine Learning in this field (Addo, Guegan, and Hassani 2018; Luo, Wu, and Wu 2017; Son et al. 2016; Khandani, Kim, and Lo 2010; Kruppa et al. 2013; Khashman 2010). A typical example is represented by the Credit Default Swaps (CDS) market. Modeling the CDS market comes down to determining the likelihood of a default credit event, as well as estimating the cost of that default in case it happens. This is a very complex problem to model from both a quantitative and computational perspective.

Luo and collaborators (2017) investigated the performance of credit scoring models applied to CDS data sets. The authors evaluated the performance of Deep Belief Networks (DBN) with Restricted Boltzmann Machines and compared it with more popular credit scoring models such as Logistic Regression, Multilayer Perceptron, and Support Vector Machine. They found that the use of DBN yields the best performance. Son and collaborators (2016) used CDS of different maturities and different rating groups to show that Deep Learning models could outperform traditional benchmark models in terms of prediction accuracy.

Other areas of credit risk, such as consumer or small business lending, have to deal with large volumes of data, and there is an increasingly reliance on Machine Learning algorithms to drive better lending decisions. Khandani and collaborators (2010) proposed a technique based on decision trees and SVM that could lead to cost savings of up to 25 percent. Another study by Figini, Bonelli, and Giovannini (2017) showed that a multivariate outlier detection technique using ML could improve credit risk estimation for small businesses lending using data from UniCredit Bank.

11.2.2 Market Risk

Market risk is generated in the process of trading and investing, and it is related to the exposure to financial markets dynamics. A report by Kumar (2018) provides an overview for the use of Machine Learning methods in market risk management. Another report by the Financial Stability Board (2017) titled "Artificial Intelligence and Machine Learning in Financial Services" provides a comprehensive overview of current applications of Machine Learning to Market risk management.

Transacting in the financial markets may also involve the risk that the trading model may be incomplete, obsolete, or just plain wrong. The market risk component is becoming prevalent in today's markets and is generally known as model risk. From this perspective ML is particularly well suited to stress test market models in order to determine unintended or emerging risk in trading behavior. Woodall (2017) published a study where he described a variety of use cases of ML for model validation. He noted that many trading forms and banks are currently using ML techniques to monitor trading within the firm and to ensure that unsuitable assets are not being used in trading models. A technology firm called *yields.io* provides real-time model monitoring, model testing, and validation using ML techniques.

Another area of interest from a market risk perspective is the understanding of the impact that trading in large volumes may have on market pricing. The entirety of Chapter 6 was dedicated to the study of the problem of Market Impact or the Optimized Trade Execution problem. Day (2017) explored how large trading firms are using ML clustering techniques to optimize the costs of execution in illiquid markets. According to this study, up to two thirds of trade profits could be lost due to market impact costs. Two ML techniques are of particular interest: cluster analysis (Cavalcante et al. 2916) and Deep Learning (Heaton, Polson, and Witte 2017).

The family of Reinforcement Learning methods gained a lot of traction recently. The use of RL endows trading algorithms with the ability to learn from market reactions to their actions and thus to adjust future trading decisions to account for how their behavior may impact market prices (Hendricks and Wilcox 2014). Chandrinos proposed a combination of neural networks and decision tree techniques to provide real-time warnings to traders about changes in underlying trading patterns while trading (Chandrinos, Sakkas, and Lagaros 2018). The use of Support Vector Machines techniques was also reported (Olson and Wu 2015) for scenarios that could provide traders with warning signals.

11.2.3   Operational Risk

Operational risk management involves the evaluation of exposure to direct or indirect financial loss emerging from a potential host of operational failures (Moosa 2007).

This category of financial risk could arise from either:

- Failures that are internal to financial institutions, like deficient internal processes, incompetent staff, operational errors, or faulty systems, or
- External factors such as fraud, system security vulnerability, or natural disasters.

Given the increased amount, variety, and complexity of operational risk exposure, Machine Learning has become the preferred methodology to build enterprise solutions to mitigate operational risk (Choi, Chan, and Yue 2017). From a risk management process perspective, ML-based solutions could identify risk exposure by estimating its potential effects (Sanford and Moosa 2015). They could also suggest the appropriate risk mitigation strategy or the instruments that could hedge this risk.

Historically the application of ML techniques in operational risk management started more than a decade ago with the development of algorithms for preventing financial losses due to credit card frauds. Nowadays the use of ML has expanded to new areas such as money laundering detection, which is a very complex process that requires the analysis of large datasets. The use of ML algorithm offers the ability to implement better process automation and thus to accelerate the pace of routine tasks, to minimize human and process errors, to parse unstructured data to detect relevant content, or to map out complex networks of individuals in order to evaluate risky clients. Network analysis techniques could be used to monitor employees and traders. Classical ML methods, such as clustering and classification, could be employed to generate behavioral profiles for traders, based on a combination of trading data, electronic, and voice communications records. All of these data enable financial firms to observe developing patterns of behavior that could eventually facilitate the prediction of latent risks.

11.2.4   Regulatory Compliance Risk and RegTech

One of the most critical consequences of the financial crisis of 2008 was a significant surge in regulatory burden. As a consequence of this post-crisis environment, being in compliance with risk management regulations has become one of the most vital obligations for financial firms. Regulatory compliance has a direct impact on each of the risk functions mentioned above, that is on credit, market, and operational risk. This regulatory load has affected substantially the profitability for financial institutions across the board.

In order to be able to handle these rapidly changing regulations, many firms have turned to RegTech (Arner, Barberis, and Buckley 2016) or regulatory technology, to help mitigate those problems. Prior to the advent of RegTech, regulatory compliance was a heavily manual process, requiring the compliance staff to review alerts related to suspicious activity or anomalies. The compliance personnel was specifically looking for emerging suspicious patterns by applying their expertise and experience to make small, incremental adjustments with the goal to improve the efficiency of the process while staying within the risk tolerance threshold imposed by their firms. This manual approach exhibits multiple shortcomings:

- The rules employed during the process were rather arbitrary and very dependent on staff's expertise and experience.
- It was a very slow changing process involving only incremental changes to rules that were typically spaced months to years apart.
- The process relied mostly on internal expertise and personnel experience and less on technology and automation.

This tediously manual approach often resulted in a significant volume of false positives, which required a nontrivial level of investigation afterwards. The last decade has seen a lot of interest from financial firms to start implementing new RegTech-based solutions. Probably the most prominent category of solutions in the RegTech space is represented by ML supervised algorithms. The use of labeled data on prior alerted activity has made possible the fine-tuning of rules and had the net effect of reducing the number of false positives. Instead of relying on cumbersome periodic reviews, this new methodology created the possibility for supervised ML algorithms to compare current rules and investigatory results and recommend the necessary changes. In the process, financial firms have gained the necessary confidence in this new methodology and the efficiency of refining the rules has increased accordingly. For the financial firms that are operating at the cutting edge of RegTech, employing unsupervised ML algorithms offers even a more promising alternative. The big advantage offered by unsupervised ML algorithms is represented by the lack of bias due to existing rules. ML algorithms are the most effective tools known for identifying new patterns and typologies. As an example, an unsupervised algorithm may identify a subset of transactions that exhibit unusual inconsistencies (like frequencies and amounts), even if no pre-existing rule would have alerted this activity.

It should be noted, however, that ML-based risk solutions are not yet fully mature and their adoption by the financial industry is still a work in progress. To reach their full potential, further research, testing, and technological progress is still required. It is also important to note that RegTech is not intended to fully replace all human involvement in the risk and compliance life cycle. RegTech is an ideal tool set for automation through the reduction and eventually the elimination of low-level, repeatable, manual processes. One of the most significant hurdles in the adoption of RegTech is the shortage of a sufficiently skilled workforce. Financial firms are in need of individuals capable of showing a strong understanding from both a technical and risk and compliance viewpoint.

11.2.5   Current Challenges and Future Directions

There are some significant practical challenges that need to be addressed before Machine Learning techniques could be applied on a large scale to risk management. Probably the most important challenge is represented by the availability of suitable data. Data is generally held in separate silos across departments and systems that face regulatory issues restricting their sharing. Another important issue is the availability of skilled staff to implement these new techniques. Last but not least there are important concerns about the accuracy and interpretability of ML solutions. Financial firms cannot simply deploy off-the-shelf risk management solutions, but they need to create a process requiring a constant evaluation of whether a particular ML solution is considered *best practice*.

When it comes to full automation of risk processes, from data gathering to decision-making, the need for human oversight becomes even more prevalent. The case of Knight Capital from 2012 serves to illustrate this type of risk (Gandel 2012). The use of a *state-of-the-art* automated stock trading set of algorithms resulting in a loss of $440 million in the space of just 45 minutes should be a stark reminder of how important it is to understand and control model risk.

Automating lending and credit risk decisions will require the assurance that such operational risks could be controlled at all times. Transparency is a particularly complex issue for some of the more modern ML techniques like the increasingly popular method of Deep Learning. A black box system of this type could not easily be subject to an effective risk oversight and can cause regulatory compliance issues especially around demonstrating model validity. Nevertheless there is a wide consensus across the financial industry that the time-consuming and costly nature of risk management could be alleviated significantly in the future by the adoption of ML techniques.

11.3   MACHINE LEARNING IN CREDIT RISK MODELING

The advent of modern ML-driven technology has compelled large banks and lending institutions to revamp their business models. As such the monitoring of credit risk and the reliability of its predictive abilities have become key factors in the decision-making process. An impressive amount of research and development resources has been dedicated to credit risk lately.

Addo and collaborators (2018) published a study about the stability of binary classifiers by comparing the performance of tree-based models with multilayer deep neural networks. The authors investigated six different ML approaches: a random forest model, a gradient boosting machine, and four deep learning models using credit data from a European bank.

Random forests is a ML methodology introduced by Leo Breiman (1997, 2000, 2004) with the goal of building a predictor ensemble from a set of decision trees that grows in randomly selected subspaces of data. A random forest is a classifier consisting of a collection of tree-structured classifiers that are parameterized by a set of iid random variables used to determine how the successive cuts are performed when building the individual trees. The accuracy of a random forest method depends on the quality of the individual tree classifiers and the dependency between them.

Gradient boosting is an ML technique applied to both Regression and Classification problems. The outcome is a prediction model that takes the form of an ensemble of weak prediction models, usually decision trees. The model is constructed in a stage-wise fashion using the idea of gradient boosting introduced by Breiman. According to the original paper, boosting could be interpreted as an optimization algorithm on a suitable cost function.

Deep Neural Networks are a family of Neural Networks that are represented by a significant number of hidden layers. The term *Deep Learning* was actually coined in 2006, when unsupervised pre-training of deep learning was made manifest through gradient enhancements and automatic learning rate adjustments while performing stochastic gradient descent optimization. As mentioned in previous chapters, Deep Learning architectures could be of different classes:

- *Convolutional Neural Networks* are standard deep NNs that could be *extended across space* using shared weights.
- *Recurrent Neural Networks* are NNs that could be *extended across time*. The network edges feed into the next time step instead of into the next layer in the same time step.

- *Recursive Neural Networks* are hierarchical networks where inputs have to be processed hierarchically as in a tree (there is no time dimension to the input sequence).

These architectures are mainly using Stochastic Gradient Descent for backpropagation, Regularization for coping with too much variance, and dimensionality reduction (max pooling). In addition to different metrics like the F-score, Recall, and Precision, the authors used several performance measures to compare the performance of the models including AUC, RMSE, Akaike information criterion (AIC), and the Gini index. Introduced by Gastwirth (1972) and extended by Yitzhaki (1983) the Gini index makes it possible to compare the performance of several algorithms. The idea was based on the decision tree methodology and the entropy measure.

11.3.1 Data

Addo and co-authors (2018) used for their analysis a data set containing more than 117,000 records, each one labeling a default binary flag (Y/N) for companies applying for bank loans. Out of this number of data records more than 115,000 records represented companies in good financial health and 1,700 were companies in default (a quite imbalanced data set). The financial health of a company was modeled using a large set of features (235) such as financial statements, balance sheets, income statements, and cash flow statements. After cleaning the data the authors decided to keep 181 features. Then the data was partitioned into three subsets: 60% for training, 20% for cross-validation, and 20% for testing. The training data set was also used to verify how balanced the data were. By using a special data-preparation algorithm, SMOTE (Chawla et al. 2002), a new balanced data set was produced (46% to 53% ratio).

11.3.2 Models

The models employed in the study were ranked with respect to the companies' creditworthiness, by using the ROC curve and the AUC and RMSE criteria. The analysis started with a 181 feature-set and then the first 10 more relevant features were selected for each model. The models were calibrated using the balanced training dataset described above. The following classes of models were considered:

- A *Logistic Regression* model M1 that was using an Elastic Net for regularization ($\alpha=0.5$).
- A *Random Forest* model M2 that was using 120 trees and a stopping criterion of 10^{-3} (if the process converged quicker than expected, the algorithm stopped and used a smaller number of trees).
- A *Gradient Boosting* model M3 employing the logistic binomial log-likelihood function $L(y, f) = \log(1 + \exp(-2yf))$, 120 trees for classification, a learning rate of 0.3, and a stopping criterion of 10^{-3};

- Four different versions of Deep Learning architectures:

  D1: having 2 hidden layers and 120 neurons. This number of neurons represents about 2/3 of the number of the initial features and corresponds also to the number of trees used by the random forest model.

  D2: employing 3 hidden layers each composed of 40 neurons, and a stopping criterion of 10^{-3}.

  D3: using 3 hidden layers each composed of 120 neurons, a stopping criterion of 10^{-3}, and type-1 and type-2 regularization functions.

  D4: Given the importance of hyper-parameter tuning for deep learning models, a grid of hyper-parameters has been specified to select the best model. The hyper-parameters included the dropout ratio, the activation functions, the type-1 and type-2 regularization functions, and the number of hidden layers. Early stopping criteria and regularization penalties were utilized to avoid overfitting, reduce the variance of the prediction error, and handle correlated predictors.

11.3.3 Results

By using the full set of 181 features, the seven models (M1-M2-M3 and D1-D2-D3-D4) were applied and the ROC curves constructed. The AUC and the RMSE performance metrics were computed for each model. The results obtained for the validation data set showed that the Random Forest (M2) and Gradient Boosting (M3) models had the best performance (AUC ~0 .99) while the more complex Deep Learning models (AUC 0.80-0.90)) were trailing in the ranking. Similar results were obtained for the test data set. Note that the model D3-DL with regularization was the closest performer with an AUC ~0.97.

Although all 7 models used the whole set of 181 features for training, the 10 most important features were different for each of the models employed. Note that 57 different features out of the whole set of 181 comprised the subset of the 10 most important features.

As such:

- The *Logistic Regression* (M1) model selected more global and aggregated financial variables like balance sheets, assets, and liabilities.
- The tree-based algorithms, Random Forest (M2), and Gradient Boosting (M3) models selected the more detailed financial variables like financial statements, equities, and debt.
- The *Deep Learning* models (D1–D4) showed a preference for more granular financial variables, usually the ones that provide more detailed information on the customer.

In summary, the tree-based algorithms (M2 and M3) outperformed the more complex Deep Learning (D1–D4) models for both the validation and test datasets using all 181 features. The tree-based models M2 and M3 were proven to be not just the best in terms of accuracy, but also the most stable binary classifiers as they properly create *split directions*, thus keeping only the efficient information. From a practical operational perspective, the set of the top 10 variables selected by model M3 could constitute the fundamental rule set for deciding whether to approve a loan or not.

The work published by Addo and collaborators (2018) was an important contribution to the study of applying modern Machine Learning techniques to credit risk modeling. The authors demonstrated the importance of the data preparation and cleaning process by filtering out redundant variables (54 out of 235) and by using the SMOTE algorithm, (Chawla et al. 2002) to balance the training dataset in order to avoid bias in respect to the majority class.

11.4 USING DEEP LEARNING FOR CREDIT SCORING

Corporate credit scoring has become a central topic in credit risk management especially after the last financial crisis. Luo and co-authors (2017) investigated the applicability of ML techniques to modeling credit scoring on CDS data sets. The authors studied the classification performance of Deep Belief Networks with Restricted Boltzmann Machines, and they compared it with other popular credit scoring models such as Logistic Regression, Multilayer Perceptron, and Support Vector Machines.

11.4.1 Introduction

A CDS contract is a derivative that protects the buyer against credit events with respect to a corporation or sovereign entity. These credit events could take the form of bankruptcy, the failure to pay or a credit rating downgrade. CDS were created in 1994 and their use drastically increased in the early 2000s. By the beginning of the 2008 financial crisis, the outstanding CDSs on the market were valued at more than $62 trillion. The CDS contracts are traded in the over-the-counter market between large financial institutions. The buyer of the contract makes periodic payments to the seller and the seller of protection pays compensation to the buyer if a credit event occurs and the contract is terminated. The CDS spread is defined as the annual premium paid to ensure this protection.

During the US subprime mortgage crisis and the European sovereign debt crisis many well-established financial institutions experienced catastrophic losses. These events raised serious concerns regarding the use of Credit Default Swaps (CDS). As a result, credit risk management started attracting significant attention from both academic researchers and market practitioners. Developing accurate credit scoring models became a major focus for financial institutions in their quest to effectively manage credit risk exposures and optimize profits. A large variety of different statistical and ML techniques were developed to build more trustworthy credit-rating models.

The last few decades have seen the rise of many statistical methods applied to credit risk assessment. These statistical models are still in widespread use by credit risk professionals, but they struggle to model effectively modern-day credit risk specifically because of the linearity of their statistical assumptions. Recent academic studies (Saberi et al. 2013) showed that ML techniques yield superior results when it comes to dealing with credit scoring problems.

One of the most frequently used statistical models for credit scoring is Logistic Regression. But other architectures such as Support Vector Machines (SVMs) and Multilayer Perceptron (MLPs) have been widely applied to credit scoring as well. These shallow architectures proved their effectiveness in solving many simple use cases. These methods are focused solely on the output of classifiers while neglecting other aspects that could carry a lot of actionable information. Because of their limited abilities to represent complex real-world situations, these models have become obsolete.

A new generation of Deep Neural Networks has been developed to tackle some of these drawbacks. One particular family of DNNs, the Deep Belief Networks (DBN) emerged (Hinton, Osindero, and Teh 2006) as a powerful ensemble technique to capture some of the rich information contained in highly dimensional data. As previously mentioned, Deep Neural Networks have been successfully applied to a variety of classification task: from Computer vision to Healthcare, or from voice translation to Natural Language Processing. One of the questions that Luo and co-authors (2017) tried to address is whether Deep architectures could hold any theoretical advantage compared to shallow architectures in problems related to credit risk assessment. The results of their study represent one of the first comprehensive reports about the use of DBN models in corporate credit rating. The authors investigated the performance of different credit scoring models by conducting experiments on a CDS data set containing information about 661 companies, using 11 features and generating 3 classification categories.

Eleven features were selected for training models: the 6-month, 1-year, 2-year, 3-year, 4-year, 5-year, 7-year, and the 10-year spreads, the recovery rate, the sector, and the region. The classifier could generate three rating categories: A, B, and C. The authors considered the outputs of the more classical ML techniques as baselines (i.e. Logistic Regression, Multilayer Perceptron, and SVM) and they compared them with the results generated by a DBN using Restricted Boltzmann Machines after applying a 10-fold cross-validation. Their findings showed that the DBN algorithm significantly outperforms the baselines.

11.4.2   Deep Belief Networks and Restricted Boltzmann Machines

Luo's study (Luo, Wu, and Wu 2017) considered a novel architecture, composed of a Deep Belief Network (DBN), which was introduced in 2006 by Hinton and collaborators (Hinton, Osindero, and Teh 2006). DBN is a multilayer generative graphical model obtained by training and stacking several layers of Restricted Boltzmann Machines (RBM) in a greedy manner (Salakhutdinov, Mnih, and Hinton 2007). An RBM is a bipartite undirected graph that is composed of two layers

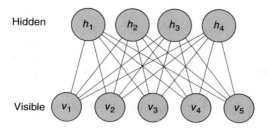

FIGURE 11.1   Restricted Boltzmann Machine concept.

of variable size. The underlying assumption for RBMs is that the hidden units are conditionally independent, conditional on the visible units and vice versa. The visible layer units are connected to the ones from the hidden layer but there are not any possible connections between units in the same layers (i.e. hidden-hidden, or visible-visible, see Figure 11.1).

A DBN is composed as a stack of RBMs where each layer is represented by a Restricted Boltzmann Machine. The hidden layer of the first RBM is considered as a visible layer for the second RBM, and so forth. The second RBM layer will learn the feature distribution of the hidden layer of the first RBM. The input layer of the first RBM is playing the role of the input layer for the whole DBN. As layers are stacked on top of each other (see Figure 11.2), the DBN starts learning increasingly complex combinations of features from the original data.

11.4.2.1   *Data*
The CDS data set consisted of 661 publicly traded companies from eight separate geographical regions including North American, Asia, Europe, and from 10 different sectors: Industrials, Consumer Services, Technology, Utilities, Telecommunications Services, Healthcare, Financials, Energy, Basic Materials, and Consumer Goods.

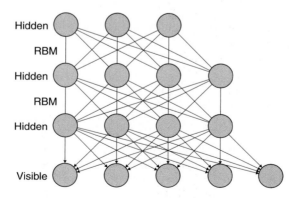

FIGURE 11.2   Deep belief network architecture.

These 661 companies were arranged into three aggregated rating categories: $A = \{A, AA, AAA\}$, $B = \{B, BB, BBB\}$, and $C = \{CCC\}$. The data set details 11 explanatory attributes for every company. Nine of these features were numerical attributes (i.e. the recovery rate and the eight different tenure spreads) and two were categorical attributes (sector and region). All categorical features were converted into numeric ones. By using the one-attribute-per-value approach, an attribute with k values is transformed into k binary attributes. Then all the numerical attributes were normalized.

11.4.3 Empirical Results

Four different algorithms were used: *Multinomial Logistic Regression* (MLR), *Multilayer Perceptron* (MLP), *Support Vector Machines* (SVM), and *Deep Belief Networks* (DBN) with Restricted Boltzmann Machines. Both a Confusion matrix and ROC methodologies were used to estimate the accuracy of these four models. To improve the reliability of the estimates, a 10-fold cross validation was employed to randomly partition the data set. In a 10-fold cross-validation process, the training set is divided into 10 subsets of equal size, and each of the 10 subsets is then tested using the classifier trained on the remaining 9 subsets. A clear advantage of using cross-validation is that the credit-scoring model is developed with a large proportion of the available data (90%). In addition, all of the data is used to train the models.

The Accuracy metric as the percentage of correctly classified instances provides a quantitative measure for the ability to make accurate predictions on previously unseen cases. The accuracy rate obtained for the DBN model with Restricted Boltzmann Machines was the highest of all 4 models, followed by the Multilayer Perceptron and the SVM (Luo, Wu, and Wu 2017). The False Positive metric is defined as the proportion of the companies that are rated higher by the model than in reality. The False Negative rate is the proportion of the companies that are rated lower than their actual rating. From all models used in this study the Multinomial Logistic Regression model had the largest false positive rate as well as the lowest accuracy. The study by Luo and collaborators brought to light a fresh new perspective on the applicability of Deep Belief Networks to the credit scoring problem. The reported results clearly indicate that DBN with Restricted Boltzmann Machines outperforms the other more classical ML algorithms.

11.5 USING ML IN OPERATIONAL RISK AND MARKET SURVEILLANCE

11.5.1 Introduction

One of the most critical requirements for operating healthy and trustworthy capital markets is to ensure the confidence of the investors in the markets themselves, as well as in their participants: exchanges, trading venues, broker/dealers, regulators, and ultimately in their operators (traders). Surveillance of trading activities and prevention of market manipulation is a very challenging and expensive process. Market abuse has become a growing concern for financial institutions during the last decade. A number of high-profile events such as the LIBOR and Foreign Exchange trading scandals and the manipulation of ISDAFIX by Deutsche bank in 2018 resulted in substantial fines (in the billions of dollars), pushing trader surveillance up the agenda.

Market operators are positioned in a quite conflicting role:

- On one hand they are the operators of the engine that generates liquidity and therefore renders markets viable.
- On the other hand they are driven by the desire to create value for themselves or for the financial firms they represent.

The line between good behavior and abuse could sometimes be blurred because of this duality of roles. The surveillance process presents many challenges, the most important ones being the extraction of actionable signals from the noise of the markets and producing the evidence of intent and market abuse. This process is driven by a variety of data, which is traditionally not well-integrated with trade monitoring systems. The amount of data that needs to be assessed when monitoring the markets is far larger than it was a decade ago.

Investigating abnormal trading activity requires a more complex analysis and significantly more time from financial firms, exchanges, and regulators, in their constant struggle to identify anomalies and separate true from false positives. Technology has become a major player in the field and its mission is to support investor confidence by providing tools to all market participants to quickly and effectively identify market abuse or operational errors. The need for surveillance tools that increase the quality and efficiency of the workflow has never been greater.

Technology firms have started to develop turnkey market surveillance solutions for exchanges, market participants, and regulators. Their offerings seek to apply modern technology to create a seamless route from early detection of market abuse to presentable evidence. To meet the demands of the modern trading industry and the ever-changing regulatory landscape, these technology solutions are not only monitoring for traditional market abuse scenarios like Spoofing, Layering, or Insider Trading, but also for abusive patterns in high-frequency trading and best execution compliance.

The surveillance process is consisting of:

- Monitoring a variety of data sources and generating alerts based on a set of predetermined abuse types.
- Building scenarios for possible investigations.
- Taking actions, either by escalating or reconciling.
- Documenting, reporting, and archiving all this information.

This surveillance process involves an incredibly large amount of data. So it is extremely important for surveillance teams to be able to prioritize their work and filter out market activity that needs immediate attention such as fat finger errors or leaks of inside information. The possibility of automating this process by extracting specific market activity could provide these teams with the opportunity to react faster to trading incidents and to identify abusive patterns in a more precise manner.

There are several important challenges related to the quality of the surveillance process:

- Relatively high rate of false positives
- Issues with data quality and coverage
- Regulatory compliance requirements
- Operation costs and personnel

The most challenging aspect by far is the availability and the quality of data. When the market surveillance process relies on rule engines and statistical analysis, it usually requires very high-quality data. These data need to be captured in a consistent format, especially when extracted from multiple sources. Mapping all data across the firm is a complex but necessary undertaking for a holistic and reliable surveillance process.

11.5.2   An ML Approach to Market Surveillance

In order to increase the accuracy of the surveillance process, better analytical tools are required to generate fewer, but higher quality alerts. Solution vendors addressed some of these requirements and proposed the use of Machine Learning algorithms to detect anomalies in a more accurate manner and match them against normal trader behavior. Supervised ML was used to improve existing reactive systems in order to provide better alerts. According to some industry reports (Chartis Research 2017), the use of Machine Learning and unstructured data analysis has reduced market surveillance false positives by as much as 50%, generating Returns on Investment (ROIs) of more than 60%.

In 2018 NASDAQ announced that Hong Kong Exchanges and Clearing Limited (HKEX) was their first customer to successfully deploy their so-called SMARTS Market Surveillance solution. By implementing ML technology, SMARTS analyzes unusual trading activities and suggests categorization to surveillance analysts. The aim of the SMARTS suite of algorithms is to predict which actions analysts are likely to take based upon their handling of historical activity as well as discovering new relationships within the data.

The Tokyo Stock Exchange also chose to apply ML-based solutions to market surveillance operations for monitoring and preventing unfair trading. As such a broad range of suspicious orders could be first identified by the surveillance systems and then surveillance personnel could conduct preliminary investigations to analyze the trading situation surrounding such orders. The deployment of ML-based technology enabled surveillance personnel with the ability to complete preliminary investigations in a timely manner and focus their efforts on the detailed investigations.

Trading Technologies (TT) is one of the best known and most valued trading platforms employed by futures and options traders. TT has adopted Machine Learning as the main approach to implement market surveillance tools. By collecting a variety of trading data from numerous sources, especially from regulatory cases, TT used these to train a suite of ML models – called TT Score to identify patterns of disruptive or manipulative trading behavior.

TT Score's clustering algorithm slices trading activity data into clusters based on time, trader ID, traded instrument, and the time proximity of other order actions. As each cluster represents a time slice of trading activity, the ML algorithm classifies this activity in a specific category that is representative of the trader's actions for that time period. These trading activity clusters may be thought of as packets of intent since each cluster contains a group of order actions (order placing, modifying, or canceling) that could be very likely related, given the time proximity of these events.

This clustering approach may offer a better view to investigators since the full context of the potentially abusive behavior is captured, analyzed, and visualized. Each ML model targets a specific category of disruptive or manipulative trading activity. Their *Spoofing Similarity* model focuses on simple spoofing behavior as well as on layering, collapsing of layers, flipping, and vacuuming. Other TT models target other types of abusive behavior, like momentum ignition, pinging, wash trading, or excessive canceling of orders.

Traditional parameter-based surveillance tools could generate massive amounts of alerts where only a small fraction might be considered true positives. TT surveillance software introduced the concept of a similarity score that addresses this problem by scoring each alert based on the degree of quantitative similarity to past actions. This similarity score is generated for each cluster on a scale of 0 to 100. The TT Score surveillance tool provides very specific guidance to its users by pointing to the clusters that have the highest risk of drawing future regulatory attention and therefore are the most important for immediate review.

11.5.3   Conclusions

The applicability of Machine-Learning techniques to market surveillance is still in its infancy. The predictive power of current ML models is sometimes difficult to gauge due to their complex black box nature. These ML models are also rather sensitive to outliers, resulting in overfitting of the data and generating counterintuitive predictions.

The adoption of ML-based technologies for regulatory compliance is very much dependent on the ability to collect, store, and properly analyze large amounts of financial data. The access to tech talent is also a major challenge to overcome.

REFERENCES

Addo, Guegan, and Hassani (2018). Credit risk analysis using machine and deep learning models. *Risks* 6 (2): 38–58.

Altman and Edward (1968). Financial ratios, discriminant analysis and the prediction of corporate bankruptcy. *Journal of Finance* 23 (4): 589–609.

Altman, Marco, and Varetto (1994). Corporate distress diagnosis: Comparisons using linear discriminant analysis and neural networks (the Italian experience). *Journal of Banking and Finance* 18 (3): 505–529.

Arner, Barberis, and Buckley (2016). The emergence of RegTech 2.0: From know your customer to know your data. *Journal of Financial Transformation* 44: 9–86.

Bigham, Nair, Soral et. al. (2018). *AI and Risk Management: Innovating with Confidence*. Deloitte Centre for Regulatory Strategy, 1. https://www2.deloitte.com/content/dam/Deloitte/global/Documents/Financial-Services/deloitte-gx-ai-and-risk-management.pdf.

Breiman (1997). Arching the edge. Technical report 486. UC Berkeley.

Breiman (2000). Some infinity theory for predictors ensembles. Technical report 577. UC Berkeley.

Breiman (2004). Consistency for a sample model of random forests. Technical report 670. UC Berkeley.

Cavalcante, Brasileiro, Souza et al. (2016). Computational intelligence and financial markets: A survey and future directions. *Expert Systems with Applications* 55: 194–211.

Chandrinos, Sakkas, and Lagaros (2018). AIRMS: A risk management tool using machine learning. *Expert Systems with Applications* 105: 34–48.

Chartis Research (2017). *The Future of Trader Surveillance*. Report. https://www.ey.com/Publication/vwLUAssets/ey-trader-surveillance-report/%24FILE/EY%20Trader%20Surveillance%20report.pdf.

Chawla, Bowyer, Hall et al. (2002). SMOTE: Synthetic minority over-sampling technique. *Journal of Artificial Intelligence Research* 16 (1): 321–357.

Choi, Chan, and Yue (2017). Recent development in big data analytics for business operations and risk management. *IEEE Transactions on Cybernetics* 47 (1): 81–92.

Day (2017). Quants turn to machine learning to model market impact. *Risk.net*. https://www.risk.net/asset-management/4644191/quants-turn-to-machine-learning-to-model-market-impact.

Figini, Bonelli, and Giovannini (2017). Solvency prediction for small and medium enterprises in banking. *Decision Support Systems* 102: 91–97.

Financial Stability Board (2017). Artificial intelligence and machine learning in financial services. https://www.fsb.org/wp-content/uploads/P011117.pdf.

Gandel (2012). *Fortune* (3 August). http://fortune.com/2012/08/02/why-knight-lost-440-million-in-45-minutes.

Gastwirth (1972). The estimation of the Lorenz curve and the Gini index. *Review of Economics and Statistics* 54 (3): 306–316.

Heaton, Polson, and Witte (2017). Deep learning for finance: Deep portfolios. *Applied Stochastic Models in Business and Industry* 33 (1): 3–12.

Hendricks and Wilcox (2014). A reinforcement learning extension to the Almgren-Chriss framework for optimal trade execution. *IEEE Computational Intelligence for Financial Engineering and Economics Conference*, 457–464.

Hinton, Osindero, and Teh (2006). A fast learning algorithm for deep belief nets. *Neural Computation* 18 (7): 1527–1554.

Khandani, Kim, and Lo (2010). Consumer credit-risk models via machine-learning algorithms. *Journal of Banking and Finance* 34 (11): 2767–2787.

Khashman (2010). Neural networks for credit risk evaluation: Investigation of different neural models and learning schemes. *Expert Systems with Applications* 37: 6233–6239.

Kruppa, Schwarz, Arminger et al. (2013). Consumer credit risk: Individual probability estimates using machine learning. *Expert Systems with Applications* 40: 5125–5131.

Kumar (2018). Machine learning for model development in market risk. GARP Institute. https://www.garp.org/#!/risk-intelligence/all/all/a1Z1W000003fM0yUAE.

Luo, Wu, and Wu (2017). A deep learning approach for credit scoring using credit default swaps. *Engineering Application of Artificial Intelligence* 65: 465–470.

Moosa (2007). *Operational Risk Management*. Palgrave Macmillan, 75–129.

O'Hara and Clark (2017). AI and deep learning in risk and investment management. *Financial Markets Insights*. The Realization Group, 3. https://verneglobal.com/uploads/TRG-AI-Deep-Learning-Risk-and-Investment-Management-2017.pdf.

Olson and Wu (2015). *Enterprise Risk Management in Finance*. New York: Springer, 119–132.

Saberi, Mirtalaie, Hussain et al. (2013). A granular computing-based approach to credit scoring modeling. *Neurocomputing* 122: 100–115.

Salakhutdinov, Mnih, and Hinton (2007). Restricted Boltzmann machines for collaborative filtering. *Proceedings of the 24th International Conference on Machine Learning*, 791–798.

Sanford and Moosa (2015). Operational risk modelling and organizational learning in structured finance operations: A Bayesian network approach. *Journal of the Operational Research Society* 66 (1): 86–115.

Son, Youngdoo, Byun et al. (2016). Nonparametric machine learning models for predicting the credit default swaps: An empirical study. *Expert Systems with Applications* 58: 210–220.

Woodall (2017). Model risk managers eye benefits of machine learning. *Risk.net*. https://www.risk.net/risk-management/4646956/model-risk-managers-eye-benefits-of-machine-learning .

Yitzhaki (1983). On an extension of the Gini inequality index. *International Economic Review* 24 (3): 617–628.

CHAPTER 12

Conclusions and Future Directions

"Live as if you were to die tomorrow.

Learn as if you were to live forever!"

– Mahatma Gandhi

12.1 CONCLUDING REMARKS

The ideas behind this book originated from three distinct, yet related sources: two decades of professional experience in quantitative trading, the current interests and needs of my students, and my desire to bring to the attention of a larger audience a series of important recent developments related to the use of *computationally intelligent* techniques in Quantitative and Computational Finance.

I had the privilege of working for more than two decades as a technologist, quant, and trader in the financial industry. During this period of time I had the extraordinary opportunity to have access to some of the most advanced High-Performance Computing and high-speed communication technology available, and to work with some of the brightest and most successful derivatives traders in the world. During the last five years I had also the opportunity of being a faculty member in one of the world's most prestigious programs in Financial Mathematics, at the University of Chicago. This affiliation gave me the chance to interact with a large and diverse group of bright and inquisitive Financial Mathematics students. Countless classroom interactions and working with them on many term projects helped me to refine the content and the structure of this book. Last but not least, I wanted to bring to the attention of more seasoned quantitative practitioners both the promises and the formidable challenges that this brave new era of intelligent computing brings about.

One of the main objectives of this book is to introduce an adequate level of engineering and scientific clarity on the usage of the term *Artificial Intelligence*,

237

especially as it relates to the financial industry. As the term is often used as an intellectual wildcard, and sometimes without much scientific rigor, I deemed it necessary to bring to the attention of the reader important aspects related to the dangers of succumbing to this hype and to separate the pop culture fantasy from the scientific and engineering reality.

An equally important objective for this book is to update the Financial Mathematics curriculum on two contemporary topics: Data-Driven decision-making (applied to trading and investing) and Computational Intelligence. Another objective is to bridge the gap between academic research and the practical needs of quantitative professionals. The second half of the book is dedicated to the presentation of a set of Case Studies that are contemporarily relevant to the needs of practitioners. As such, Chapters 6 through 11 of this book illustrated the applicability of Machine Learning techniques to a plethora of practical problems: from trade execution optimization and price dynamics forecast, to portfolio management, market making, derivatives valuation, and risk management.

The three principal objectives of this book are:

- Describing the new paradigm of Data-Driven trading and the application of Computational Intelligence techniques to implement it.
- Analyzing from both a scientific and an engineering perspective, the current state of and attempting to demystify its hype factor.
- Popularizing the advent of new engineering discipline, a discipline that will be at the same time data-focused and learning-focused and that I label *Quantitative and Computational Engineering*.

Today we are witnessing the onset of a major transformation within our culture that is driven by the groundbreaking technological achievements of the last decade, as well as by the emergence of a new paradigm of scientific inquiry, called the fourth paradigm. These new developments will fundamentally change the way many industries operate, but they will particularly revolutionize the structure of the workforce for generations to come. Dr. James Gray, one of the greatest American computer scientists of the twentieth century and Turing award recipient, predicted the advent of this new era more than a decade ago. He called it the *data exploration* era, or a time where theory, experimentation, and simulation will come together to solve some of the most important problems of our time.

The maturation of some of the major technological achievements of the last decade contributed to the generation of vast amounts of data, and the birth of what is called the age of *Big Data*. Recent advances in High-Performance Computing and hardware acceleration (e.g. GPUs and FPGAs), coupled with new discoveries in algorithmic processing, created the conditions to apply complex machine learning algorithms to a variety of practical problems. All these new technological developments are going to have a revolutionary impact on many industries, and as usual the financial industry will be one of the first ones to take advantage of them. A new concept is already making its way in today's financial world: *data-driven decision-making*. Today both high-frequency trading and longer time horizon investing are increasingly driven by large-scale data analysis, while the use of *alternative data* is becoming ubiquitous.

12.2   THE PARADIGM SHIFT

"Without change there is no innovation, creativity, or incentive for improvement. Those who initiate change will have a better opportunity to manage the change that is inevitable."

– *William Pollard, theologian*

One of the main objectives of this book is to inform the reader about a paradigm shift that is happening before our eyes. This is the dawn of a new era where business decisions are going to be driven by data and powered by algorithms. This new paradigm is very different from the ones that preceded it, because it is actually a combination of various models and archetypes from different domains. The fourth paradigm of scientific discovery was introduced in 2007 by Dr. James Gray, who was then a senior researcher at Microsoft. In his last public talk (Hey, Tansley, and Tolle 2009) Dr. Gray described his vision of the fourth paradigm, which in his opinion is similar in importance to the invention of the printing press.

More than 400 years ago Johannes Kepler used Tycho Brahe's catalog (Verbunt and van Gent 2010) of systematic astronomical observations and discovered the laws of planetary motion. This historical event represented the first documented usage of data mining of experimental data for the creation of scientific theories. If many thousands of years ago the scientific method of inquiry was empirical in nature, during the Renaissance a new scientific paradigm appeared, and it was characterized by the use of models and generalizations based on experiments. As a result of this paradigm, many theories have been created, from Newton's Laws of Motion, to Maxwell's equations, to mention just a few.

The advent of computers makes possible a new type of scientific method – the *in silico* simulation of phenomena that may occur very infrequently or that are just too complex or too expensive to study in the real world. Nowadays, vast volumes of scientific, industrial, and commercial data are captured on a real-time basis. Along with synthetic information generated by computer models, this enormous amount of data is likely to reside in a live, readily accessible, curated state for the purposes of continued analysis. And this analysis will most likely result in the development of many new theories.

The world of science and engineering has changed substantially in the last 50 years. Data is either captured by instruments and sensors or generated by simulations before being processed into information or knowledge that could be digitally stored (Bell, Hey, and Szalay 2009). This new set of technologies and approaches employed in data-intensive scientific research are at the origins of the *fourth Paradigm* (Hey, Tansley, and Tolle 2009). The last decade has seen the parallel evolution of two distinct, yet related branches in major scientific disciplines: there is Medicine and there is Computational Medicine, as there is Biology and Computational Biology.

And in our own industry, there is Theoretical Finance and there is Computational Finance. The idea of *computational thinking* originated with Jeannette Wing (2006) and addressed the representation of information (structured from data) in an algorithmic way, such that one could objectify Knowledge for different problem domains. The work and ideas of Dr. Gray illustrated the profound impact that Information Technology had on science and engineering. One of this book's main objectives is to illustrate the progress achieved in the field of Quantitative and Computational Finance as a result of the onset of the fourth paradigm.

12.2.1 Mathematical Models vs. Data Inference

"All models are wrong but some are useful."

                                                    – George Box, distinguished statistician

Since data was first used for scientific inquiry, Statistical modeling has been the main tool set used by both scientists and practitioners. It is fascinating to explore the two schools of thought that have contributed so much to the progress of Data Science.

Leo Breiman (2001) is the author of a seminal paper on this subject. Professor Breiman was a very distinguished statistician at UC Berkeley, and the inventor of Random Forests and Bootstrap Aggregation (which are fundamental methods in modern ML). In this paper, Breiman described in rather stern terms the opposition between the two cultures (see Figure 12.1) that employ statistical modeling to reach conclusions from data. The data modeling school assumes that data is generated by a given (parametrized) stochastic process. The algorithmic culture uses algorithmic models inferred from data without making any assumptions on the mechanism that generates this data. Statisticians have been committed to an almost exclusive use of data models, and according to Professor Breiman, this commitment has led to "irrelevant theory, questionable conclusions, and has kept statisticians from working on a large range of interesting current problems." On the other hand, Algorithmic modeling has developed very rapidly in fields outside the realm of Statistics (like Computer Science).

The Data modeling culture starts with the assumption of a stochastic data model that resides inside a gray box. The main goal is to be able to predict the values of response variables by using a parametrized function that uses input (predictor) variables and eventually to include some random noise. These models are validated by using goodness-of-fit tests and by examining the residuals.

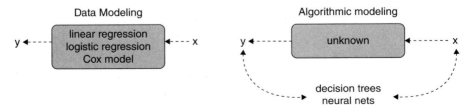

FIGURE 12.1   The two cultures of statistical modeling. **Source:** Adapted from Breiman (2001).

The algorithmic culture considers the inside of the box too complex to be modeled and thus it labels it as black (unknown). Their approach is to find a functional representation f(x) that is an algorithm that operates on x to predict the responses y. The validation of this model is done by estimating the predictive accuracy in a fashion that is similar to supervised ML training. A very important difference in the way these two cultures approach the process of learning from data is related to the interpretability of the models they construct. Within the algorithmic culture there is a school of thought that completely trusts the black-box models (i.e. Deep Learning models), without any regard for their interpretability. For this tribe, the correlation inferred from very large amounts of data is considered to be enough to be able to train models that display a high predictability score. This culture believes that by consuming more and more data, one augments the complexity of the hypothesis space, and therefore one could make up for its lack of interpretability.

But there is a branch of the algorithmic culture that is looking for interpretability and it believes that causal inference is far more important in the learning process than just finding correlations. This school of thought is looking to devise methods that will work for problems that cannot benefit from the availability of huge amounts of data, simply because there is not enough of it available. They are looking for algorithms that decompose a problem into smaller pieces, easier to solve; they are seeking for structural interpretability. According to this camp, the biggest challenge ahead is to be able to devise new learning techniques that do not rely solely on massive amounts of data, but also on some other human intelligence techniques. After all, we should address the Intelligence dimension of AI? This school of thought is a firm believer in delivering on the promise of understanding and implementing truly intelligent machines.

Both Mathematical modeling and Machine Learning modeling are dealing with similar objects and processes, but they are dealing with them in very different ways. There are many problem domains (such as healthcare, finance, and military) where users of ML algorithms need to be able to interpret their decisions; unfortunately, most of the advanced ML models are not designed to provide this feature. The main selling point of Deep Learning is represented by its automatic feature extraction. Given a large data set and a combination of linear and nonlinear transformations that take place within the neural networks, a resulting vector, also called an embedding, is produced at the output.

As a result, the main challenges associated with the use of Deep Learning methods are:

- *Interpretability* – The output vector does not carry any information about why some particular decisions were taken during the learning process.
- *Data needs* – DNNs require a lot of data.
- *The zero-shot reuse* – A Deep Neural network trained on one data set could be rarely applied directly on another similar data set without proper retraining.
- *Theory* – There is not much of a theoretical foundation on explaining why DL works so well in some situations, and not at all in others.

By comparison mathematical modeling presents a series of advantages like:

- *Interpretability* – Mathematical models are created with a clear motivation and understanding. For example, when describing physical motion, the embedding will consist of the object mass, its speed, and its coordinates – there are no abstract vectors involved.
- *Data needs* – Most of scientific discoveries did not require very large data sets.
- *The zero-shot reuse* – The same stochastic differential equation, like for example the geometric Brownian motion, could be applied in finance, biology, or physics by just renaming its parameters.
- *Theory* – benefits of many centuries of scientific output.

The natural question that ensues is why not use partial differential equations for everything? The obvious answer is that the simulation of complex phenomena and the use of very large data sets render impossible the use of classical mathematical models mainly due to computational performance issues. A lot of effort has been put more recently into combining the discriminative and predictive power of ML with the interpretability of human-based modeling. The concept of disentangled representations has become a popular topic in this respect (Higgins et al. 2018).

The discriminative power of Deep Learning in image processing is due to its ability of transforming pixel level features (like color or shape) into more complex ones, such as *eyes*, *petals*, or *wheels*. Using these high-level representations makes it easier to explain and classify the content of a digital image. The lack of interpretability comes from the mixing of these representations in a spaghetti-like fashion. Anecdotally, Yoshua Bengio, one of the creators of DNN, once said that "if we can take that spaghetti and disentangle it, that would be very nice" (Bengio et al. 2019). The main idea behind *disentangled representations* is to come up with algorithms that discover high-level features like *eyes*, *petals*, or wheels that are *separable* in an *unsupervised* manner. The Variational Autoencoder (VAE) is a deep generative model and it has been shown to be able to disentangle simple data generating factors from a highly complex input space. After training is completed, one can vary each of the hidden variables and observe its effect on the output, thus determining what kinds of features the model has learned.

The importance of this result at the present time can not be overstated. The complexity of the problems at hand and the expectations that surround them are going to fundamentally change the educational process that is responsible for training the future workforce. As a result the transition to this new paradigm will trigger the emergence of new approaches in educating the future hi-tech workforce.

12.3   DE-NOISING THE AI HYPE

"A lot of what we call 'smart-systems' are derailed from the reality of the empirical process ... ."

– Jaron Lanier, computer scientist and philosopher

Large companies are currently placing big bets on the AI buzz. Some of them like Apple, Google, Microsoft, Intel, Uber, Facebook, or Amazon have their own research labs where large teams of scientists and engineers are dedicated to the application of technologies to their current product lines. The big question that needs to be answered is two-pronged: How mature has AI become and how do we prepare the workforce for its widespread adoption?

In that respect it is worth mentioning a few interesting statistics:

- According to Element AI, an independent lab in Montreal, fewer than 10,000 people in the world have the skills necessary to tackle AI research.
- According to some reports in 2017, Google DeepMind's staff costs were at the level of $138 million for about 400 employees (an average of $345,000 per employee).
- Top academic talent has moved massively into the private sector. As an example Uber hired 40 people from Carnegie Mellon's groundbreaking AI program in 2015 to work on its self-driving-car project. Four of the best-known academic AI researchers have left or taken leave from their professorships at Stanford.

Venture Capital firms are flocking into this field at an unprecedented rate. Merger and acquisition activity in this sector reached an all-time high (see Figure 12.2).

Questions about both the affordability and feasibility of AI remain open. The hype generated by the so-called Artificial Intelligence revolution is nothing but the most noticeable manifestation of a systemic failure to understand the technical complexity

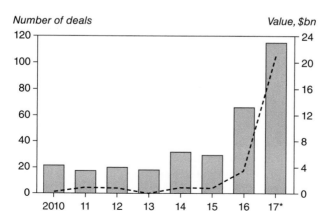

FIGURE 12.2   AI-related investments. **Source:** Based on data from PitchBook.

of this topic. This effect is enhanced by a profit-making impulse that exploits any opportunity to promote products and services that could benefit from the use of the term. This hype-factor is always elevated for new technologies emerging from the research labs into the public domain. But given the weight of the expectations placed on AI a bit more scrutiny is to be expected.

12.3.1   Why Intellectual Honesty Should Not Be Abandoned

Major practical achievements like DeepMind's victory over the world's Go champion have fed into the frenzy of the AI-era as a time where *one does not need to work any longer and all societal problems will be magically resolved*. This hype feeds also the opposite view that humanity is inching a step closer into some sort of Matrix-like enslavement.

But fortunately there is also another camp, albeit smaller, that is more reluctant to accept at face value the bold promise of *Artificial Intelligence*. One of the most critical voices is that of computer scientist and virtual reality pioneer, Jaron Lanier (92nd Street Y 2016; Greenemeir 2016). He believes that the Go world's champion was not playing just against an algorithm, but also "against the aggregate of 30 million moves made during previous games by human players." The victory of the algorithm over the human was the result of many Go gamers informing the Go algorithm through the availability of massive amounts of data. DeepMind's success was not related to any magic algorithm that emulates human Intelligence, either artificially or computationally. The same reasoning goes for the possibility of doing real-time Skype translation, for example. "The only way we do it is by scraping the efforts of millions of translators who don't even know what's happening to them to get the examples." Lanier is just one of the many researchers who are warning against this hype that it seems to become more of a religious movement than an engineering discipline. He calls this hype a cultural fantasy, a promise that is not grounded, at least not currently, on scientific discoveries or engineering realities. As long as there is no clear understanding of how the human brain works, and therefore the emulation of human intelligence is not yet possible, "pretending to have something working when one really does not," is an intellectually dishonest exercise, which Lanier labels as "premature mystery reduction."

This type of dealing with extreme complexity, such as the one represented by human intelligence, is a reflection of poor scientific discipline. For many centuries the most valuable best practice of scientists was their ability to accept and deal with a certain level of ignorance. Discounting the unknown before discovering it could have major negative consequences in the field of Sciences, from creating confusion and false promises, to generating a false representation of the reality, and ultimately to hampering the scientific progress. What is nowadays called the *AI revolution* may qualify for what Lanier calls "premature mystery reduction." The vast majority of the so-called AI-driven software was developed using massive data sets representing specific types of human activity. This is similar to "pretending that there is some AI behind the curtain that is freestanding when in reality there are also millions of people there, as well." Jaron Lanier (92nd Street Y 2016; Greenemeir 2016)

As mentioned in Chapter 3, there are some very distinguished academics, like Professor Michael Jordan from Berkeley, who are looking critically at the current state of affairs in AI. Many of them agree that in order to realize the full promise of AI, some very daunting challenges need to be addressed. Some of the most pressing challenges are engineering challenges in nature, and they are related to systems and infrastructure. For AI to become applicable to real-world problems, especially for domains such as financial trading and investing, or healthcare and medicine, AI systems will need to make decisions that are not just faster, but also safer and interpretable by human operators.

When it comes to interpretability, the debate within the ML community is even more divisive. On the practical side there are many current and potential users of ML algorithms who would want to get a basic understanding of how data should be collected, how features should be engineered from the data, and eventually of how the algorithms are generating the end results. Just consider applications where human well-being is involved, like self-driving cars, medical applications, and financial decisions. In all these situations, the human operator needs to trust the algorithms. The best way to do this is to make the computer explain its decision-making process in a way that humans could understand. The European Union passed a law in 2016 that it will require the right to explanation from any algorithm that is used for making predictions based on user-level predictors.

Until research in Cognitive sciences makes more tangible progress in the understanding of how human intelligence works and how it can be emulated, we will need to focus our efforts to the development of Computational Intelligence methods, concentrating on improving the Automation aspects and making more progress on Meta-Learning (Vanschoren 2018).

12.4 AN EMERGING ENGINEERING DISCIPLINE

"We should embrace the fact that what we are witnessing is the creation of a new branch of engineering. In the current era, we have a real opportunity to conceive of something historically new – a human-centric engineering discipline."

– *Professor Michael I. Jordan, UC Berkeley*

As someone who has been engaged for more than 20 years in the field of Quantitative and Computational Finance, from architecting and leading the development of firm-wide software systems, to developing valuation and risk models as a quant, or employing them as a trader, I especially appreciate the importance of the quantitative and computational financial education. During my career in quantitative trading I have interviewed hundreds of candidates and I have hired many of them. I always recruited candidates who had a great formal education that was complemented by the necessary passion for solving real-world problems. Today's generation of Quants and Financial Engineers are facing brand-new challenges. They are the quants of the Post-Crisis generation and new sets of skills and knowledge are required from them. This is a new era, one of risk aversion and frugality. Many firms and jobs have disappeared in the last decade.

A brand-new set of expectations are emerging. The most important trend is the great convergence between the quantitative and the computational domains. The most looked-after role has become recently the one called quant-developer. Pretty much two experts for the price of one: a great quant and a very capable software engineer in one person. Even the recruiting process has changed significantly. The interviewing process is a lot more challenging and it definitely requires a better preparation and a lot of stamina.

The most important lesson that I have learned in my career is that the potential to solve complex business problems depends predominantly on being able to recruit, train, and develop the necessary talent that could apply efficiently the latest technology available.

12.4.1   The Problem

There is a widespread perception that the current higher education system is technically outdated, costly, inefficient, and often irrelevant to the needs of the financial industry. The current models are in dire need of feedback from an industry where tech recruiting and continuous education has become very costly and inefficient. While technology firms are spending massive amounts of resources on recruiting and corporate training, the learners are incurring ever-increasing costs to attend educational programs that are not meeting the norms and the needs of the tech industry. Educating the twenty-first century hi-tech workforce will require a brand-new approach, one that is more Relevant, Modern, and Efficient, for both the tech firms and their current and future workforce. Current research in Neuropsychology, Human Cognition, and Cognitive Computing points to the fact that the learning process should not be devoted principally to content acquisition, but it should be focused on ways and means to efficiently apply the acquired knowledge to solve *real-world* problems. The efficiency of the learning process must be quantitatively assessed, in ways that will allow *actionability* to be quantified via a cost function score.

12.4.2   The Market

The global markets for professional education and talent management are two extremely large markets estimated at about $250 billion to $300 billion annually. Their identified inefficiencies are so large in scope and so critical to the success of the current industrial revolution that they will require adopting a brand-new paradigm in professional education: shifting the emphasis from content acquisition to experiential learning. This paradigm shift will require adopting modern quantitative models to continuously evaluate the efficiency of the educational process and develop the algorithms to optimize it. Technology companies in general, and trading and asset management firms in particular, need to gain the ability to have a quantifiable measure of the *in-house* resident knowledge, as well as a framework of well-defined metrics to be used in the recruiting process to seamlessly match business needs to talent.

12.4.3   A Possible Solution

Financial firms are looking for candidates who are mastering an ever-increasing set of tools, from Financial Mathematics, to Computer Science, from Big Data Analytics to

Machine Learning and Blockchain technology. But no matter how extensive the tool set is, what they are especially looking for is the ability to solve problems. This brave new world will require a new breed of quant workforce: one combining classical quant skills with deep knowledge of Computer Science and hands-on knowledge of modern HPC technologies. We have recently stepped into the era of data-driven intelligent computing, a new realm where the most coveted prize is Innovation. And because Innovation is principally driven by technological developments, being cognizant of the latest tech developments becomes a hard-core prerequisite that requires life-long education. The life cycle of modern technologies is averaging about 2.5 years today. Next year it may be even shorter. Quants should be ready to embrace and thrive in a life-long cycle of learning. Educators should be prepared to nurture an innovative Engineering Mind that is driven by a powerful Mathematical Engine, supported by a vigorous Research Impetus and guided by a strong Technology background. All of these components have to be present, have to be nourished, and have to grow and develop you the reader into the quant of the twenty-first century.

The main purpose for this new breed of engineering is to address the needs of the current industrial revolution by making itself available to a variety of industries, way beyond the realm of the finance. Fields like Computational Medicine (Johns Hopkins n.d.), Healthcare, Education, or the Internet of Things are going to be big consumers of this modern profession. Since the whole society is so immersed in and dependent on data and the methods to extract actionable information from it, the twenty-first-century quants will position themselves at the core of the system that drives the most important business decisions.

12.5   FUTURE DIRECTIONS

The success of the current industrial revolution and the achievement of the *AI* dream will heavily depend on the ability to thoroughly modernize the Education system and to restore Scientific Research to its glory days. The AI-research labs are currently being depleted of their talent that is massively migrating into the private sector. Doing research in a proprietary environment is not conducive to sharing scientific results or engendering collaboration with other scientists around the world. And the fundamental challenges that the field of AI is currently facing cannot be easily addressed by isolated groups, even if they are backed by tech giants like Google, Microsoft, or Amazon. This is in my opinion the most serious impediment in advancing the current state of AI research.

Moving from the current paradigm of *Representation Learning* (or learning by imitation from data) to a paradigm of *Machine Consciousness* (where the agent will be able to make decisions based on independent thinking by using an approach that is more akin to human behavior) is still a distant milestone. This paradigm shift will require some major scientific and technological breakthroughs, and they will most likely happen in a more collaborative setting, that is, in publicly funded research labs and not in confined, proprietary corporate environments.

But even if this singularity point could be reached any time soon, who is going to implement the new theory into real-world products and services? What kind of engineers are going to be able to do this work? How are business decision-makers going to select the right tools for their given problems? This desired disruption will require novel approaches to educate the future workforce and to train the existing personnel.

Until these much anticipated scientific and technological breakthroughs occur, the best course of action is to continue to make steady progress on automating some of the most complex tasks at hand and in finding new ways of learning from data by using the great computational tools already available. At the same time we would need to redirect the focus of the education process from mastering ever-more complex tools and frameworks, to the development of solid and scalable *problem-solving* skills.

One should hope that this quantitative accumulation of knowledge will one day mutate into the great discovery that will trigger the singularity point.

Until then, happy reading, but especially happy Intelligent Computing!

REFERENCES

Bell, Hey, and Szalay (2009). Beyond the data deluge. *Science* 323 (5919): 1297–1298.

Bengio, Deleu, Rahaman et al. (2019). A meta-transfer objective for learning to disentangle causal mechanisms. https://arxiv.org/abs/1901.10912.

Breiman (2001). Statistical modeling: The two cultures. *Statistical Science* 16 (3): 199–215.

Greenemeir (2016). Is artificial intelligence being oversold? *Scientific American* (10 March). https://blogs.scientificamerican.com/observations/is-artificial-intelligence-being-oversold/

Hey, Tansley, and Tolle (2009). Jim Gray on eScience: a transformed scientific method. In *The Fourth Paradigm: Data-Intensive Scientific Discovery* (ed. Hey, Tansley, and Tolle). Redmond, WA: Microsoft Research. http://itre.cis.upenn.edu/myl/JimGrayOnE-Science.pdf.

Higgins, Amos, Pfau et al. (2018). Towards a definition of disentangled representations. https://arxiv.org/abs/1812.02230.

Johns Hopkins University (n.d.). Computational medicine. *Johns Hopkins Biomedical Engineering.* https://www.bme.jhu.edu/research/computational-medicine-2/.

92nd Street Y (2016). IQ2 Debate: Don't trust the promise of artificial intelligence. https://youtu.be/Qqc0t8ghvis.

Vanschoren (2018). Meta-learning: A survey. https://arxiv.org/abs/1810.03548.

Verbunt and van Gent (2010). Three editions of the star catalog of Tycho Brahe. https://arxiv.org/abs/1003.3836.

Wing (2006). Computational thinking. *Communications of the ACM* 49 (3): 33–35.

Index